PERSPECTIVES

ON dEVIANCE

Allen E. Liska

State University of New York at Albany

Prentice-Hall, Inc., Englewood, New Jersey 07632

Library of Congress Cataloging in Publication Data

LISKA, ALLEN E
    Perspectives on deviance.

    Includes bibliographies and index.
    1. Deviant behavior.   I. Title.
HM291.L56   302.5   80-27493
ISBN   0-13-660373-4

Editorial production/supervision and
interior design by *Edith Riker*
Cover design by *R L Communications*
Manufacturing buyer *John Hall*

Printed in the United States of America

10 9 8 7 6 5 4 3 2 1

Prentice-Hall International, Inc., *London*
Prentice-Hall of Australia Pty. Limited, *Sydney*
Prentice-Hall of Canada, Ltd., *Toronto*
Prentice-Hall of India Private Limited, *New Delhi*
Prentice-Hall of Japan, Inc., *Tokyo*
Prentice-Hall of Southeast Asia Pte. Ltd., *Singapore*
Whitehall Books Limited, *Wellington, New Zealand*

CONTENTS

two

three

four

five

six

seven

eight

Grateful acknowledgment is made for the use of material as follows:

Page 18   Box 1.2. "The criminal patterns of Boston since 1849," in American Journal of Sociology, 73, 1967 by T. N. Ferdinand. Copyright 1967 University of Chicago. Used by permission of the publisher.

Page 34   Box 2.1. Robert K. Merton, "Social Structure and Anomie," ASR, Vol. 3, 1938, p. 676. Used by permission of the publisher.

Page 39   Box 2.3. Capote, Truman. In Cold Blood. New York: Signet, 1965.

Page 41   Box 2.4. "The social functions of the career fool," in Psychiatry, 27, 1964, by A. K. Daniels and R. R. Daniels. Copyright 1964 by Psychiatry. Reprinted by permission of the publisher.

Page 61   Figure 3.1. C. R. Shaw, F. M. Zorbaugh, H. D. McKay, and L. S. Cottrell. Delinquency Areas. Chicago: University of Chicago Press, 1929. Used by permission of the publisher.

Page 128   Table 5.1. Richard D. Schwartz and Jerome H. Skolnick, "Two Studies of Legal Stigma," Social Problems, 10:2 (Fall, 1962) p. 137. And "Delinquency and Stigmatization," by W. Buikhuisen and P. H. Dijksterhuis in British Journal of Criminology, 11 April 1971, p. 186. Copyright 1971 by British Journal of Criminology. Reprinted by permission.

Page 133   Table 5.2. "Rejection: a possible consequence of seeking help for mental disorders," in American Sociological Review, Vol 28, 1963 by D. Phillips. Copyright by American Sociological Association. Reprinted by permission of the publisher.

Page 154   Table 6.1. J. L. Simmons. Deviants. San Francisco: Boyd and Fraser Publishing Company, 1969. Reprinted by permission of the publisher.

Page 155   Table 6.2. "Typifications of Homosexuals," in The Sociological Quarterly, 20, 1979 by Russell Ward. Copyright 1979 by Midwest Sociological Society. Reprinted by permission of the publisher.

Page 159   Box 6.2. "Police encounters with juveniles," in American Journal of Sociology, 70, 1964 by I. Piliavin and S. Briar. Copyright 1964 University of Chicago. Reprinted by permission of the publisher.

Page 163   Box 6.3. John I. Kitsuse, "Societal Reactions to Deviant Behavior," Social Problems 9:3 (Winter, 1962), pp 251, 253.

pREfACE

Most present textbooks on the sociology of deviance can be classified into two distinct organizational styles: topical and theoretical.

A topical style focuses on different patterns or topics of deviance, such as delinquency, drugs, alcohol, prostitution, and crime. Typically, one chapter is devoted to each topic. It is generally organized into a descriptive section detailing the extent and distribution of the deviance, an explanation or theory section, and a section advocating some form of social action. The major disadvantage of this organizational style is that it does not facilitate the learning of sociological theories or explanations of deviance. While sociological explanations are included, they are adapted to the unique aspects of the specific topic of each chapter, such as delinquency or drugs. In some chapters bits of two or three different explanations are merged, and their inconsistencies and contradictions are ignored. While learning about specific patterns of deviance is important, learning sociological explanations of deviance is also important and should be the mainstay of a course in the sociology of deviance.

Recent textbooks on the sociology of deviance have explicitly introduced students to theories of deviance. Two formats are popular. One divides the textbook into two sections. The first section is theoretically organized, briefly discussing different sociological theories of deviance; the second section is topically organized, discussing various types of deviance such as drugs or delinquency. While this format is an improvement over the simple topical organization, in my experience students have difficulty learning theories of deviance abstractly and briefly presented in an introductory section. Furthermore, the theoretical introduction is frequently not well integrated with the topically organized body of the book. The theories described in the introduction tend to be ignored or deemphasized in the topically organized chapters. The other popular format organizes the textbook from the viewpoint of one theoretical perspective. This format overcomes most of the disadvantages of both the topical and theory/topical formats. A sociological theory of deviance is coherently and systematically presented and applied to various topics. Yet the presentation of only one perspective is too limiting for an introductory course in deviance. A beginning course should expand a student's horizons, not limit them to one perspective.

A multiple theory format is needed. This textbook *Perspectives on Deviance*, is organized to introduce the student to the major theoretical perspectives in the sociology of deviance. Each chapter describes one of six theoretical perspectives. It is divided into four sections: one on theory, one on research, one on social policy, and a final section summarizing and criticizing the perspective. The theory section describes the assumptions, concepts, and propositions of the perspective. The research section discusses various studies selected to illustrate the theory and to demonstrate the scope and range of the theory's application to specific patterns of deviance (drugs, prostitution, and so on). Hence, the theory is not discussed in the abstract. The social policy section discusses the implications of the theory and research for social policy, as well as specific policies and programs. The final section summarizes the first three sections and discusses the limitations of the perspective. Additionally, each chapter includes two to four boxes emphasizing a particular point or topic, two to four illustrations or diagrams, and two or three photographs of leading proponents of the perspective. Hence, while the book is theoretically organized, it is not exclusively theoretical. It discusses research and social policy as well as theory, and emphasizes the logical interrelationships among theory, research, and social policy. This organizational format facilitates thinking about deviance in a coherent and systematic fashion, not in terms of just one perspective but in terms of six different perspectives.

Allen E. Liska

Acknowledgments

It is difficult to recall everyone, including undergraduate and graduate professors who contributed, directly or indirectly, to this book. There have been many. However, there are a few whose contributions can easily be identified. First, I would like to acknowledge the contributions of Marshall B. Clinard. As a teacher and mentor at the University of Wisconsin—Madison, he stimulated my interest and directed my studies in the sociology of deviance; and as a colleague, he provided valuable criticism and comments on the book. I would also like to acknowledge the contributions of Bernard N. Meltzer and Nanette J. Davis; both read the entire manuscript and provided valuable insights and editorial comments. I would like to acknowledge the contributions of various colleagues who reviewed specific chapters. Marshall B. Clinard reviewed Chapter Three; Charles R. Tittle reviewed Chapter Four; Victoria L. Swigert and Ronald A. Farrell reviewed Chapters One, Five, and Six; and Richard Quinney reviewed Chapter Seven. Their comments and insights are very much appreciated. I would also like to acknowledge several typists, including Eileen Crary, Gloria Swigert, Barbara Kapelle, and particularly my wife, Jean Liska, who have typed and retyped the manuscript with care and concern. Finally, I would like to acknowledge the contributions of the editors at Prentice-Hall: Edward Stanford, Sociology Editor; Edith Riker, College Production Editor; and Susan Sandler, Copy Editor. Thank you.

Allen E. Liska

cHApTER ONE

iNTRodUCTioN

SUBJECT MATTER OF STUDY

To the general public, the term "deviance" refers to knavery, skulduggery, cheating, unfairness, crime, sneakiness, malingering, cutting corners, immorality, dishonesty, betrayal, graft, corruption, wickedness, and sin (Cohen, 1966). Although the commonality underlying these behaviors is difficult to identify, sociologists have attempted to formally demarcate an area of study which captures the common meaning of the above patterns.

> Dinitz, Dynes, and Clark (1969:4): Regardless of the specific content of behavior, the essential nature of deviance lies in the departure of certain types of behavior from the norms of a particular society at a particular time.
>
> Clinard (1968:28): Deviant behavior is essentially a violation of certain types of group norms; a deviant act is behavior which is proscribed in a certain way. . . . Only those deviations in which behavior is in a disapproved direction and of sufficient degree to exceed the tolerance limit of the community, constitute deviant behavior as it will be used here.
>
> Matza (1969:10): According to any standard dictionary—still the best source of clearly stated nominal definitions—to deviate is to stray as from a path or standard.

Marshall B. Clinard, born 1911, received his B.A. in 1932 and M.A. in 1934 from Stanford University, and his Ph.D. in 1941 from the University of Chicago, and has just recently retired as a Professor of Sociology at the University of Wisconsin. He has been a major contributor to the study of deviance for over three decades and published the first textbook in the contemporary field, *Sociology of Deviant Behavior*, 1957. (Courtesy of Marshall B. Clinard, reprinted by permission.)

While different in some respects, these definitions describe deviance as norm or rule violations, particularly violations which are negatively evaluated in society. Since the 1960s sociologists have also studied deviance as a social definition.

Becker (1963:9): The deviant is one to whom that label has successfully been applied; deviant behavior is behavior that people so label.

Schur (1971:24): Human behavior is deviant to the extent that it comes to be viewed as involving a personal discreditable departure from a group's normative expectations and it elicits interpersonal or collective reactions that serve to isolate, treat, correct, or punish individuals engaged in such behavior.

These definitions shift attention from deviance as a pattern of behavior to deviance as a social definition or label which some people use to describe the behavior of others. The study of deviance as a norm violation and as a social definition constitutes the sociology of deviance.

Deviance as a Norm Violation

To be a bit more precise, the study of norm violations refers to the study of behavior which violates social rules and of the individuals who violate them. In principle the violation of all rules of social behavior is the subject of study: rules against socially harmful behavior, such as homicide, as well as rules against relatively innocuous behavior, such as spitting in public; and rules adhered to by most members of society as well as rules adhered to by small groups or single organizations, such as the work rules at Ford Corporation. In practice, however, research has focused on rules adhered to by most members of society, particularly by the middle and upper class.

The study of norm violations can be classified into the study of norm violation rates and the study of individual norm violations. The former refers to norm violations summed for social-political units (wards, cities, counties, states, and countries), and generally expressed as the number of violations per 1000 population. Various questions about norm violation rates can be asked. 1. What are the rates? Are they higher in some wards, cities, and states than others? Are they increasing or decreasing? 2. What are the social correlates of high and low rates and of increasing and decreasing rates? Do norm violation rates, for example, correlate with the age structure, or the racial, ethnic, and social class composition of a city or state? 3. What are the consequences of high and low norm violation rates on community life? Can a high crime rate, for example, disrupt community life by creating fear in people, or can it build community solidarity by constituting a common problem to which community action can be directed? 4. Finally, why are rates higher in one city, state, or country than another? Why, for example, is the homicide rate generally higher in southern than northern United States cities? Why is it higher in the United States than in Canada or Japan? Why is it increasing in some countries and decreasing in others?

The second major area of study concerns individual norm violations. Generally, the same types of questions are asked. Given that norm violation rates are high or low, who is the norm violator? What characterizes people who violate norms (alcoholics, drug addicts, child molesters, tax evaders)? Are they males or females, old or young, black or white, rich or poor? Most significantly, why do people violate social norms? Why, for example, do different people violate different norms to different degrees? Why do some people violate a norm only once or sporadically, while others are regular or systematic violators?

Norm Violations and Related Areas of Study. Courses in a sociology curriculum are related and frequently overlap. It is difficult for students, and in some cases professors, to clearly differentiate between courses entitled ''Deviance,'' ''Social Problems,'' ''Criminology,'' and ''Mental Illness.'' This section further demarcates the study of norm violations by distinguishing it from the study of social problems, crime, and psychological abnormality.

Social problems are social conditions which the public or government agencies evaluate negatively and wish to change. While numerous norm violations are regarded as social problems, such as delinquency, drug addiction, prostitution, and robbery, norm violations and social problems are not equivalent. On one hand, many social problems do not involve norm violations. For example, traffic congestion, water and air pollution, residential slums, disease, migration, economic depression, and war are certainly social problems, but do not involve norm violations. On the other hand, many norm violations are not considered serious enough to be social problems, such as conversational discourtesy, jaywalking, and profanity.

Crime refers to that behavior which violates the law. Although numerous norm violations are law violations, such as homicide, assault, and rape, norm violations and law violations are not equivalent. Given the process by which laws are formulated in the United States (and most legal entities), the equivalence between laws and norms is a subject for study. Many crimes are not norm violations, such as nonmarital sex, driving over fifty-five miles per hour on highways, price fixing, lobbying, and gambling. Alcohol prohibition during the 1930s is particularly illustrative. The buying and selling of alcohol was illegal, although alcohol drinking approximated a national norm, especially in urban areas. Marijuana smoking may be a comparable contemporary case. On the other hand, many norm violations are not law violations, such as expelling air through the mouth (belching) while in the presence of others, using profane language, interracial marriage, and marriage between people of widely different ages, especially when the male is younger.

Definitions of psychological abnormality are shaped by general theoretical frameworks. Psychoanalysts define abnormality in terms of emotional problems; cognitive theorists define abnormality in terms of nonrational decision making; and behaviorists discuss abnormality in terms of behavior which is nonproductive for the individual. Whatever the exact definition, psychological abnormality is not equivalent to norm-violating behavior. One can suffer from emotional problems and make nonrational decisions but still conform to social norms of behavior. In fact, some psychiatrists talk of compulsive conformity. On the other hand, one can violate social norms without being psychologically abnormal. Many sociologists argue that the vast bulk of norm violations are committed, not as a result of emotional problems, cognitive distortions, or faulty decision making, but by emotionally healthy people making rational decisions, frequently for political, social, and economic gains (robbery, burglary, tax evasion, and false advertising).

To summarize, deviance as norm violations refers to actions which can be studied in other sociology courses and under other conceptual rubrics. Some norm violations are law violations; some are social problems; and some reflect psychological abnormalities. Conceptual overlap, however, is not equivalence. Many norm violations are not law violations and many law violations are not norm violations; many social problems are not norm violations and many norm violations are not social problems; and while psychological abnormality may be reflected in norm violations, the vast number of norm violators are not psychologically abnormal.

Deviance as a Societal Definition

The study of deviance as a social definition centers on two questions: *What* is labeled deviance and *who* is labeled deviant? The former refers to the study of the emergence and development of social norms and social labels for describing norm violations and violators and the latter refers to the study of how such labels are used in specific cases and situations.

What is Labeled Deviance? While the norm violations approach to deviance assumes that norms vary and change, it does not conceptualize normative change as an object of study. Norms simply constitute a reference point from which behavior is judged to be deviant or nondeviant; and when the norms of the different segments of society conflict (lower class versus middle class; black versus white; young versus old), the norms of the more powerful segments tend to be accepted as reference points.

Recently, sociologists have emphasized the emerging, changing, and conflicting character of norms. Some have focused on the historical emergence of general societal norms, asking, for example, why the norms of alcohol consumption in Italy are different from those in the United States, and why the norms of sexual behavior in Mexico are different from those in the United States. Other sociologists have focused on the situational emergence of norms, arguing that general norms of behavior are frequently very ambiguous as behavioral directives in specific situations. For example, norms governing alcohol consumption vary, not only from country to country and from region to region within a country, but also within very limited space-time contexts. The norms of proper drinking depend on the day of the week (weekend, weekday), the time of day (morning, evening), and even the duration of time elapsed at a party. Greater freedom is frequently permitted as a party goes on. The same is true of sexual behavior. Flirting with someone's spouse may be permissible at one A.M. at a party, but not during the morning while grocery shopping.

Sociologists have also examined the historical emergence of social labels used to describe norm violations and violators. This is not just a question of semantics, but involves the issue of how norm violations and violators are socially treated. The category "mental illness" is instructive. Today people who experience emotional problems and cognitive distortions are treated in many ways like people with a physical illness (Scheff, 1966). They are treated by experts trained in medicine (psychiatrists) and are frequently treated in hospitals. This social response has not always been the case in the United States and presently is not the case in all parts of the world. In the United States at one time or another such people have been labeled as evil, lazy, and witches, and, accordingly, have experienced a very different social response.

A special case of the question (what is labeled deviance?) is the study of legal norms (laws) and the categories used to describe law violations and violators. Special attention has focused on studying how some norms are transformed into laws, thus making some norm violators law violators (Quinney, 1970). For example, marijuana smoking is illegal, but cigarette smoking and alcohol use are not. Why? Prostitution is illegal in most but not all states and cities. Why? The emergence of categories to describe law violations and violators is also studied. For example, juvenile norm violators constitute a formal legal category in the United States. They are treated under a special set of legal procedures (juvenile court) and are subject to a special set of court dispositions. Why?

Who is Labeled Deviant? This question refers to the study of how existing categories for describing norm violators and violations are applied in specific situations (Lemert, 1967). Of all individuals who violate norms only some are socially identified and labeled by their families, friends, colleagues, the public, and organizational authorities. Others somehow escape the social label. Their norm violations remain socially unnoticed. Why? Under what circumstances are people identified as norm violators (delinquents, drug addicts, witches, mentally ill)? On the other hand, some nonnorm violators are falsely identified as norm violators. Why? Under what circumstances are people falsely labeled as norm violators?

These concerns are important because of the psychological and social consequences of being publicly identified—correctly or falsely—as a norm violator (drug addict, alcoholic, tax evader, embezzler). A considerable amount of study has been directed toward discovering the extent to which such public labels affect people's social relationships (family relations, friendship patterns, and economic opportunities), and the extent to which this in turn influences future norm violations.

As a special case of this question (who is labeled?), attention has been directed toward the study of how existing legal categories are applied to individuals and the consequences of such applications. Like norm violators, only some law violators are publicly identified; of those who violate laws only some are arrested; of those arrested, only some are prosecuted; and of those prosecuted, only some are sentenced. What affects the degree to which law violators get involved in the legal process and become officially labeled, and what are the psychological and social consequences of different degrees of involvement? To what extent, for example, does imprisonment or prosecution affect psychological dispositions and social relationships, and to what extent do the latter in turn affect future law violations?

Generally, the social definitional approach to the sociology of deviance focuses on the following questions:

1. What is labeled deviance?
   a. What are the general and situational social norms, and how have they emerged?
   b. What are the social categories and labels for describing norm violators and norm violations, and how have they emerged?
   c. As a special case of the above, what are the legal norms (laws) and legal categories for describing law violators and violations, and how have they emerged?
2. Who is labeled deviant?
   a. Who is socially labeled a norm violator?
   b. What are the consequences of being labeled a norm violator?
   c. As a special case of the above, who is labeled a law violator, and what are the consequences of being so labeled?

LEVELS OF EXPLANATION

Now that the subject matter of the sociology of deviance has been defined, this section presents a brief examination of biological, psychological, and social levels of explanation.

Biological Theories

Biological theories ignore the study of deviance as a social definition and focus on norm violations. In one manner or another they assume that certain biological structures or processes cause norm violations. The specific underlying structures or processes vary from theory to theory and are frequently quite complex. Two simple examples are diagrammed in Figure 1.1, where X (a biological process or structure) causes certain physical characteristics and norm violations (diagram A), and where X causes certain physical and psychological characteristics, the latter of which causes norm violations (diagram B).

Up until the last decade little research focused on directly linking biological structures or processes with norm violations. Instead, research focused on the relationship between certain physical characteristics and norm violations, mainly

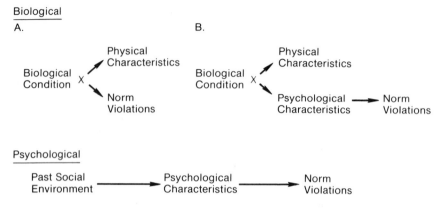

Figure 1.1. Causal Logic Underlying Biological and Psychological Theories of Norm Violations

law violations. For example, Cesare Lombroso (1876) argued that criminal behavior is a manifestation of a "lower" position on the evolutionary scale (see Wolfgang, 1960). Criminals are evolutionary throwbacks (atavists), a biological state manifested in a variety of physical or anatomical characteristics, such as protruding jaws and high cheekbones found in animals low on the evolutionary scale. Since this underlying biological state (atavism) was not clearly defined or measurable, Lombroso's research attempted to link observable physical characteristics with criminal behavior. Other students of the time (such as Enrico Ferri, a student of Lombroso) suggested that such biological states are inherited. As evidence for these theories has not been found, today they are only of historical interest.

The work of William Sheldon (1949) is one of the most popular extensions of past biological theories. While there is no concern with evolutionary throwbacks or inheritance, the general logic is similar to that of earlier biological theories. Essentially, Sheldon argues that certain types of germ plasm (not identified or measured) produce physiological and chemical states which are manifested in anatomical and psychological characteristics. He classifies people into various physiological and psychological types, and associates criminal behavior with a muscular and energetic physical type (mesomorphic) and an assertive and vigorous psychological type (somatotonic). Like most earlier biological theories the supporting evidence is weak and controversial.

During the mid-1960s and 1970s interest emerged in chromosomal abnormalities as a cause of norm- and law-violating behavior. The normal male complement is 46XY chromosomes and the normal female complement is 46XX chromosomes. An additional Y is quite rare (1.3 times per 1000 cases). Research has focused on the 47XXY complement (also known as the Klinefelter's syndrome) and the 47XYY complement. Reports in the mid and late 1960s noted that 47XYY males are tall, aggressive, and have histories of criminal behavior (Shah and Roth, 1974). Some studies, for example, reported that a relatively high proportion of imprisoned males have an XYY chromosome complement, well-developed genitalia, are quite tall, and show signs of mental deficiency. Additional studies have reported that males with an extra Y are more prone to psychopathology and are convicted of crimes at a young age. Because of these studies, some investigators have concluded that an extra Y chromosome in some manner and via some causal process predisposes males to engage in antisocial behavior. This research was publicized during the trial of Richard Speck, who was accused and convicted of murdering eight nurses in 1968. His attorney claimed that Speck had an XYY chromosome complement, thereby suggesting that he was not responsible for his actions; however, it was later concluded that Speck was a normal XY.

More recent studies in the 1970s (see Shah and Roth, 1974) suggest more cautious conclusions. In fact, various studies report no relationship at all between an extra Y chromosome and law-violating and antisocial behavior. Yet, even if such a relationship could be demonstrated, what does it prove? It does not suggest how or why a chromosome abnormality affects behavior generally or law-violating behavior specifically. Various social explanations have been suggested. Taylor et al. (1973) have argued that perhaps the tallness of XYY individuals excludes them from conventional friendship groups and occupations, which in turn may cause them to violate norms. Furthermore, XYY researchers (like so many biological researchers) ignore the fact that the XYY complement (like most other abnormal states) is rare, and thus could account for only a microscopic proportion of the volume of deviance in contemporary America.

In an extensive review of the biology literature, Shah and Roth (1974) discuss the following areas of contemporary biological research:

1. Tumors and other destructive or inflammatory processes of the limbic system.
2. Epileptic seizures, including those behaviors occurring during a seizure, between seizures, and after a seizure, and electroencephalogram abnormalities with or without seizures.
3. Endocrine abnormalities, especially levels of testosterone (male hormone) or progesterone and estrogen (female hormone).
4. Prenatal birth complications.
5. Brain dysfunction in children and adolescents, especially as related to EEG and other neurological abnormalities, hyperkinesis, and reading disorders.
6. Genetic research on the inheritable components in personality disorders.
7. Chromosomal abnormalities.
8. The association between physique, temperament, and behavior.

Criticism of biotheories includes the following: 1. Supporting research is meager. 2. Biotheories fail to examine the processes by which biological states cause norm violations. Why or how does atavism, mesomorphism, or XYY chromosome complements cause psychological states or norm violations?

3. Biotheories tend to focus on biological inferiority or abnormality, thereby restricting their application to a limited portion of the American population. Yet official records and self-report surveys show that norm and law violations are widespread throughout the American population. Hence biotheories remain largely irrelevant in explaining the bulk of law and norm violations in the United States. 4. Biotheories do not examine deviance as a social definition, for questions of social definition and meaning are not well suited to explanation on the biological level.

Psychological Theories

Psychological theories also ignore the study of deviance as a social definition and focus on norm violations. They explain norm violations in terms of processes and structures of the individual psyche, which in turn are generally explained in terms of past social experiences. The general causal logic is described in Figure 1.1.

As a subtype of psychological theories, personality theories have been very significant. They analyze people in terms of general psychic characteristics (tendencies, needs, motives, and drives) assumed to affect behavior over a variety of social situations. A considerable amount of effort has gone into constructing personality scales, such as the Minnesota Multiphasic Personality Inventory (MMPI), examining how people develop certain personality characteristics like aggressiveness and sociability, and studying how such characteristics influence behavior in a variety of social situations. The immediate social situation is viewed as having relatively little influence on behavior other than in providing a medium for the expression of general personality characteristics.

In respect to norm violations, personality theories can be classified into two general types. One type explains norm violations as an outcome of normal personality characteristics which also cause conformist behavior. For example, homicide is sometimes explained as a manifestation of an aggressive personality, and homosexuality is sometimes explained as a manifestation of psychological dependency. These theories, however, do not clearly explain why only a small percentage of aggressive personalities commit homicide and why only a small percentage of dependent personalities become homosexuals. To circumvent this problem, some theorists have argued that only certain personalities violate certain norms in certain social situations, while in other situations the same personalities manifest conformist behavior. For example, sexuality as a personality characteristic may be expressed in homosexual behavior in social situations where heterosexual contacts are restricted, such as prisons, but where heterosexual contacts are available, sexuality is expressed in heterosexual behavior.

The McCords' (1960) theory of alcoholism is another such example. They argue that all people have dependency needs, generally satisfied during childhood in parent-child relationships, although in some cases these needs are not satisfied and must be satisfied in adolescence and adulthood. This is particularly a problem in the United States, where adolescent and adult males are expected to be independent. The personality need for dependence clashes with the social demands for independence, creating a psychological conflict. Alcoholism relieves the associated guilt and anxiety, and relaxes social inhibitions, thereby permitting the expression of dependency needs.

A second type of personality theory explains norm violations as expressions of abnormal personalities, termed psychopathic and sociopathic personalities. The meaning of these concepts is vague (Hakeem, 1958; Mechanic, 1969), generally referring to a variety of "undesirable" psychological characteristics, such as acting on impulse, misrepresenting reality, and lacking the capacity to feel shame and remorse. Cason (1943) recorded fifty-five such characteristics in the literature and Cleckley (1950) recorded sixteen. The link between these characteristics and norm and law violations is equally vague. Frequently, norm violations are used to infer the existence of psychopathology and sociopathology, which are then used to explain norm and law violations! Some psychiatrists thus consider psychopathology and sociopathology as "wastebasket" or "residual" concepts, referring to no clear psychological entities and used to describe a variety of otherwise unclassifiable psychological states and socially problematic behaviors.

Generally, efforts to explain norm violations in terms of personality characteristics, normal or abnormal, have not been very successful, although relationships between norm violations and personality characteristics are frequently reported. Schuessler and Cressey (1950), examining 113 studies using 30 different personality tests, report that 42 percent of the studies found some personality differences between criminals and noncriminals. Updating this study, Waldo and Dinitz (1967) examined ninety-four studies using twenty-nine tests between 1950 and 1965, and report that 81 percent of the studies found some differences between these two groups. These reports, however, are not very convincing, for in many of the studies the differences are quite minor, and in most it is not clear whether the personality characteristics existed before the violations and thus may be a cause of them, or after the violations and thus may be an effect of them. For example, being publicly identified and convicted as a regular drug user may cause a good deal of anxiety and psychological disorder, thereby producing a relationship between anxiety and drug use.

Generally, personality theories have been criticized for emphasizing rare and abnormal personalities in explaining norm violations, for ignoring or at least deemphasizing the present social situation in explaining norm violations, and for ignoring the study of deviance as a social definition.

This discussion does not thoroughly review biological and psychological theories and research. Some theories are far more sophisticated and complicated than those discussed (Eysenck, 1970), and some incorporate social variables. This review only describes the general logic of biological and psychological theories of norm violations as a point of departure and comparison for the discussion of social theories.

Social Theories

Whereas biological and psychological theories emphasize biological and psychological processes and structures in explaining deviance as a norm violation (particularly individual norm violations rather than group rates), social theories emphasize social processes and structures in explaining deviance as a norm violation (individual violations and group rates) and as a social definition (group definitions and individual applications).

Social theories which focus on norm violations can be classified into those which emphasize structure and those which emphasize process. Theories which explain norm violations in terms of repetitive stable patterns of social interaction are referred to as structural. Merton's (1938) theory of anomie, for example, is a structural theory. He argues that norm violations are a direct result of the degree of continuity between cultural goals into which people are socialized and structural opportunities to achieve these goals; cultural-structural discontinuity produces stress in people, which in turn is expressed in norm violations. Societies with a high level of discontinuity should show high rates of norm violations; and those individuals most exposed to the discontinuities should show the highest level of norm violations. Durkheim's (1951) theory of suicide is another example of a structural theory. Durkheim explains differences in suicide rates between countries by differences in the level of social cohesion (the strength of social ties or relationships) between countries. He argues that as social cohesion decreases, the level of dissatisfaction with life increases (expressed as stress, alienation, and disorientation) and suicide rates consequently increase.

Social process refers to a continuing change or development of social interaction over time. Processual theories explain norm violations in terms of a sequence of stages by which the violations develop. Becker's (1963) theory of regular marijuana use examines the sequence of stages by which people become regular marijuana users. He argues that people must first learn to correctly smoke the drug, then to identify its effects, and finally to define them as pleasurable. Becker links these stages of learning to a network of interpersonal relationships. In one sense, the final stage (defining the effects as pleasurable) is the immediate "cause" of regular marijuana use; processual theories, however, emphasize the sequence of steps by which people become involved and arrive at that final stage.

Theories of deviance as a social definition can also be classified as structural or processual. Structural theories attempt to explain social definitions of deviance in terms of repetitive stable patterns of social interaction. Quinney (1977), for example, argues that the behavior which becomes defined as crime in a society depends on the economic structure of society. Certain patterns of behavior become criminalized in a capitalist society, whereas others become criminalized in a socialist society. He further argues that position within the social structure (upper class or lower class) of a capitalist society strongly affects who is defined or labeled a criminal.

Processual theories have come to be particularly significant in explaining deviance as a social definition. At the societal level, research has traced the development of various social definitions of deviance (such as mental illness and alcoholism) over decades and even centuries, and has examined the stages by which social definitions are transformed into legal definitions. At the individual level, theories have outlined the interaction sequences or stages by which a person's social identity is transformed from that of a nondeviant to that of a deviant. Scheff (1966), for example, specifies the stages by which a public identity is transformed from normal to mentally ill.

Generally, in contrast to biological and psychological theories, social theories examine deviance as a social definition as well as a norm violation at the macro as well as the micro level, and explain deviance in terms of social structures and processes rather than psychological and biological structures and processes. Like biological and psychological theories, social theories are subject to criticism. Concepts, for example, are frequently vaguely defined and measured, and the supporting research is frequently weak. These criticisms will be discussed in the chapters to follow.

In sum, it is not always easy to distinguish theories by the level of explanation. Many theories are biopsychological, including both biological and psychological conditions in their explanation; and many theories are social-psychological, including both social and psychological conditions in their explanation. Yet even these tend to emphasize one rather than another level of explanation. For the most part, biological and psychological theories restrict their focus to norm violations; questions of social definition tend to be ignored. Biological theories explain norm violations at the biological level, in terms of genes and chromosomes; psychological theories explain norm violations in terms of psychological factors, such as personality types; and social theories explain both norm violations and social definitions in terms of social processes and structures.

A THEORETICAL PERSPECTIVE

A theoretical perspective is a conceptual scheme which functions as follows:

1. It defines some part of the social world as problematic, that is, deserving of study, and specifies certain questions for study (subject matter).
2. It provides answers to these questions (theory).
3. It includes empirical tests of the theory (research).
4. Based on theory and research, it suggests directions for social policy.

This book, then, while theoretically organized, is not exclusively theoretical; it emphasizes the integration of subject matter, theory, research, and social policy.

Subject Matter

Previous sections have described the subject matter of the sociology of deviance as the study of norm violations and social definitions. This discussion need not be repeated here, except to note that each perspective specifies and highlights different aspects of these two general areas of study. The structural/functionalism, Chicago, and social control perspectives focus on norm violations, each specifying somewhat different questions for examination; and the labeling, ethnomethodology, and conflict perspectives focus on social definitions, each also specifying different questions for examination.

Theory

Of the four components of a perspective, theory is the most difficult to define, as the concept is used in different ways by different sociologists (see Gibbs, 1972; Stinchcombe, 1968; Blalock, 1969). Here the term is used to mean an interrelated set of statements or propositions used to explain the events or things which constitute the subject matter of a perspective. Explanation is the key term in the definition, but like the term "theory" it, too, is vaguely defined and loosely used by sociologists (Brown, 1963).

Many sociologists subscribe to the deductive interpretation or meaning of explanation. An event is said to be explained when it is deduced from a set of statements or propositions. Consider the following:

For countries, if unemployment increases, norm violations increase.
In country "A" unemployment increased from 1960 to 1970.
Therefore, in country "A" norm violations should increase from 1960 to 1970.

If norm violations increase in country "A" from 1960 to 1970, this fact is then said to be explained, as it is deduced from a set of propositions (major and minor premises in a deduction system). The major premise (if unemployment increases, norm violations increase), then, becomes the subject of explanation. It too is said to be explained when it is deduced from an even more general set of propositions.

For countries, if status changes increase, norm violations increase.
Unemployment is a status.
Therefore, if unemployment increases, norm violations should increase.

This logical process is continued until all the events and things defined as the subject matter of the perspective are deduced, and until all the major premises are accepted as needing no further explanation.

While explanation as logical deduction is accepted by some sociologists, others are concerned less with the logical form of an interrelated set of statements and more with the substance of what is asserted. Some sociologists argue that statements must assert something about the values or motives of people to constitute an explanation, while others argue that statements must assert something about causality to count as an explanation. The latter is particularly important as many—if not most—sociologists adhere to it in their everyday work. In effect, they argue that an event or thing is explained when its cause is identified. "Cause," however, is a vaguely defined concept.

While the debate over the properties—logical and substantive—of an explanation is interesting and worthy of consideration, it need not be the focus of attention of a textbook on the sociology of deviance—even one organized by theoretical perspectives. Explanation will generally be defined here as an answer to the question: why do the events occur and the things exist which constitute the subject matter of a perspective? A theory is, then, defined as an interrelated set of statements used to answer this question. By using a broad definition, the theory of each perspective can be described and evaluated in its own terms. Some perspectives attempt to answer the "why" question by deducing the events and things in question; some attempt to answer the "why" question with assertions about causality; and others employ still different criteria in answering the "why" question.

In describing a set of interrelated assertions it is worthwhile to distinguish between those which are testable (subject to empirical observation) and those which are not. (The former will be discussed in the research section.) The latter are frequently referred to as theoretical assumptions; some are explicitly stated, and some are unstated but implicit assertions of the theory.

All six theoretical perspectives make assumptions about the extent to which society is orderly. Some theoretical perspectives assume—implicitly or explicitly—that society is essentially orderly, that the norms of behavior are clear, consistent, and stable; other perspectives assume that society is essentially disorderly, that the norms of behavior are vague, inconsistent, and unstable. These assumptions are important. They affect the subject matter of study and the nature of the testable propositions. Perspectives which assume society to be essentially orderly tend to define norm violations as significant and as the proper subject matter of the sociology of deviance. However, if norms are assumed to be vague, inconsistent, and unstable, norm violations are difficult—if not impossible—to define, and, consequently, difficult to study. Perspectives which view society as essentially disorderly tend to study the emergence of norms and social definitions of deviance.

All six perspectives also make assumptions about the link between the individual and society. Some perspectives assume that individuals are passive in their interaction with society, implying that individuals are acted upon by the social environment and come to reflect the objective characteristics of that environment.

Other perspectives assume that individuals act upon the social environment. They select environments in which to behave; they select aspects of the environment toward which to direct their attention; they interpret the environment; and they attempt to change the environment. With the possible exception of the Chicago School, the perspectives which focus on norm violations (structural/functionalism, and social control) tend to view individuals as more passive than active. They generally explain norm violations in terms of the influence of objective social environments. Social definitional perspectives are more difficult to locate on this dimension. The ethnomethodology perspective takes an active conceptualization of individuals, leading to the study of how people and organizations construct social norms and categories for describing norm violators (Cicourel, 1968). The conflict perspective (particularly traditional Marxism) takes a somewhat more passive conceptualization, leading to the study of how the economic and political order of society affects social definitions of deviance.

Assumptions about the nature of society (orderly or disorderly) and nature of the relationship between individuals and society (active or passive) influence the substance of testable assertions and even the subject matter of study; and the latter in turn influences the nature of these assumptions.

It is not necessary to disentangle the degree of mutual influence here; it is important, however, to appreciate the significance of identifying the untestable and sometimes implicit assertions of a theory.

Research

Sociologists generally define research as the systematic observation of the social world. They disagree, however, upon the techniques for making valid observations and types of observations necessary to validate theories.

Observing Norm Violations. Considerable debate has ensued as to the most valid techniques for systematically measuring norm violations. These techniques can be classified under three general categories: official records, self-reports, and direct observations.

Records of socially problematic norm violations, such as alcoholism, drug use, suicide, mental illness, and crime, are maintained by various public and private agencies. Crime statistics, for example, are maintained by police departments and courts at the municipal, county, state, and national levels. Since the 1930s the FBI has attempted to organize these statistics into reasonably comparable categories, referred to as the Uniform Crime Reports. These records are generally used to estimate the volume of crime, the degree to which it is increasing or decreasing, and its distribution in geographical and social space, and to test various theories.

Are the records valid? In answering this question one must critically review the components in their construction. Official records include only those norm violations known to authorities. Violations become known to authorities by two routes:

either the public observes and reports them or authorities detect them. This process suggests two types of errors. Official records probably underestimate the real rates, for many norm violations are neither reported to the recording agency by the public nor detected by the agency. Perhaps more important, the underestimations may also be biased in unforeseen directions. The level of public reporting or official detection may be higher in some areas, for some time periods and for some social categories than for others.

For example, official records show that norm violations are generally higher in urban than rural areas. Does this difference reflect differences in real rates, differences in reportability, or differences in detectability? As to reportability, research suggests that the level of informal social control is considerably lower in urban than in rural areas; urbanites are prone to rely on formal social control agencies. Detectability may also be higher in urban than rural areas. Studies suggest that urban social control agencies are better equipped and considerably larger per capita than rural social control agencies. Hence, if the level of norm violations is similar for urban and rural areas, we should expect official records to show that norm violations are higher in urban than rural areas.

Historical comparisons are also problematic. Official statistics frequently show that norm violations have increased over the last twenty or thirty years. Perhaps only reportability and detectability have increased. As the United States has become more urban, informal social control processes have become less effective; consequently, formal social control agencies have expanded, thereby increasing reportability and detectability. Hence, even if the level of norm violations has remained constant over this time span, official records would probably show that violations have increased.

Generally, official rates reflect three components: real rates, reportability, and detectability. Until reportability and detectability effects can be estimated, the extent to which official records reflect real rates cannot be known. (See Box 1.2.)

In an effort to solve some of these issues, sociologists have turned to self-reports of norm violators and of the victims of norm violators. Bypassing official agencies, self-reports avoid some of the problems associated with detectability and reportability.

Victimization studies involve a face-to-face interview in which members of a household or a business are asked to reveal what crimes have been committed against them over some time period, generally the last six months or year. In the United States these studies were first initiated by the Bureau of Social Science Research in a study of Washington, D.C., in 1966, and by the National Opinion Research Center in a national study. Subsequently, a National Crime Panel was formed within the U.S. Department of Justice to regularly conduct victimization studies. During the early and middle 1970s the Panel conducted a continuous national survey and periodic surveys of certain urban areas directed by the Bureau of the Census.

Box 1.2 CRIMES IN BOSTON FROM 1849 TO 1951

The Uniform Crime Reports were first assembled in the 1930s; thus, most trend studies examine rates from the 1930s to today. However, some cities, mainly in the East, have kept records from much earlier periods. Ferdinand (1967), in a study of Boston from 1849 to 1951, reports that crimes have regularly decreased since 1849, although there are various minor counter trends. Perhaps the time period measured by the UCR simply reflects such a counter trend and the United States is experiencing a long-term decrease in crime!

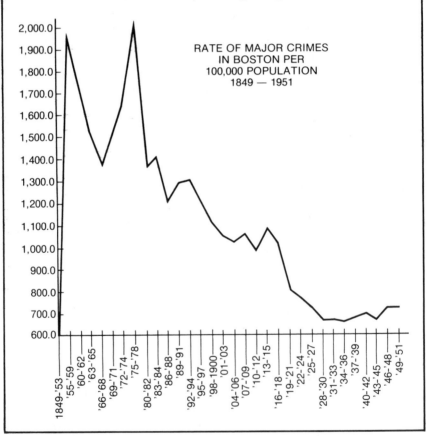

RATE OF MAJOR CRIMES
IN BOSTON PER
100,000 POPULATION
1849 — 1951

What have these studies discovered about crime, particularly regarding the issues of underestimation and biased estimation of the Uniform Crime Reports? Regarding the former, the victimization surveys suggest that the UCR vastly underestimates the level of crime. The figures in Table 1.1 compare the results of the National Opinion Research Center survey and the UCR for one year. The victimization survey shows about double the amount of crime shown in the UCR,

Table 1.1 ESTIMATED RATES OF CRIMES (1965)

Crime	NORC SAMPLE Estimated rate per 100,000 population	Uniform Crime[a] Reports: 1965 total per 100,000 population	Uniform Crime[b] Reports: 1965 (individual or residential rates) per 100,000 population
Homicide	3.0	5.1	5.1
Forcible rape	42.5	11.6	11.6
Robbery	94.0	61.4	61.4
Aggravated assault	218.3	106.6	106.6
Burglary	949.1	605.3	296.6
Larceny ($50+)	606.5	393.3	267.4
Vehicle theft	206.2	251.0	226.0[c]
Total	2,119.6	1,434.3	974.7
		N . . (32,966)	

[a] Crime in the United States, 1965 Uniform Crime Reports, Table 1, p. 51.

[b] Crime in the United States, 1965 Uniform Crime Reports, Table 14, Page 105, shows for burglary and larcenies the number of residential and individual crimes. The overall rate per 100,000 population is therefore reduced by the proportion of these crimes that occurred to individuals. Since all robberies to individuals were included in the NORC sample regardless of whether the victim was acting as an individual or as part of an organization, the total UCR figures were used as comparison.

[c] The reduction of the UCR auto theft rate by 10 percent is based on the figures of the Automobile Manufacturers Association (Automobile Facts & Figures, 1966), showing 10 per cent of all cars owned by leasing-rental agencies and private and governmental fleets. The Chicago Police Department's auto theft personnel confirmed that about 7–10 per cent of stolen cars recovered were from fleet and rental sources and other non-individually owned sources.

although the exact difference depends on the type of crime. Forcible rape is four times higher in the survey than in the UCR, but the level of vehicle theft is the same in both. (While women may be reluctant to report being raped to the police, people generally report vehicle theft, as insurance reimbursement requires a police report.) Note, however, that the ranking of the crimes by their rate of occurrence is the same for both the UCR and the NORC survey. It is highest for burglary and lowest for homicide. Do the victimization reports suggest any differences in the spatial and social distribution of crime than suggested by the UCR? One approach to this question is to compare the ranking of cities by crime rates as yielded by the UCR and the surveys. Clarren and Schwartz (1976) report that the similarity in the rankings depends on the type of crime. It is quite strong for property crimes (robbery, burglary, and auto theft), but quite weak for personal crimes (rape and aggravated assault).

Victimization surveys, while avoiding some of the problems associated with official statistics, have their own validity problems. They are surveys and are thus hampered by the problems associated with all surveys. There are problems with the use of households and commercial establishments as the sampling units. As the victimizations of transients are ignored, crime in cities with a high transient population is underestimated. There are memory problems. People forget what has happened to them, and are frequently unable to place victimizations within the time frames asked for by the interviewer. People also lie. Many people may not wish to admit being victimized for certain types of crimes; others may wish to indulge the interviewer by admitting acts that have not happened. Most importantly, victimization studies provide very little information about offenders.

This brings us to the use of offender self-reports. Sociologists have used both face-to-face interviews and anonymous questionnaires in asking people what norms they have violated over some period of time. For example, an interviewer may ask, "Over the last six months how many times have you stolen things valued over two dollars (do not remember, never, once, twice, three or more times)." Hundreds of such studies have been conducted, although none is of the scope of the recent victimization studies.

What do these studies show? They support the victimization studies, showing that official records strongly underestimate the volume of crime and delinquency; and they suggest some bias in official records. For example, official records strongly show that blacks are far more delinquent than whites. This finding is not clearly confirmed by self-reports (Hirschi, 1969; Gould, 1969). The fact that self-reports are much more ambiguous about the race-delinquency relationship should make us cautious in accepting the validity of official records.

In considering the validity of offender self-reports the following should be noted. As surveys they are susceptible to some of the same types of problems as victimization studies: transients are ignored and respondents have memory lapses and they lie. The latter may be more important in offender than victim self-reports. While people may be willing to admit being the object of a serious offense, they may be much less likely to admit committing one. How many people would admit, even on a seemingly anonymous questionnaire, to having committed rape and homicide? Self-reports, therefore, may be limited to the study of nonserious norm violations. Clark and Tifft (1966) argue that for nonserious delinquency (about 90 percent of all delinquency) self-reports are a reasonably valid technique; for the ranking of juveniles on a delinquency scale, using their self-reports and using a polygraph (lie detector) examination give very similar results.

To circumvent the problems encountered with official records and self-reports, some sociologists advocate the direct observation of behavior. In discussing the advantages and disadvantages of direct observation it is useful to distinguish between natural observation and experiments.

Natural observation refers to the observation of norm violations in the day to day situations in which they normally occur. Sociologists distinguish between participant and nonparticipant observation. The nonparticipant observer locates himself or herself so as to be in a position to observe ongoing behavior. For example, in the study of interaction between homosexuals, the researcher might spend time in homosexual bars; in the study of prostitution the researcher might spend time at certain street corners and bars; and in the study of juvenile delinquency the researcher might spend time with juvenile gangs. Such observational techniques, however, can sometimes alter the course of the interaction. A heterosexual in a homosexual bar may well be noticed and consequently affect the interaction patterns; and an observer on a street corner or bar may well be noticed and defined by prostitutes as a plainclothes detective or a journalist, thereby altering the interaction between prostitutes and clients. To avoid being an intruder, the observer must blend into the action. One strategy is to participate in the action (participant observation) whenever possible. The observer can thus get very close to the action without being intrusive, learning things that might not be revealed to outside researchers.

While natural observations allow sociologists to get very close to the action and perhaps to observe things which might not be revealed in self-reports and official records, like most other techniques they too have their limitations. Natural observation cannot be used to examine norm violation rates across political and geographical units. Given the time involved in the observation of each case, natural observation is limited to very small samples in small geographical areas. Natural observation can also be quite unreliable, as the observations can easily reflect the values, concerns, and biases of the observer. Finally, the type of norm violations which can be observed is limited. Many norm violations do not occur frequently and others are committed so as to go undetected, such as rape, homicide, suicide, and child molesting. The limitation is particularly true for participant observation; it is certainly not the recommended method for studying suicide!

Many sociologists have argued that norm violations can be reliably observed under specially constructed circumstances designed to induce them, termed social experiments. In these circumstances various observers can simultaneously observe the behavior, record its occurrence, and continually reproduce it. Social experiments have been conducted in both field and laboratory settings. For example, to study the relative honesty of Parisians, Athenians, and Bostonians, Feldman (1968) had shoppers overpay cashiers and recorded the percentage in each country who kept the money. In a series of laboratory studies, Bandura and his associates (1973) studied the effect of aggressive models on physical aggression in children. Children observed different forms of aggressive behavior (such as aggression in face-to-face situations and on television); researchers then observed the extent to which these children manifested physical aggression in subsequent play sessions.

There are also disadvantages with experiments. For example, since experiments induce people to violate norms, only nonserious norm violations can be studied. Sociologists cannot induce people into suicide, homicide, rape, drug addiction, or alcoholism for the benefit of their research. Experimenters, however, argue that the processes which account for nonserious forms of norm violations (keeping the change when overpaid) are the same or similar to those which explain more serious types (auto theft). This point has yet to be proven. Also, as we are not sure how much experimentally induced behavior is simply a response to the fact that people know they are being studied, it is difficult to generalize laboratory findings to norm violations in natural settings.

To summarize, techniques of observing norm violations can be classified into three categories: official records, self-reports, and direct observations. Each has a unique set of advantages and disadvantages, making it suitable for the study of some research questions and norm violations but not others. As all of the measurement techniques include some degree of error, it is the responsibility of the researcher to know which techniques will minimize error in the study of particular issues and norm violations.

Theoretical Correspondence. In addition to accurately describing the subject matter of study, to validate a theory, observations must correspond to the assertions of the theory. For causal theories the rules of observational correspondence can be briefly summarized as follows:

1. When the causal events or things occur, then the events or things to be explained should occur; and when the causal events and things do not occur, then the events or things to be explained should not occur. To support a causal theory, observations should correspond to this pattern, thereby showing a relationship between cause and effect. In social research this rule is generally interpreted within a probabilistic framework. For example, if unemployment is asserted to be the cause of drug addiction, when unemployment occurs the probability of drug addiction should be significantly higher than when unemployment does not occur.

2. In addition to showing a relationship between cause and effect, observations should show that the causal event or thing occurs before the occurrence of the event or thing to be explained. In regard to the previous example, drug addiction may cause unemployment or unemployment may cause drug addiction. To support the latter assertion, observations must show that unemployment temporally precedes drug addiction.

3. Observations must show that other events or things do not cause the relationship between the hypothesized cause and effect. For example, unemployment and drug addiction may be related, not because one causes the other, but because another factor, low education, causes both.

The description of these observational correspondence rules is simplified, ignoring complications and complexities which occur because of multiple causes, measurement errors, and sampling errors. Numerous sampling, measurement, and statistical techniques have been developed to deal with these complexities. They need not be discussed here. At this time it is only necessary to know that to validate a theory, observations must not only accurately describe the subject matter, but must correspond to the assertions of the theory.

Social Policy

The term "social policy" refers to a directed course of action to change people or society. Concerning norm violations, actions are directed toward the prevention of norm violations and the treatment or rehabilitation of norm violators; and concerning societal definitions, actions are directed toward changing various social norms (drinking norms), changing the categories used to describe norm violators (medical versus criminal terms), and reducing the consequences of being publicly labeled a norm violator. While government policies are of central importance, the policies of other organizations and of concerned individuals should not be ignored. Business corporations have formulated programs to reduce norm violations (absenteeism and alcoholism of employees); specific organizations have been formed by concerned citizens to reduce norm violations (neighborhood groups and vigilante committees); and organizations have been formed by norm violators themselves to reduce norm violations (Alcoholics Anonymous).

For each of the six theoretical perspectives implications of theory and research for social policy and efforts at implementation are discussed. While most, if not all, theories have implications for social policy, the implications of causal theories are most easily explicated. Quite simply, the causal conditions need to be changed. For example, if a theory specifies social conditions X and Y as causing suicide, to reduce suicide the theory implies changing conditions X and Y. Although it is not unusual to be able to alter problematic physical, biological, psychological, and social conditions without understanding why the course of action is effective, this book is concerned with how theory can assist in the construction of effective social policy. Policy implications provide the practical justification for theory and research.

Such implications are always moderated by social research. Policy makers are not interested in just theories; if they are interested in theories at all, they are interested in those supported by social research. This raises the question: how much supporting research is enough before a theory can be used to guide the construction of social policy? No clear answer can be given. On one hand, it makes no sense to construct social policy, the implementation of which is expensive, unless the guiding theory is well proven. Yet, on the other hand, theories are never completely proven, especially social theories, and social conditions are frequently of such concern that policy makers must act. It is thus incumbent on sociologists to marshal whatever the state of knowledge and suggest the best course of action. Clearly, the sensible position lies somewhere in between. Policy makers cannot wait until all the facts are in; if they do, they may never act. On the other hand, sociologists cannot suggest policy until some minimal level of knowledge is achieved.

Generally, the link between policy implications and implementation is mediated by social technology, social values, and social power. Concerning social technology, theory and research may identify as the cause of norm violations social conditions which sociologists do not know how to change. For example, research may identify economic crises in a society as the major cause of suicide. The policy implications are clear: reduce economic crises. Yet sociologists, as well as economists, may not know how. Theory and research may identify as the cause of norm violations social conditions which people are unwilling to change. For example, if research shows that a certain set of religious beliefs cause delinquency, what should be done? The policy implications are clear—change the religious beliefs; yet Americans believe in religious freedom. This example illustrates a conflict of values, where the assumed causal conditions are valued more than the norm violations are disvalued. Finally, theory and research may identify as the cause of norm violations social conditions which contribute to the positions and careers of institutional and organizational authorities. If research shows, for example, that the rate of property crime is caused by the level of income inequality in a society, what should be done? Will those with high incomes (generally in positions to influence social policy) sponsor social programs to equalize income? It seems unlikely.

The student should thus be aware that, while theory suggests social policy guidelines, the implementation of social policy is constrained not only by supporting research but by what is tractable to policy manipulation. In fact, policy makers are frequently more concerned with theory that suggests ''practical'' courses of action than with theory that is well-supported by research but suggests ''impractical'' courses of action, ones that are difficult to implement, violate social values, or adversely affect institutional and organizational authorities.

Integration

To summarize, a theoretical perspective is here defined as an integrated conceptual scheme which includes subject matter, theory, supporting research, and social policy implications. The diagram in Figure 1.2 illustrates the various paths of influence between the components.

Direct paths of influence flow from left to right. The subject matter influences the construction of theory by specifying the significant questions—the objects of theorizing; theory influences research by specifying the testable propositions; and both theory and research suggest guidelines for social policy. This flow of influence is frequently not always adhered to in practice. Some of the components are frequently circumvented. The subject matter is sometimes perceived as so problematic that research is initiated without the benefit of well thought out theory or that social action is initiated without the benefit of either theory or research. Both theory and research take time; yet social problems are frequently of such concern that action is demanded immediately.

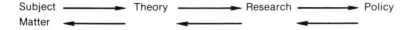

Figure 1.2. Components of a Theoretical Perspective

Additionally, direct paths of influence flow from right to left. The assumptions a theory makes about the nature of society and about the relationship between individuals and society shape the subject matter of study. The study of norm violations is premised on the assumption that society is essentially orderly, that social norms are clear, consistent, and stable, thus making it possible to define norm violations. Research also shapes both theory and subject matter. Nonsupportive research can be used to reject or reformulate theories, and available research techniques affect what aspects of the social world can be studied. For example, available government statistics have facilitated the study of some types of norm violations (such as drug addiction), whereas certain areas of study have been retarded because empirical observations are difficult to make. Finally, social policy—the presumed end product of theory and research—frequently affects theory and research. As previously stated, various government programs exist because they are popular, beneficial to the interests of the powerful, or simple to implement. Government funds for research are frequently made available to evaluate and in some cases to justify such programs.

Summary

Each of the next six chapters examines one perspective of the sociology of deviance. Each chapter is organized into three major sections (theory, research, and social policy) and a section critically evaluating the perspective. The book concludes with a summary chapter, which reviews all six perspectives and then compares them in terms of theory, research, and social policy.

REFERENCES

BANDURA, ALBERT. *Aggression: A Social Learning Theory* (Englewood Cliffs, N.J.: Prentice-Hall Inc., 1973).

BECKER, HOWARD S. *Outsiders: Studies in the Sociology of Deviance* (New York: Free Press, 1963).

BLALOCK, HUBERT. *Theory Construction* (Englewood Cliffs, N.J.: Prentice-Hall Inc., 1969).

BROWN, ROBERT. *Explanation of Social Science* (Chicago: Aldine 1963).

CASON, HULSEY. "The psychopath and the psychopathic," Journal of Criminal Psychopathology 4 (Jan. 1943): 522−27.

CICOUREL, A.V. *The Social Organization Of Juvenile Justice* (N.Y.: John Wiley, 1968).

CLARK, J. and L. L. TIFFT. "Polygraph and interview validation of self-reported deviant behavior," American Sociological Review 31 (Aug. 1966): 516–23.

CLARREN, SUMNER N. and ALFRED I. SCHWARTZ. "Measuring a program's impact: A cautionary note," in, *Sample Surveys of the Victims of Crime,* ed. Wesley G. Skogan (Cambridge, Mass.: Ballinger, 1976).

CLECKLEY, HENRY M. *The Mask of Sanity* (St. Louis, Mo.: C.V. Mosby, 1950).

CLINARD, MARSHALL B. *Sociology of Deviant Behavior* (New York: Holt, Rinehart & Winston, 1968).

COHEN, ALBERT. *Deviance and Control* (Englewood Cliffs, N.J.: Prentice-Hall, Inc., 1966).

DINITZ, SIMON, RUSSELL R. DYNES, and ALFRED C. CLARK. *Deviance: Studies in the Process of Stigmatization and Societal Reaction* (New York: Oxford University Press, 1969).

DURKHEIM, EMILE. *Suicide: A Study in Sociology,* trans. J.A. Spaulding and G. Simpson (New York: Free Press, 1951).

ENNIS, P. H. Criminal Victimization in the United States: A Report of a National Survey, The President's Commission on Law Enforcement and Administration of Justice (Washington, D.C.: Government Printing Office, 1967).

ERIKSON, KAI. *Wayward Puritans* (New York: John Wiley, 1966).

EYSENCK, HANS. *Crime and Personality* (London: Paladin, 1970).

FELDMAN, R. E. "Response to compatriots and foreigners who seek assistance," Journal of Personality and Social Psychology 10 (1968): 202–14.

FERDINAND, THEODORE N. "The criminal patterns of Boston since 1849," American Journal of Sociology 73 (July 1967):84–99.

FERRI, ENRICO. *Criminal Sociology,* trans. Joseph Kelly and John Lisle (Boston: Little, Brown, 1917).

GIBBS, JACK. *Sociological Theory Construction* (Hinsdale, Ill.: Dryden, 1972).

GOULD, LEROY. "Who defines delinquency: A comparison of self-reported and officially-reported indexes of delinquency for three racial groups," Social Problems 16 (Winter 1969):325–35.

HAKEEM, MICHAEL. "A critique of the psychiatric approach to crime and corrections," Law and Contemporary Problems 22 (1958):681–82.

HAWKINS, RICHARD and GARY TIEDEMAN. *The Creation of Deviance* (Columbus, Ohio: Charles E. Merrill, 1975).

HIRSCHI, TRAVIS. *Causes of Delinquency* (Berkeley, Calif.: University of California Press, 1969).

LEMERT, EDWIN M. *Human Deviance, Social Problems and Social Control* (Englewood Cliffs, N.J.: Prentice-Hall, Inc., 1967).

MATZA, DAVID. *Becoming Deviant* (Englewood Cliffs, N.J.: Prentice-Hall, Inc., 1969).

McCord, William and Joan McCord. *Origins of Alcoholism* (Stanford: Stanford University Press, 1960).

Mechanic, David. *Mental Health and Social Policy* (Englewood Cliffs, N.J.: Prentice-Hall, 1969).

Merton, Robert K. "Social structure and anomie," American Sociological Review 3 (Oct. 1938):672–82.

Nettler, Guwyn. *Explaining Crime* (New York: McGraw-Hill, 1974).

Quinney, Richard. *Class, State and Crime* (New York: David McKay, 1977).

―――. *The Social Reality of Crime* (Boston: Little, Brown, 1970).

Riesman, David (with Nathan Glazer and Reuel Denney). *The Lonely Crowd* (New Haven: Yale University Press, 1961).

Sagarin, Edward. *Deviants and Deviance* (New York: Praeger, 1975).

Sarbin, Theodore and Jeffrey E. Miller. "Demonism revisited: The chromosomal anomaly," Issues in Criminology 5 (Summer 1970):195–207.

Scheff, Thomas. *Being Mentally Ill* (Chicago: Aldine, 1966).

Schuessler, Karl F. and Donald R. Cressey. "Personality characteristics of criminals," American Journal of Sociology 55 (March 1950):476–84.

Schur, Edwin. *Labelling Deviant Behavior: Its Sociological Implications* (New York: Harper & Row, 1971).

Shah, Saleem A. and Loren H. Roth. "Biological and Psychophysiological Factors in Criminology," in *Handbook of Criminology,* ed. Daniel Glaser (Chicago: Rand McNally, 1974).

Sheldon, William H. *Varieties of Delinquent Youth: An Introduction to Constitutional Psychiatry* (New York: Harper & Row, 1949).

Stinchcombe, Arthur. *Constructing Social Theories* (New York: Harcourt, Brace, 1968).

Sutherland, Edwin and Donald Cressey. *Principles of Criminology* (Philadelphia: J. B. Lippincott, 1970).

Taylor, Ian, Paul Walton, and Jock Young. *The New Criminology* (New York: Basic Books, 1973).

Waldo, Gordon P. and Simon Dinitz. "Personality attributes of the criminal: An analysis of research studies, 1950–1965," Journal of Research in Crime and Delinquency 4 (July 1967):185–202.

Whyte, William H. *The Organization Man* (New York: Simon & Schuster, 1956).

Wolfgang, Marvin E. "Cesare Lombroso," in *Pioneers in Criminology* ed. Mannheim (Chicago: Quadrangle Books, 1960).

CHAPTER TWO

THE STRUCTURAL / FUNCTIONAL PERSPECTIVE

THEORY

Generally, structural/functionalism conceives of society as well oiled, integrated, and orderly. It assumes that people generally agree on appropriate values and behaviors (social consensus) and that the social structure or persistent patterns of behavior (roles, formal organizations, and institutions) function to realize society's values and goals.

Assuming that patterns of behavior do not persist unless they perform some social function, structural/functionalism explains the persistent patterns of behavior in society by identifying their social function. Some studies analyze how one institution contributes to the functioning of another institution. For example, how does the Protestant religion contribute to the functioning of the American economic system? How does serial monogamy contribute to the functioning of the economic system? How does the American economic system contribute to the functioning of serial monogamy? Other studies examine how particular institutions contribute to the attainment of general social values and goals. For example, how do different institutions (capitalistic economic system, democratic political system) and different groups (organized labor) contribute to economic opportunity and productivity as American values?

Structural/functionalists distinguish between manifest and latent functions. The former refers to those functions of persistent patterns of behavior which are intended and readily recognized by most members of society. For example, to most Americans it seems readily apparent that stable religious institutions function to maintain social morality in society. Latent functions refer to those consequences of persistent patterns which are neither commonly apparent nor recognized, and frequently are unintended. Merton (1957), for example, has suggested that contrary to public opinion, political machines perform many significant functions in society. They organize political activity and provide services and social mobility opportunities to those people (lower-class ethnics) unable to utilize formal bureaucracies. Structural/functionalists attempt to identify these functions and analyze the mechanism by which they operate.

How is social deviance studied from this general perspective? As structural/functionalism assumes a high level of social or normative consensus, norm violations, assumed to be definable, are the central focus of study, although social deviance as a social definition is not ignored. Two major themes can be identified. In perhaps the major thrust of the perspective, norm violations are conceptualized as reflecting disruptions of the social order, specifically, breakdowns in social consensus and integration. A second theme treats norm violations as any other persistent pattern of behavior; they are viewed as normal and are studied in terms of their functions in maintaining the existing social order. Remember, in terms of structural/functionalism, patterns of behavior that persist are assumed to have a function.

Social Deregulation: Historical Development

Structural/functional theories of norm violations can be historically traced to the writing of Emile Durkheim, a French sociologist writing in the latter part of the nineteenth and early twentieth centuries. His work provides a general analysis of society and constitutes the historical foundations of a general approach to deviance. Durkheim was concerned with the transformation from rural agricultural societies to urban industrial societies occurring in Western Europe during the last century. In rural agricultural societies people are generally involved in similar activities; the division of labor is minimal. Consequently, people tend to form similar ideas, goals, and values—a strong collective consciousness. It is the social force which holds the society together. With industrialization and urbanization comes a division of labor, which weakens the collective consciousness. People who hold different social positions and statuses come to hold different thoughts, ideas, interests, and values. A weak collective consciousness in turn brings about a decrease in social control. In an agricultural society the social consensus about what is proper and appropriate clearly defines reality for the individual, as there are no alternative realities of right and wrong from which to choose. With the division of labor this changes. The emergence of different interest groups fosters the emergence of different and competing realities of right and wrong, each having minimal control over the individual. This thesis has come to be labeled Durkheim's theory of social deregulation.

While Durkheim described the social change experienced by Europe during the end of the last century, his analysis seems applicable to contemporary America. Processes of socialization seem more effective in isolated rural communities where there exists only one reality of right and wrong. This reality is learned as the only reality. In urban communities, exposure to diverse values of right and wrong leads people to question the values of their group.

In positing a theory of suicide, Durkheim examined two sources of social deregulation: egotism and anomie. Egotism refers to a relationship between the individual and society where the individual is relatively free, independent, and nonintegrated in society, and thus not well regulated by society. For example, Durkheim stated that unmarried people are less integrated in society than married people. Married people are involved with spouses, children, and in-laws. These relationships are sources of social regulation. The married man, for example, has numerous social responsibilities (to his wife, children, etc.) which control and limit his behavior, while the unmarried man is free of these entanglements, and, consequently, of social control. Additionally, he argued that Catholics are more regulated than Protestants. The Catholic religion provides extensive rules governing thoughts and behavior, and ceremonial occasions where such thoughts and behavior are reinforced. The Protestant religion, on the other hand, is more individualistic, emphasizing an individual's direct relationship to the Almighty. It provides few rules of thought and behavior, and few ceremonial occasions in which rules are socially reinforced.

Throughout *Suicide* Durkheim discussed various psychological and social processes by which social disintegration or deregulation produce suicide. Generally, he suggested that group integration, by providing clear guidelines to behavior, makes life simpler and less stressful, and by providing a sense of social responsibility and social support during times of despair, moderates stress and deters its expression in suicide. For example, while both married and unmarried individuals may entertain suicidal thoughts, the married have more social responsibilities, which deter suicide, than the unmarried, who have no one to worry about and live for; and because Catholics are socially integrated, they experience social support (comfort, understanding, and sympathy), which deters suicide in times of despair.

Durkheim also argued that rapid social change (economic, political, technological) is a cause of suicide (anomic suicide). He observed, for example, that the rate of suicide follows the economic cycle. It is highest during economic contractions and expansions. During economic depressions people lose their economic means: unemployment increases and wages decrease. As the discrepancy between peoples' goals and means increases, stress increases, manifested in a high rate of suicide. During economic expansion a similar phenomenon occurs, although via a different process. Rapid economic expansion allows people to achieve their goals. However, people do not stop aspiring and striving. Having realized their socially inculcated goals, their aspirations are without limit. Anything becomes possible in an era of rising expectations, whereas during normal economic times society regulates people's goals. Durkheim thus argues that economic expansion, similar to contraction, increases the discrepancy between ends and means, which increases stress, manifested in the rate of suicide.

Note the similarity between egotistic and anomic suicide. Both emphasize deregulation. The former examines the relationship between certain social statuses and deregulation, and the latter examines the relationship between social change and deregulation. This theme in *Suicide* reflects Durkheim's general concern with the link between deviance and deregulation developed in the *Division of Labor*. Historically, it is not important whether Durkheim was right or wrong, or even whether he was explicit. Whatever the case, his work directed the sociology of deviance away from individual psychological causes of suicide (idiosyncratic personalities and interpersonal environments) toward the properties of society or small groups which reflect persistent social relationships. Durkheim's work on the relationship between social deregulation and suicide stimulated sociological research on suicide, as well as on other patterns of deviance and socially problematic behavior.

Social Deregulation: Contemporary Work

Durkheim's work on social deregulation has been developed by various contemporary sociologists. Andrew F. Henry and James F. Short (1954) have focused on states of the economic cycle as a cause of homicide and suicide; Jack P. Gibbs and Walter T. Martin (1964) have focused on inconsistencies in social regulations as a cause of suicide; and Ephraim H. Mizruchi and Robert Perrucci (1968) have focused on proscriptive social regulations as a cause of heavy drinking.

Henry and Short (1954) argue that suicide and homicide are functional psychological equivalents, both being behavioral expressions of extreme frustration. The specific expression is determined by the external restraint (regulatory) system. People subject to social constraints and controls are prone to blame others for their problems, and thus are prone to express frustration outwardly in homicide. People not subject to external restraints cannot easily blame others for their frustrations, and thus are prone to express frustration inwardly in suicide.

Social constraints exist in relation to social status. High-status people are not constrained; they are more often the initiators of social rules and constraints than the subject of them. Low-status people, on the other hand, are the subject of social constraints; they are regularly told by authorities what they can and cannot do.

Thus, when frustrated, high-status people are prone to suicide and low-status people are prone to homicide.

Like Durkheim, Henry and Short further argue that economic contraction and expansion are major sources of frustration. Giving Durkheim's theory a different twist, they argue that during economic contractions high-status people are the most frustrated, for compared to low-status people they have the most to lose. Therefore, since high-status people express frustration in suicide, during economic contractions the suicide rate should be higher than the homicide rate. On the other hand, because economic expansion benefits high-status people more than low-status people, during economic expansions low-status people experience relative deprivation and frustration. Therefore, since low-status people express frustration in homicide, during economic expansion the homicide rate should be higher than the suicide rate. Thus, suicide and homicide rates should vary inversely. When the economy contracts suicide should increase, and when the economy expands homicide should increase.

Gibbs and Martin interpret Durkheim's concept of social deregulation in terms of status integration. Some people occupy an integrated status set, that is, the role demands of different statuses are consistent; other people occupy a disintegrated status set, that is, the role demands are inconsistent. Consider, for example, a woman with aging parents, young children, and a demanding occupation; assume also that she is unmarried and trying to maintain a social life. Can she possibly meet the social demands of her parents, children, lover, and employer? Low conformity to some roles is inevitable. According to Gibbs and Martin, this situation leads to unstable social relationships, which in turn frequently lead to suicide. Succinctly, the theory is expressed as follows:

status disintegration ⟶ inconsistent role demands ⟶ low conformity ⟶
unstable social relationships ⟶ suicide,

where status disintegration causes inconsistent role demands, which cause low conformity, which causes unstable social relationships, which in turn cause suicide.

Whereas Durkheim focused on the degree of social regulation, Mizruchi and Perrucci (1968) focus on qualitatively different patterns of social regulation: prescriptive norms and proscriptive norms. The former inform people how to behave in certain situations and toward certain social objects, whereas the latter inform people how not to behave in certain social situations and toward certain social objects. For example, Protestant drinking norms are traditionally proscriptive. They inform people not to drink. Judaism, on the other hand, is characterized by prescriptive drinking norms, defining when drinking is proper, with whom, and under what circumstances. Mizruchi and Perrucci argue that proscriptive norms lead to behavioral extremes. They limit the number of people who engage in the prohibited behavior; but once the norm is violated, they provide little social control over the behavior. For example, abstinence and alcoholism are higher for Protestants than for Jews. Proscriptive norms deter many Protestants from drinking, but for those who for one reason or another do drink, there is little social control over the extent and pattern of drinking. For Jews, drinking is a meaningful part of religion and culture. Social rules regulate the pattern and extent of drinking. Countries can also be characterized by whether the drinking norms are proscriptive or prescriptive. Italian drinking norms are prescriptive. Drinking is interwoven into the fabric of social life; norms govern how, when, and with whom people drink. Both the abstinence and alcoholism rates are low in Italy compared to some Northern European countries (such as Ireland) where the drinking norms are proscriptive.

To summarize, Durkheim focused the attention of sociologists on the pattern of social regulations. Henry and Short argue that the level of external constraints (regulations) affects the behavioral expression (suicide and homicide) of frustration. Gibbs and Martin focus on inconsistencies, rather than breakdowns, in social regulations. And Mizruchi and Perrucci focus on qualitatively different patterns of social regulation. Although not tied together into a general theory of norm violation, these theories are linked by the concept of social deregulation. They suggest that the level and pattern of norm violations are affected by the nature of the social regulatory system.

Regulation and Strain

Robert K. Merton's (1938) theory dominated the sociology of deviance during the 1950s and is still important today. It constitutes a major effort to extend Durkheim's theory of suicide into a general systematic theory of norm violations. Like Durkheim, Merton argues that ends-means discrepancy is linked to the social order. However, influenced by contemporary social psychology, Merton refutes Durkheim's argument that people naturally aspire high and that social regulation is thus necessary to control aspirations. Instead, he asserts that both ends and means are learned. Some people aspire high and some do not, depending on cultural socialization.

American culture, for example, emphasizes economic achievement and extols high aspirations. Children learn, informally and formally, from the mass media and schools that everyone can be President (figuratively speaking) and that everyone should aspire and work to be economically successful. However, as economic opportunities are limited, only a few can achieve and satisfy their culturally induced aspirations; others must settle for something less. Thus, frustration levels will be high as people confront economic realities. Since structural opportunities and cultural values are not integrated, Merton describes American society as structurally dysfunctional. (See Box 2.1.)

Perhaps one example of a structurally functional society is pre-World War II India. The culture did not extol economic achievement as a universal goal; rather, economic goals were culturally stratified, consistent with economic opportunities.

Box 2.1 MERTON'S THEORY OF DEVIANCE

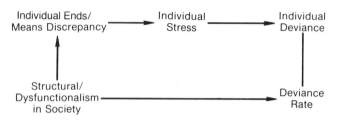

The diagram illustrates that structural/dysfunctionalism in society causes ends/means discrepancy in people, which in turn causes stress, which is expressed in deviance. Hence, a society with a high level of dysfunctionalism should show a high rate of deviance.

Those who did not achieve by the standards of the upper castes were not necessarily judged by those standards; their accomplishments and achievements were evaluated by their own subcultural standards. In terms of Merton's logic, since the level of cultural/structural integration was high, frustration should have been low, even though the level of poverty may have been high by Western standards.

Clearly, contemporary America does not perfectly illustrate the case of universal cultural goals, and pre-World War II India does not perfectly illustrate the case of stratified cultural goals. Numerous Americans do not aspire high and numerous pre-World War II Indians of the lower caste probably did aspire high. Merton, however, is not concerned with individual cases, but with societal characteristics.

The economic opportunity structure is a special case of the social regulatory system, constituting regulations which govern economic opportunities. Deregulation, however, is not Merton's major concern; rather, he is concerned with the degree of integration between the system of norms which regulates economic activity and the cultural imperatives or ideals. Merton argues that low integration causes stress and that people respond by violating cultural goals or structurally acceptable means. Societies with a high level of structural dysfunctionalism should show a high rate of norm violations, and, conversely, societies with a low level of structural dysfunctionalism should show a low rate of norm violations.

Merton enumerates five modes of stress resolution: conformity, innovation, retreatism, ritualism, and rebellion. (See Figure 2.1.)

The conformist is a person who responds to ends-means discrepancy by doing nothing—a person who grins and bears it but carries on. It is a response, not a resolution. The plus signs in Figure 2.1 mean that the conformist adheres to cultural goals and conventional means.

Much of Merton's attention centers on the innovator, who, not being able to achieve success via conventional or legitimate avenues of opportunity, achieves

Robert K. Merton, born 1918, received his B.A. in 1931 from Temple University, and his M.A. in 1932 and Ph.D. in 1936 from Harvard University, and is presently a University Professor Emeritus and Special Services Professor at Columbia University. Professor Merton has published widely; in the sociology of deviance he is best known for his paper, "Social Structure and Anomie." (Courtesy of Robert K. Merton, reprinted by permission.)

success through the violation of social norms. The plus sign under goals in Figure 2.1 means that the innovator adheres to the appropriate cultural goals. He or she tries to achieve. The minus sign under means implies that he or she violates the accepted opportunity structure in achieving socially acceptable goals. The archetype is the racketeer, who achieves financial success by illegal activities, frequently from selling products (drugs) or services (gambling or prostitution) that are in demand. In some ways the successful racketeer manifests the characteristics of the legitimate businessperson: ambition, drive, hard work, and intelligence.

Ritualism refers to a psychological process of goal de-escalating, whereby frustration and stress are reduced by aligning goals with what is possible. An example of this pattern of resolution is the low-level bureaucrat who is aware that he or she is no longer going to make it to the top of the organization and has come to accept this. He or she no longer tries, but simply comes to work each day and does his or her job. Many people do this; perhaps we all do to some extent. While no behavioral rules are violated, Merton argues that the ritualist is deviant nevertheless, for in the United States people are culturally expected to strive to achieve. To do otherwise is deviant. Ritualism is symbolized in Figure 2.1 by a minus sign under cultural goals (designating that goals are violated) and a plus sign under means (designating that conventional means are adhered to). As a pattern of deviance which causes few problems for other people and organizations, it has generated little discussion and research.

Retreatism refers to a stress adaption whereby both the culturally approved goals and socially acceptable means are rejected. In Figure 2.1 a minus sign appears under both cultural goals and means. In a sense, retreatists drop out of society and are in a different social world. Mental illness, drug addiction, and alcoholism may be forms of social retreatism.

Ends	Means	Resolutions
+	+	Conformity
+	−	Innovation
−	+	Ritualism
−	−	Retreatism
±	±	Rebellion

Each resolution is an adaptation to high ends-means discrepancy.

Figure 2.1. Merton's Five Adaptations

Rebellion refers to a stress adaptation whereby cultural goals and acceptable means are rejected, like retreatism; but unlike retreatism, new goals and means are advocated. The rebel does not drop out of society, but tries to change it. He or she has an image—however vague—of the "good" society. The minus signs in Figure 2.1 refer to the rejection of both cultural goals and conventional means, and the plus signs refer to the advocacy of alternative goals and means.

While formulating a system for classifying norm violations, Merton is somewhat vague in explaining why one adaptation occurs rather than another. He generally suggests that when people experience a discrepancy between goals and means, their first inclination is to achieve their goals through the use of illegitimate means (innovation). Those people socialized against the use of illegitimate means reduce stress by deescalating their goals (ritualism). Merton links these resolutions to positions in the social structure. He argues that lower class people are not morally committed to the legitimate opportunity structure; upon experiencing ends-means discrepancies, they are thus prone to become innovators. Middle class people are more thoroughly socialized into accepting the legitimacy of the opportunity structure; hence, upon experiencing stress they are prone to de-escalate their goals—to become ritualists.

In general, Merton presents a theory of stress, a system for classifying deviant adaptations, and an incipient theory of deviant adaptations. He argues that when cultural goals exceed structured opportunities people experience a discrepancy between their ends and means, a stressful psychological state. Norm violations are conceptualized as a resolution to stress.

Richard A. Cloward and Lloyd E. Ohlin (1964) apply Merton's general theory of deviance to delinquency, extending and further developing the theory. Their primary contribution is an explicit theory of deviant adaptations. Merton implicitly assumes that people who do not have access to legitimate means have access to illegitimate means. Cloward and Ohlin argue, to the contrary, that to innovate with any degree of success requires more than motivation; it also requires the opportunity to learn and use illegitimate means. A juvenile must learn how to be a successful thief. What houses are easy and safe to burglarize? How to avoid being caught? How to dispose of stolen merchandise? What to say and do if caught by the police? Juveniles differ not only by their opportunities to learn legitimate means, but by their opportunities to learn illegitimate means as well. Not all people who lack legitimate opportunities possess illegitimate opportunities. Some lack both. Cloward and Ohlin refer to those who fail in both systems as "double failures."

Based on this critique of Merton, Cloward and Ohlin formulated a theory of adaptations. They argue that most juveniles who are unable to innovate (double failures) express their frustration in interpersonal aggression (note that this resolution is not suggested by Merton). Some double failures, however, have internalized prohibitions against violence and still others do not possess the necessary physical ability. These juveniles adapt to frustration by goal deescalation (retreatism), manifested in drug use. Hence, Cloward and Ohlin offer a theory of juvenile theft (innovation), aggression, and drug use (retreatism). Merton's ritualistic and rebellion adaptations are not included. (See Box 2.2.)

Cloward and Ohlin are primarily concerned with subcultural or collective adaptations, specifically adaptations which characterize neighborhoods rather than individuals. They argue that in neighborhoods which lack legitimate opportunities, innovation becomes a subcultural adaptation when a high proportion of juveniles have opportunities to interact with successful adult criminals who provide illegitimate learning and role models. The latter in turn is dependent on the level of integration between criminal and conventional business activity, on ties and links between criminals and retail outlets for stolen goods, between criminals and lawyers, between criminals and police, and between criminals and politicians. When these conditions do not prevail in a neighborhood that also lacks legitimate opportunities, Cloward and Ohlin predict a high level of either aggression and gang violence, or drug use (retreatism). Lacking alternative avenues of success, juveniles associate status with physical prowess and violence.

Box 2.2 CLOWARD AND OHLIN'S THEORY

Goals	LEGITIMATE Means	ILLEGITIMATE Means	VIOLENCE Accepted	PATTERN OF Adaptation
+	+			Conformity
+	−	+		Innovation
+	−	−	+(Yes)	Aggression
+	−	−	−(No)	Retreatism

The table describes Cloward and Ohlin's extension of Merton's theory. Row one shows that those who have access to the legitimate means (+ +) become conformists. Row two shows that those who lack legitimate means but have access to illegitimate means (+ − +) become innovators. Of those who lack both legitimate and illegitimate means, some (+ − − +) express frustration in aggression (row three), but some having internalized prohibitions against violence (+ − − −) become retreatists (row four).

To summarize, Cloward and Ohlin question Merton's implicit assumption that all who lack legitimate opportunities have access to illegitimate opportunities; arguing instead that people vary in their access to illegitimate learning and performance opportunities, they construct a theory of individual and collective deviant adaptations.

Functions of Deviance

Interest in Merton's and Cloward and Ohlin's theories of deviance peaked in the early 1960s. Recent interest within the structural/functional perspective has focused on the functions of deviance.

Durkheim (1951) reasoned that, if patterns of norm violations persist, perhaps, like persistent patterns of normative behavior, they perform certain functions for society. For example, the violation of commonly held values and sentiments (the rape of an elderly lady, the kidnaping and molesting of a young child, the murder of a respected citizen) may unite people in an expression of common outrage and contempt. As the mass media publicize the case and as people talk to each other about it, common values about what is good and bad are reconfirmed. The deviant is the common enemy who in a sense integrates and unites the society. (See Box 2.3.) Durkheim (1960:102) states:

> Crime brings together upright consciences and concentrates them. We have only to notice what happens, particularly in a small town, when some moral scandal has just been committed. They stop each other on the street, they visit each other, they seek to come together to talk about the event and to wax indignant in common.

Kai Erikson (1966) has extended and elaborated this thesis in an examination of small interpersonal groups and the Puritan society of the Massachusetts Bay Colony.

Richard A. Cloward, born 1926, received his B.A. in 1949 from the University of Rochester, and his M.S.W. in 1950 and Ph.D. in 1959 from Columbia University, and is presently a Professor at Columbia University. He is well known for his book (co-authored with Lloyd E. Ohlin) *Delinquency and Opportunity: A Theory of Delinquent Gangs*, 1960. (Courtesy of Richard A. Cloward, reprinted by permission.)

Box 2.3 THE SOCIAL FUNCTIONS OF A HIDEOUS CRIME

The social functions of a hideous crime are noted in Truman Capote's *In Cold Blood*. The following excerpt illustrates the social process by which such a crime can build social cohesion in a small town. Describing the composition of a crowd awaiting the arrival of two confessed murderers on the sidewalk in front of the county jail, Capote (1965:279–80) writes:

> Indeed, the congregation in the square might have been expecting a parade, or attending a political rally. High school students, among them former classmates of Nancy and Kenyon Clutter, chanted cheerleader rhymes, bubbled bubble gum, gobbled hot dogs and soda pop. Mothers soothed wailing babies. Men strode about with young children perched on their shoulders. The Boy Scouts were present —an entire troop. And the middle-aged membership of a women's bridge club arrived en masse. Mr. J. P. (Jap) Adams, head of the local Veterans Commission office, appeared, attired in a tweed garment so oddly tailored that a friend yelled, "Hey, Jap! What ya doin' wearin' ladies' clothes?"—for Mr. Adams, in his haste to reach the scene, had unwittingly donned his secretary's coat. A roving radio reporter interviewed sundry other townsfolk, asking them what, in their opinion, the proper retribution would be for "the doers of such a dastardly deed," and while most of his subjects said gosh or gee whiz, one student replied, "I think they ought to be locked in the same cell for the rest of their lives. Never allowed any visitors. Just sit there staring at each other till the day they die." And a tough, strutty little man said, "I believe in capital punishment. It's like the Bible says—an eye for an eye. And even so we're two pair short!"
>
> Although none of the journalists anticipated violence, several had predicted shouted abuse. But when the crowd caught sight of the murderers, with their escort of blue-coated highway patrolmen, it fell silent, as though amazed to find them humanly shaped. The handcuffed men, white-faced and blinking blindly, glistened in the glare of flashbulbs and floodlights. The cameramen, pursuing the prisoners and the police into the courthouse and up three flights of stairs, photographed the door of the county jail slamming shut.

Dentler and Erikson (1959) have studied small friendship groups of army recruits and various Quaker work groups. These groups functioned as if they were organized to encourage or sustain deviance. In most of the groups one or two people violated the norms by not doing their share of the work. Yet the other group members did not isolate or ostracize them; rather, they sustained them by doing their assigned work and by covering up their mistakes, and, frequently, they united to bring them back into the fold. Why? Dentler and Erikson suggest a functional explanation. The deviants were sustained by the group because of what they contributed to the group. In a sense, the deviants created for the other group members a sense of common pursuit, a common goal. In responding to the norm violations, the group members were reminded of what they have in common.

Additionally, Erikson (1966) argues that deviance clarifies norms. Frequently, the general norms of correct and proper behavior are vague. The reaction to some people as rule violators functions to clarify the meaning of the norm. Others learn "how far they can go." Consider the rule, "do not cheat on examinations." What does it mean for specific examination situations? In the case of a take-home examination, it clearly means that a student should not copy another student's answer. Does it also mean that students should not work together, nor talk over the assignment at all? How does the rule apply to term papers? Does it mean that students should not seek assistance from other students or other professors? Does it mean that one term paper should not be submitted in two classes? When some students "go too far" and exceed the academic community's boundaries or tolerance limits, a societal reaction occurs, which defines specific situational meanings of the rule.

Erikson has applied this functional analysis to the Puritan society of the Massachusetts Bay Colony. During the 17th century the Bay Colony was undergoing a transformation from a group of revolutionaries searching for a new spiritual world to an established community. In such social transformations the virtues of revolutionaries (freedom, expression, individualism) embodied in the community's values and norms also undergo a transformation in situational meaning. What do such values and norms mean when the revolutionaries become authorities and must administer an established order? Erikson argues that in the Massachusetts Bay Colony, deviants played a vital role in this transformation. By their behavioral expressions of the traditional revolutionary values, they elicited societal reactions, which redefined the situational meaning of these values in the emerging new community.

Durkheim and Erikson also suggest that deviance highlights and accentuates the rewards for conformity. Punishing some people for norm violations reminds or makes salient to others the rewards for conformity. What social respect is given to saintly behavior in a community of saints? A little deviance by some makes saintly behavior stand out and become the object of respect. Additionally, people can feel virtuous about their conformity by contrasting themselves to norm violators.

Kai T. Erikson, born 1931, received his B.A. from Reed College in 1953, and his M.A. in 1955 and Ph.D. in 1963 from the University of Chicago, and is currently a Professor at Yale University. He is most well known for his book *Wayward Puritans: A Study in the Sociology of Deviance*, 1966. (Courtesy of Kai T. Erikson, reprinted by permission.)

Box 2.4 THE SOCIAL FUNCTIONS OF THE FOOL

Arlene and Richard Daniels (1964) nicely illustrate the functions of deviance in their research on Air Force basic training. The second author lived in a barracks with sixty recruits, referred to as a "flight." Their training schedule consisted of thirteen weeks of drill, firing range, field marches, bivouacs, lectures, and films on military topics. The schedule of training was of such a nature that everyone made mistakes and foolish errors; yet, with time all but a few mastered the necessary techniques and skills. This research is about one exception, Axel, and the social functions of his errors.

From the beginning, the flight marchers had singled him out as the essence of recruit stupidity; they liked to use him as a model in illustrating blunders and inexperience. By making a fool of Axel before his comrades and using his performance as an example of their gaucherie, the flight marchers amused the recruits with their own weaknesses and, presumably, hoped to embarrass them into improving. In time this practice resulted in the development of a rudimentary joking relationship between Axel and the two flight marchers. They tacitly encouraged his eccentricities for, by commission of them, Axel afforded further pedagogical materials. Thus, among other things, he was permitted to caper a bit, talk out of turn, and make mild rejoinders to their denunciations of ignorance. The effect of his levity was to turn situations of tension, which potentially could result in punishment for the whole group, into cathartic situations in which the conflict between the group and its leaders was reduced through comic relief.

Frequent recollections of his escapades by others helped him assume the status of a small-time legend. Axel was an important personage in the group with which he trained. For one thing, he managed partially to convert a rigid, tight, authoritative institution into one which could, at times, be magnanimous. By joshing with the flight marchers, throwing precedence to the wind in his familiarities, he narrowed the social distance between the recruits and the noncoms.

Axel thus performed a valuable service for this group of recruits. In return, the men enabled Axel to give the appearance of meeting minimum requirements by doing for him what he could not do for himself. The exchange was one in which both parties benefited.

Building on the work of Durkheim, Erikson directs our attention to three functions of deviance: 1. deviance increases group cohesion; 2. deviance clarifies the situational meaning of general values and norms; and 3. deviance highlights rewards for conformity. Generally, sociologists emphasize the positive consequences of conformity and the negative consequences of deviance. They note that deviance can produce disorder, reduce trust, and generate fear. Agreed, it can do all of these and more. Yet there is no reason to assume that it cannot produce positive consequences as well.

Summary

Structural/functionalism assumes that societies are orderly, characterized by social consensus, integration, and functionality. Within this general framework, Durkheim developed ideas about deviance. He focused on breakdowns in the social order, arguing that a division of labor, rapid social changes (such as economic contractions and expansions) and individualism weaken the social control of the community, leading to norm violations. Different variants of this theme have been developed by Gibbs and Martin, Henry and Short, and Mizruchi and Perrucci. Merton is particularly noteworthy. Rather than focusing on breakdowns in the social order as the cause of deviance, he focused on inconsistencies in the social order—inconsistencies between cultural goals and structural opportunities—as the cause of deviance. This theme has been developed and extended by Cloward and Ohlin and others. Durkheim also examined how norm violations function to stabilize and maintain the social order, a theme recently developed by Erikson.

RESEARCH

Structural/functionalism has stimulated research on a variety of norm violations. Suicide and drug use are discussed in this section.

Suicide

Durkheim's work on structural integration and regulation initiated a tradition of research. Some studies have examined general structural characteristics (urbanization, industrialization, economic expansion and contraction) and others have examined specific positions in the social structure (marital status, race, social class, sex, and religion) as indicators of social integration and regulation. Research on economic change, marital status, and status disintegration is discussed here.

Durkheim was one of the first to study the relationship between the economic cycle and suicide. Using data on Western Europe around the turn of the last century, he reported that suicide rates rise in periods of depression (as measured by bank failures and bankruptcies) and prosperity (as measured by productivity). For example, between 1874 and 1886 the average yearly increase in the French suicide rate was 2 percent; in 1882, the year of an economic crash, the rate increased by 7 percent. Industrial expansion in Italy started in approximately 1870 with sharp increases in the number of steam boilers, horsepower, salaries, and in the general standard of living; from 1866 to 1870 the suicide rate was stable but from 1871 to 1877 it increased by 36 percent and from 1877 to 1899 it increased another 28 percent. Durkheim provided numerous other examples. For the most part, however, the research findings are more illustrative than conclusive. Cases which disprove his theory are frequently explained away or even ignored. Pope (1976) has recently reanalyzed much of Durkheim's data and finds that the support is much more marginal and less conclusive than Durkheim suggested.

Henry and Short systematically examined economic cycles, using the Ayres index of industrial activity, in the United States from about the turn of the century to the end of World War II. The suicide rate increased for 82 percent of the years in which the Ayres index fell, supporting Durkheim; but, contrary to Durkheim, the suicide rate only increased for 42 percent of the years in which the index rose. Concerning the latter, close inspection of the data shows that the suicide rate decreased during the early years of business expansion, but increased in the final months of expansion. Henry and Short argue that this pattern is also nonsupportive of Durkheim's theory, as the early years show the greatest expansion. Yet, in support of Durkheim, it could be argued that in the early years people's goals may not exceed their means; this seems more likely when expansion reaches its final stages. People's goals continue to rise but the expansion slows down

The psychological effect of economic expansion and contraction may be cushioned because it is experienced by individuals as part of a societal change; others experiencing the same phenomena are available for comfort, support, and advice. When experienced alone the effect may be more deleterious. If so, then socially mobile people (those moving from low to high statuses and those moving from high to low statuses) in a stable economy should experience high levels of stress and show high rates of suicide.

Examining this hypothesis, Warren Breed (1963) has compared the level of social mobility of 103 New Orleans white males who committed suicide to the social mobility of a sample of New Orleans white males who resided on the same blocks as the suicides. Social mobility was measured by comparing present income and occupation with income and occupation two years prior (intragenerational mobility) and with father's income and occupation (intergenerational mobility). The findings suggest that only downward mobility is linked to suicide. As to intergenerational mobility, 58 percent of the suicides but only 31 percent of the controls were downwardly mobile; 22 percent of the suicides and 31 percent of the controls were immobile; and 25 percent of the suicides and 38 percent of the controls were upwardly mobile.

Similar results are reported by Jack Gibbs and Austin L. Porterfield (1960) in a study of 955 suicides in New Zealand. Comparing present occupation and father's occupation, they found that, while both upward and downward mobility are associated with suicide, downward mobility is more highly associated with suicide than is upward mobility.

The studies by Gibbs and Porterfield, and Breed showing that downward mobility is more highly related to suicide than is upward mobility, are consistent with Henry and Short's findings, showing that economic contraction is more highly related to suicide than is economic expansion. In sum, the studies suggest that Durkheim may have overemphasized the deleterious effect of economic expansion.

Turn now to marriage. Durkheim assumed that marriage is socially integrating. He summarized statistics from various countries during the latter part of the nineteenth century, showing that married people had much lower suicide rates than unmarried people (single and widowed). Only married men under twenty were an exception. The stress of being married at an early age may have overcome the benefits of integration. Furthermore, the rate difference between married and unmarried men was greater than the rate difference between married and unmarried women, suggesting that men benefited more than women from marriage. Children were also a critical factor. Married people without children showed much higher suicide rates than married people with children. Interestingly, these relationships are equally true of the United States one hundred years later. (See Table 2.1.) Married people, with the exception of those who marry young, show much lower rates of suicide than unmarried people; and marriage is more beneficial for men than women. Note the extremely high rates of suicide for widowed and divorced men.

The fact that certain age-marital status combinations (married, male, fifteen years of age) show particularly high or low suicide rates is central to Gibbs and Martin's theory of suicide. To reiterate, they argue that when a set of statuses is disintegrated, the occupants experience an inconsistent set of role demands, which generates a high level of stress. For example, being married at age sixteen is a disintegrated status set. The role demands of adolescence (such as school) are inconsistent with the role demands of spouse and parent. On the other hand, it is also difficult to remain single too long. Since people are expected to marry, social activity is centered around the family after age thirty-five. Those who remain single beyond age thirty-five or forty experience difficulties meeting the social demands of their age group. Early widowhood is also a problematic status set.

Table 2.1. SUICIDE BY MARITAL STATUS AND AGE GROUPS IN THE UNITED STATES, 1959 (RATES PER 100,000 POPULATION).

Age Group		Total	Single	Married Males	Widowed	Divorced
15−24	. . . . . .	7.4	6.8	8.4	—	19.7
25−34	. . . . . .	14.5	23.2	11.1	95.8	66.7
35−44	. . . . . .	20.5	29.8	16.7	81.7	112.6
45−54	. . . . . .	30.3	39.0	25.6	58.3	111.7
55−64	. . . . . .	39.1	58.3	32.4	65.0	80.4
65−74	. . . . . .	45.5	82.0	33.6	79.6	152.5
75 and over	. . . . . .	54.6	85.3	34.5	79.2	140.0
				Females		
15−24	. . . . . .	2.1	1.7	2.4	—	12.4
25−34	. . . . . .	5.5	9.2	4.7	7.2	17.8
35−44	. . . . . .	6.9	9.4	5.9	10.2	24.4
45−54	. . . . . .	8.5	8.8	7.5	12.0	17.4
55−64	. . . . . .	9.8	12.3	8.0	12.4	19.6
65−74	. . . . . .	9.7	9.6	7.5	11.3	25.8
75 and over	. . . . . .	6.4	4.0	4.6	6.9	18.4

Source: National Office of Vital Statistics, unpublished data.

Young widows experience difficulties not experienced by those widowed at the "normal" time (age sixty-five). They frequently have children to rear and demanding economic responsibilities to bear; further, there are few other widows in their age group to console them. Those widowed in their later years are beyond these responsibilities, and generally know other widows in their age group who may console them.

Gibbs and Martin employ a systematic although somewhat cumbersome technique for measuring status set disintegration. They argue that people avoid status sets which generate stress: people do not move into them, and if in them, they move out. Thus, the occupancy rate of status sets can be used as a measure of status set disintegration. Table 2.2 examines age and marital statuses for white males. Marital status is divided into four categories (single, married, widowed, and divorced) and age is categorized into five-year intervals, starting with fifteen to nineteen through eighty-five plus. Each age-marital cell includes two numbers. The top number refers to the suicide rate per 100,000; and the bottom number refers to the percentage of people who fall into that cell of all those in the age column. For example, in the upper left-hand corner cell (age 15−19 and single), 5.4 persons per 100,000 commit suicide and 96.1 percent of that age group are single. For the 15−19 age category, the 96.1 percent occupancy level of the single status indicates that it is a low stress category, and the 3.8 percent occupancy level of the married category indicates that it is a high stress category. For the 60−64 age category, the 7.6 percent occupancy level of the single category indicates that it is a high stress category, and the 83.5 percent occupancy level of the marriage category indicates that it is a low stress category. Note that for each age status the high occupancy categories generally show the lowest suicide rates, supporting Gibbs and Martin's theory. For example, for the 15−19 age status the single category shows the highest occupancy rate (96.1 percent) and lowest suicide rate (5.4); and for the 25−29 age status the married category shows the highest occupancy rate (78.1 percent) and the lowest suicide rate (9.3). Of the sixty cells (four rows and fifteen columns), 72 percent conform to this principle.

Recently, Miley and Micklin (1972) have used the Gibbs and Martin technique of measurement to investigate the relationship between status integration (sex and labor force participation) and suicide rates across countries. They argue that if labor force participation is restricted to either males or females but not both, sex role expectations are clear and simple. On the other hand, if both males and females participate in the labor force more or less equally, then sex role expectations are ambiguous. Females, for example, are not sure whether to enter the labor force or remain in the home; they face ambiguous and conflicting role demands. In the language of Gibbs and Martin, sex and work statuses are disintegrated. Following Durkheim, Miley and Micklin identify social change (population change, technology development, and increasing division of labor) as the cause of social disintegration. Using twenty-four countries, they tested the theory for 1950 and 1960, and report that the relationship between status disintegration and suicide

Table 2.2. AVERAGE ANNUAL SUICIDE RATES PER 100,000 POPULATION, 1959–61, BY MARITAL STATUS AND AGE, WHITE MALES IN THE UNITED STATES.

Marital Status	AGE GROUPS															
	15–19	20–24	25–29	30–34	35–39	40–44	45–49	50–54	55–59	60–64	65–69	70–74	75–79	80–84	85+
Single:															
SR	5.4	13.1	23.9	31.3	35.9	38.6	43.8	52.4	55.9	57.4	61.6	74.2	84.5	90.2	72.6
M	96.1	52.6	20.0	11.3	8.3	7.1	7.0	7.5	8.0	7.6	7.8	7.9	8.1	7.6	7.2
Married:															
SR	8.3	8.4	9.3	12.0	15.6	20.3	25.1	30.5	33.3	32.9	32.1	33.5	37.1	46.1	43.1
M	3.8	46.3	78.1	86.4	89.0	89.6	88.9	87.5	85.5	83.5	80.0	73.5	65.0	53.7	38.3
Widowed:															
SR	26.0	142.3	95.7	83.7	121.0	92.8	91.6	100.8	88.1	82.5	72.3	78.7	80.3	83.4	82.3
M	0.0	0.1	0.1	0.2	0.4	0.7	1.2	1.9	3.4	6.0	9.6	16.2	24.9	37.1	53.0
Divorced:															
SR	6.8	34.1	50.2	77.6	87.9	104.4	107.0	111.0	118.0	118.8	92.5	108.6	125.9	116.6	101.8
M	0.1	1.0	1.8	2.1	2.3	2.6	2.9	3.1	3.1	2.9	2.7	2.4	2.1	1.6	1.4

Note: SR = suicide rate; M = the percentage of the age category which falls into the particular marital status.

Source: J. P. Gibbs. "Marital status and suicide in the U.S.: A special test of the status integration theory." American Journal of Sociology, 74, 1968. Copyright 1969 by University of Chicago. Reprinted by permission of the publisher.

is strongly positive for both years. Stack (1978), in a recent study of forty-five nations, also reports a strong relationship between status disintegration and suicide for 1970. While the results of both studies are not clear on the causes of status disintegration, the strong relationship between status disintegration and suicide is consistent with Gibbs and Martin's research in the United States and supports Durkheim's theory.

To summarize, stimulated by Durkheim, sociologists have published a considerable volume of work on the relationship between social structure and suicide. While the work can be criticized (Pope, 1976; Chambliss and Steele, 1966) and sometimes does not show strong relationships (Henry and Short, 1954), it suggests that the nature of the social order is important in understanding suicide rates in both the nineteenth and twentieth centuries. This is not to say that suicide is not also affected by interpersonal relationships and psychological factors; however, in emphasizing these factors psychologists and psychiatrists have frequently neglected the social order. Durkheim and his contemporaries remind us that the nature of the social order and people's relationship to it are equally important.

Drug Use

Merton conceptualizes drug use, particularly addiction, as a form of retreatism; he argues that retreatism comes about when cultural prescriptions for success are blocked and when cultural inhibitions against the use of illegitimate or criminal means are internalized. Modifying this thesis, Cloward and Ohlin argue that the fact that drug addicts usually have criminal records suggests that they have not internalized social inhibitions against the use of illegitimate means. They argue that drug addiction is an adaptation to failure to achieve success via both legitimate and illegitimate means—the double failure hypothesis. While the ideas of Merton and Cloward and Ohlin may be applicable to many, if not most, forms of drug use, the thrust of their work has focused attention on "hard" addicting drugs, such as heroin.

Before examining this research, it may be useful to examine some of the procedures for measuring the critical concepts. Procedures for measuring ends-means discrepancy can be classified into two types, referred to as objective and subjective measures. The former infers the level of ends-means discrepancy from opportunities associated with objective social statuses. For example, as low educational attainment and minority group statuses generally afford few legitimate opportunities, it is assumed that people who occupy these statuses will experience a relatively high level of ends-means discrepancy. Some researchers have attempted to measure the level of ends-means discrepancy in interviews and questionnaires (subjective measures). One format asks respondents to indicate the probability of achieving their aspirations. For example, "On a scale of one to ten, how confident are you of being able to reach your goals?" Another format asks respondents to indicate income, education, and occupation levels which they seriously would like to achieve, and to also indicate that which is available or possible. The realistic expectation levels are subtracted from the aspiration levels. For example, a person aspiring to earn $30,000 a year but expecting only $10,000 a year probably experiences a higher ends-means discrepancy than one aspiring to earn $15,000 and expecting $14,000.

There are, of course, some problems with this research technique. To some extent, the reported aspirations may reflect fantasies—not aspirations for which people are striving. If so, the calculated ends-means discrepancies may not be valid indicators of stress and frustration. Nevertheless, this procedure provides some indication of the psychological distance between people's aspirations (goals) and realistic expectations (means).

Now, do people with a high ends-means discrepancy show a relatively high level of drug addiction or use? Lindesmith and Gagnon (1964) report that clearly this was not the case in the nineteenth century. Summarizing various research studies, they report that during the nineteenth century drug (opiate) addiction mainly occurred among middle-aged, middle-class whites and females—hardly the social statuses associated with blocked opportunities.

Remnants of this pattern are also present today, as evidenced by the high addiction rates among physicians, nurses, and pharmacists—people who by all objective standards should be able to achieve their economic goals legitimately. Winick (1961), in an interview study, reports that physician addicts are as successful professionally as are physicians who are not addicts, and that physicians frequently use drugs not to retreat from life but to enhance their performance as physicians by reducing the fatigue and anxiety associated with their work.

While Merton and Cloward and Ohlin may not be able to explain the pattern of drug addiction in the nineteenth century and even the drug addiction rates of some groups and classes in the twentieth century, this is not their major concern. They are concerned with explaining addiction among urban, young, nonwhite males, a distinct pattern since World War II. Various studies (Chein et al., 1964) have examined this pattern in Merton's terms, as a retreatist response to structured inopportunities.

This research has been criticized on various counts. DeFleur (1975) has argued that official statistics of drug arrest, used in many of these studies, may be more a function of police policy and practices than a reflection of underlying patterns of drug addiction and use. Yet the fact that studies using self-reports and observational techniques (Chein et al.) also report a similar pattern suggests that police practices and policies may only aggravate rather than produce the pattern. Lindesmith and Gagnon (1964) have argued that, while this pattern of drug use may exist, it may be accounted for by social factors other than blocked opportunities. They suggest that drugs are generally available in the geographical areas (inner urban neighborhoods) in which young, urban, nonwhite males reside, and that availability may be the common element that explains the drug habits of these users and certain professionals (physicians, nurses, and druggists).

A recent study by Glaser et al. (1971) attempts to isolate the effects of blocked opportunity from the effects of availability on drug use. Using a large sample, they were able to locate thirty-seven siblings residing in the same household in an urban slum, one of whom had used heroin and the other had not. Since both resided in the same neighborhood and in the same household, it seems safe to assume that drugs were equally available to both. The findings seem to support anomie theory, as the drug-using siblings had slightly higher occupational aspirations and lower levels of both educational performance and employment than the nonusing siblings.

The major problem with this type of research is that it does not establish the time sequence between blocked opportunities and drug use. While they may correlate, the latter may cause the former rather than the reverse, for it seems reasonable to argue that drug use can lead to both a low educational attainment and a poor employment record. In an attempt to establish this time sequence, DeFleur et al. (1969) examined the career patterns of fifty addicts. Approximately 43 percent of them started using drugs while in school; thus occupational failure could not account for their use. Unfortunately, they do not report data on educational failure. Also suggesting that occupational failure may not be as important as suggested by Merton, 17 percent of the drug users had been permanently employed since high school.

Box 2.5 STRESS AND DELINQUENCY

Various studies of drug use examine ends and means, but do not critically examine the discrepancy between them. Liska (1971) has located and critically reanalyzed three such studies of general delinquency (Clark and Wenninger, 1963; Short, 1964; and Spergal, 1964). The level of delinquency is reported for four categories of adolescents: those with high aspirations and high expectations of future success (low stress); those with high aspirations and low expectations (high stress); those with low aspirations and high expectations (a combination which rarely occurs and should not cause stress); and those with low aspirations and low expectations (low stress). All three studies show that the level of delinquency is higher for adolescents with high aspirations and low expectations of future success than for those with both high aspirations and high expectations, supporting Merton's theory. Merton's theory also implies that juveniles with low aspirations and low expectations should show the same level of delinquency as those with high aspirations and high expectations. Both experience low discrepancy, and thus should experience low stress. Yet the data for all three studies show that the delinquency level is considerably higher for juveniles with low aspirations and low expectations than for those with high aspirations and high expectations. In support of Merton it could be argued that the juveniles with low aspirations and low expectations are retreatists; according to Merton, retreatists should show a low level of theft and a high level of drug use. However, the three studies suggest that juveniles with low aspirations and expectations show a high level of theft, and provide little information on drug use. Generally, the three studies provide only marginal support for Merton's theory.

In addition to not establishing the time sequence between drug use and blocked opportunities, this line of research has not come to grips with the double failure hypothesis, that addiction is an adaptation to failure in both the legitimate and illegitimate opportunity sectors. To support Cloward and Ohlin's theory, research must show that prior to drug use, users tried and failed at innovation (property crime) as well as at legitimate endeavors.

What constitutes failure at property crime? Lindesmith and Gagnon report that in the early 1960s an addict needed $10 to $50 per day, seven days a week, to support a drug habit. Since stolen goods are discounted, if a user needed $25 per day, he or she would have had to steal $75 to $100 per day. Because of inflation these figures may have doubled and tripled today. Glaser et al. (1971) report that, while some addicts support their habit by pimping and pushing drugs, most do so simply by theft. Lewis (1970) suggests that supporting a habit requires hard work, ingenuity, and organizational skills, not only to secure goods but to locate and maintain markets for stolen goods. Can such addicts be labeled double failures?

Box 2.6 NEIGHBORHOOD ORGANIZATION AND PATTERNS OF DEVIANCE

Cloward and Ohlin also emphasize how the adaptations which characterize neighborhoods (collective adaptations) are affected by the legitimate or illegitimate opportunity structure of neighborhoods. Tackling this question, Spergal (1964) studied a racket, a theft, and a conflict neighborhood. He used the following data collection procedures: two to six months of field observation in the neighborhoods, formal interviews with 125 residents of the neighborhoods, and an analysis of neighborhood agency records. In the racket neighborhood, criminal and noncriminal activities were integrated; that is, the numbers bankers, loan sharks, and other racketeers worked closely with legitimate businessmen, politicians, and police. One racketeer financed both legitimate and illegitimate enterprises. Additionally, age integration was evident, with older youths serving as role models for younger youths. The conflict neighborhood showed a high level of social disorganization, with little evidence of organized crime, integration between criminals and conventional institutions, and contact between delinquents and successful criminals. The theft neighborhood was somewhere in between the organization of the racket neighborhood and the disorganization of the conflict neighborhood. The pattern of neighborhood delinquency fits Cloward and Ohlin's theory. In the racket neighborhood, juvenile delinquency was linked to organized crime, including policy and loan shark operations, and there was little juvenile gang conflict. On the other hand, juveniles in the disorganized neighborhood participated in inter-gang fighting on a full-time basis. Social status was linked to prowess in fighting. Delinquency in the theft neighborhood was somewhere in between. Youths participated in car theft (joy riding and burglary), but property crime was less organized than in the racket neighborhood, and gang fighting was less intense than in the conflict neighborhood.

Also, contrary to Cloward and Ohlin's thesis, Chein et al. (1964) report that in areas where drug use is high delinquency is more profit oriented than in areas where drug use is low, and that those drug users not engaging in delinquent activities tend to come from upper social class families and tend to be psychologically disturbed. Hence, when retreatism occurs it appears to be less likely in slums than in middle-class neighborhoods where legitimate opportunities exist.

To summarize, of the research directions suggested by Merton's and Cloward and Ohlin's theories only a few have been explored. In respect to drug use and addiction, the following questions have been a focus of concern. (1) Is there a relationship between blocked legitimate opportunity and drug addiction? (2) If there is, which is the cause and which is the effect? (3) Is there a relationship between double failure and drug addiction? (4) Is drug addiction a form of retreatism? It is difficult to draw simple conclusions from this research; but on the whole it is not very supportive of Merton's and Cloward and Ohlin's theories. In respect to innovation, retreatism, and rebellion the conclusion is similar. Yet the idea of linking the degree and pattern of deviance to the level of cultural/structural discontinuity still seems challenging.

SOCIAL POLICY

Given contemporary American values, existing technology for social engineering, and existing power structures, can structural/functional theory and research be translated into social policy?

Durkheim argued that social disintegration or deregulation causes norm violations. The policy implications are reasonably clear: increase social integration and regulation. This implies an extensive restructuring of American society—a restructuring which may conflict with existing social values and the interests of authorities, and which may not be technically feasible. For example, Durkheim identified Protestantism and being unmarried as statuses providing relatively low levels of social regulations; as Americans value freedom of religion and marriage, they would be unlikely to support policies which advocate changes in religious and marital institutions to maximize social integration and regulation. Durkheim also argued that economic expansion and contraction are stress generating, and Henry and Short have extended this thesis into a comprehensive theory of suicide and homicide. What would be done, if the evidence strongly supported the theory? While Americans may agree that economic contraction is undesirable, they strongly agree that economic expansion is desirable; and even if most Americans supported a policy of economic stability, economists do not agree on how to manage the economy. Hence, the theory and research closely tied to Durkheim's ideas of societal disintegration and deregulation have not been a source of social policy.

Merton suggests that the societal rate of deviance is directly linked to the level of cultural/structural integration; thus, to decrease the rate of deviance, policy makers need only increase the level of culture and social integration! In this regard some policy discussion has focused on increasing economic opportunities to correspond to cultural values. To do this, either the economy must be expanded, creating more goods and services, or the available goods and services must be redistributed so that the poor get more, which, of course, implies that others get less. Expanding the economy has proven to be difficult, and for the most part those who effectuate economic policy have shown little interest in redistributing economic resources to any significant degree.

Some policies have emerged, however, which redistribute resources and opportunities to a limited degree, although the basic economic order remains undisturbed. The most well known of these is the Mobilization for Youth Program, thought to be logically derived from Merton's anomie theory. In fact, the program was partially organized by Richard Cloward. It began in the 1960s and was financed by the National Institute for Mental Health, the Department of Health, Education and Welfare, the New York School of Social Work, and the Ford Foundation. Based on the theoretical proposition that economic and social obstacles to goal achievement are the causes of crime and delinquency, the program sought to expand work and educational opportunities in a sixty-seven-block area in the lower east side of Manhattan—an area composed of poor nonwhites. It proposed vocational training for hard-to-place juveniles and employment of social utility for those without jobs. To overcome educational barriers confronting the slum student, it proposed educational laboratories and the use of high school students to tutor low-income elementary school children. In addition, it proposed to assist slum dwellers to organize themselves to solve their own problems.

How did the program work in practice? Arnold (1964) reports that it was a failure. The political aspects of the program produced considerable controversy and turmoil (Quinney, 1975), preventing its full implementation. For example, the community organization program helped generate rent strikes, demonstrations, marches, lawyers for welfare clients, and the collection of data on landlord violations. Much of this activity disturbed local and state authorities. Monies for the program were sometimes impounded, the FBI began an investigation into the program, and program files were confiscated (Quinney, 1975). In addition, considerable distrust developed between those who organized the program and those who were supposed to benefit from it (Arnold, 1964). For the most part, the program has all but disappeared, and there has been little analysis of its effect on the rate of deviance in the area. This situation is not unusual. Activities designed to change slum conditions meet with considerable resistance from those who benefit politically and economically from them. Generally, changing social conditions means changing the lives of those in power, and they resist.

Assume for a moment that programs like this are successful at increasing the educational and work skills of slum dwellers. What effect would this have on the norm violation rate? The proposition that increasing educational and economic skills should reduce norm violations assumes that the economy can absorb these people. This may be true of an expanding economy; but what about an economy that is stagnant or even contracting? Consider the issue in these terms. If an economy generates jobs for 95 percent of those who wish to work, 5 percent must be unemployed. These people will probably be the least educated, the least motivated, and the least skilled. Increasing their education and skills may not reduce the rate of unemployment; rather, making these people more employable only shifts the people who are employed. If the economy generates jobs for only 95 perent of those who wish to work, some people will remain unemployed. Thus, if successful, these programs may not lower the rate of norm violations; they may only shift the propensity for norm violations from some people to others.

Generally, social policies like these assume that economic opportunities exist but that some people are not trained to take advantage of them. Social policy is thus directed to training people in educational and technical skills. However, the implications of Merton's theory for reducing norm violations appear to be far more radical. The theory suggests changing the economic order so that substantial economic opportunities are available to all, which, of course, implies that economic resources be reallocated more equally. However, those who are doing well in the present economic system (and who also control social programs) have little interest in radically changing the system. Hence, if Merton and Cloward and Ohlin are correct, high norm violation rates will remain with us for some time to come.

CRITIQUE AND SUMMARY

Theory

Since the mid-1960s structural/functionalism has been the subject of considerable criticism. Various sociologists (Lemert, 1964) have questioned the assumption that American society is characterized by value and normative consensus, consistency, and integration. They have argued, instead, that the United States is characterized by value pluralism, dissensus, and conflict, noting differences and conflicts between social classes, ethnic groups, racial groups, geographical regions, and age groups.

This criticism carries significant implications for theories of deviance built on the assumption of societal consensus and integration. First and foremost, if this assumption is invalid, the definition of deviance as a norm violation becomes problematic, for conformity from the viewpoint of one group then constitutes a norm violation from the viewpoint of another group. Structural/functionalists sidestep this issue by implicitly assuming the normative perspective of middle-class whites. This criticism may account for the decline of structural/functional theories since the mid-1960s.

As Merton's theory has been the most prominent of the structural/functional theories of deviance, it has elicited the most rigorous criticism (Cohen, 1965).

1. Merton, assuming that most people value economic success, focuses on differences in economic opportunity. Since the upper class possess economic opportunities, few studies of upper-class norm violations have been generated by Merton's theory. The theory has, thus, been criticized for ignoring upper-class deviance.

2. Merton has been criticized for not providing a theory of deviant adaptations. While classifying patterns of deviance (innovation, retreatism, ritualism, and rebellion), Merton does not clearly indicate the conditions under which each of these adaptations occur. Why does one person become a retreatist and another a ritualist? To some extent, Cloward and Ohlin address this problem, specifying the conditions under which innovation and retreatism occur. Yet they, too, do not suggest the conditions under which ritualism and rebellion occur, rather than innovation and retreatism.

3. The theory has been criticized for making faulty psychological assumptions. It assumes a direct relationship between the level of ends/means discrepancy and the level of stress. However, much psychological research suggests that the level of stress experienced from any level of ends/means discrepancy depends on what is "normal" in a person's past and present social environment. People tend to compare themselves to others. If everyone in a neighborhood or family experiences a similar level of ends-means deprivation, the deprivation may have little psychological effect. For example, a man residing in a lower-class neighborhood and holding a working-class job may well experience a high discrepancy between his ends and means. It may be much higher than that experienced by most middle-class men, but it may be much lower than that experienced by his everyday associates with whom he compares himself. Compared to his fantasies and dreams, he may be doing poorly; but compared to his friends he may be doing well.

4. Merton's anomie theory has been criticized for failing to examine the

Albert K. Cohen, born 1918, received his B.A. in 1939 from Harvard University, his M.A. in 1942 from Indiana University, and his Ph.D. in 1951 from Harvard University, and is presently a Professor of Sociology at the University of Connecticut. He is well known for his theoretical work on juvenile delinquency, *Delinquent Boys: The Culture of the Gang*, 1955, and for his critique of anomie theory. (Courtesy of Albert K. Cohen, reprinted by permission.)

processes which intervene between the first act of deviance and a deviant career. A high ends-means discrepancy may lead to stress, which in turn may lead to an act of deviance; but not all people who commit an act of deviance commit a second, third, etc. The theory does not explain why some people simply stop, why some become episodic deviants, and why others become systematic career deviants.

Durkheim's theory of suicide has also been criticized. Pope (1976), for example, states that the theoretical link between deregulation and suicide is vague. Exactly how is deregulation experienced by people so as to produce suicide, or how is regulation experienced so as to deter suicide? Pope argues that throughout Durkheim's monograph, *Suicide*, a variety of unintegrated and sometimes contradictory explanations are given, such as ends-means discrepancy, stress, meaninglessness, and social irresponsibility, which are induced by social deregulation and culminate in suicide.

Theories of the functions of deviance have been criticized on various counts. Importantly, they ignore the dysfunctions of deviance. If some people do not play their roles, an interdependent society may not survive. For example, a strike by certain occupational groups can just about bring the United States economy to a halt. Also, the deviance of some may motivate others not to play their roles. A comprehensive theory of the consequences of deviance should include both functions and dysfunctions, specifying the conditions under which deviance is functional and the conditions under which it is dysfunctional for society. The proposition that deviance shores up social consensus and collective boundaries has also been criticized for assuming some level of social consensus to shore up. Consider behaviors characterized by social dissensus or open conflict, such as drug use, pornography, and homosexuality. What are the consequences of deviance in these areas? An increase in homosexuality, for example, may not strengthen the conventional norm; it may strengthen the subcultural norm of homosexuality and weaken the conventional norm. Generally, while the violation of high consensus norms (like child molesting and homicide) may bolster social consensus and social cohesion, the violation of low consensus norms may foster social conflict.

Research

Many of the central concepts of structural/functional theories have not been measured and many others have not been validly measured. Perhaps the most obvious example is "stress," a central concept in Durkheim's and Merton's theories. Very few researchers have measured it. Rather, they have measured the hypothesized causes of stress (economic crises, marital status, status disintegration, and social class) and the outcomes of stress (suicide and drug addiction). Criticism has also been leveled on the tendency of structural/functional research to use official records (police files, court records, etc.) without due consideration for their validity. For example, Durkheim, in support of his theory, reported that Catholics show a lower suicide level than Prostestants. Douglas (1967) argues that this finding may simply reflect a bias in official records. Suicide is regarded as more sinful in the Catholic than the Protestant religion. In some Catholic countries, for example, a suicide victim cannot be buried within the church. Thus, Catholic families and friends may cover up suicides, disguising them as natural deaths (accidents and disease). These actions may produce the official statistics which show Protestants to have a higher suicide rate than Catholics.

Time order is another important problem. Some research suggests a relationship between ends-means discrepancy and norm violations. Researchers frequently assume that the ends-means discrepancy occurs first and causes norm violations. Yet the reverse may be true in many cases. Norm violations may lower economic and educational opportunities. Alcoholics or drug addicts, for example, may have little time available for educational and economic pursuits and may be discriminated against in educational and economic organizations.

Measurement and time order deal with the quality of research. The quantity of research is also important. Generally much more research is needed before we can have confidence in structural/functional theories of norm violations; yet in recent years research has shifted away from these theories. Thus, many of the questions posed here probably will not be answered for some time to come.

Policy

Concerning social policy, a theoretical perspective can be criticized on two counts: one, the policy implications are vague, and two, the policy implications are not subject to implementation. Structural/functional theories are subject to criticism on both counts. Those who have extended Durkheim's social deregulation theory tend not even to discuss social policy, perhaps because of the drastic changes in society that their theories imply are necessary to reduce suicide or other norm violations. The same is equally true of the functions of deviance thesis. It is not likely that policy makers would be interested in increasing norm violations, specifically those which violate the common social consciousness, to strengthen social cohesion and moral boundaries. Merton's theory, on the other hand, has generated discussions of social policy, although these discussions have ignored what might be called the "radical" implications of the theory. Generally structural/functionalists have not seriously discussed the societal or macro social policy implications of their work. They have either ignored policy or couched it in individualistic terms, such as the Mobilization for Youth Program, which was directed toward changing individuals rather than the social structure of society.

REFERENCES

ARNOLD, ROBERT. "Mobilization for youth: Patchwork or solution?" Dissent 11 (Summer 1964):347–54.

BELL, DANIEL. "The racket ridden longshoremen," in *End of Ideology*, ed. Daniel Bell (New York: Free Press, 1960).

BREED, WARREN. "Occupational mobility and suicide among white males," American Sociological Review (April 1963):179−88.

CHAMBLISS, WILLIAM and M. STEELE. "Status integration and suicide: an assessment," American Sociological Review 31 (Aug. 1966) 524−33.

CAPOTE, TRUMAN. *In Cold Blood* (New York: Signet, 1965).

CHEIN, ISIDOR, DONALD L. GERAND, ROBERT S. LEE, and EVA ROSENFELD. *The Road to H: Narcotics, Delinquency and Social Policy* (New York: Basic Books, 1964).

CLARK, J. P. and E. P. WENNINGER. "Goal orientation and illegal behavior among juveniles," Social Forces 42 (Oct. 1963):49−59.

CLOWARD, RICHARD A. and LLOYD E. OHLIN. *Delinquency and Opportunity* (New York: Free Press, 1964).

COHEN, ALBERT K. "The sociology of the deviant act: Anomie theory and beyond," American Sociological Review 30 (Feb. 1965): 5−14.

DANIELS, ARLENE and RICHARD DANIELS. "The social functions of the career fool," Psychiatry 27 (Aug. 1964):219−29.

DEFLEUR, LOIS B. "Biasing influence on drug arrests records: Implications for deviance research," American Sociological Review 40 (Feb. 1975):88−103.

DEFLEUR, LOIS B., JOHN BELL, and RICHARD W. SNARR. "The long-term social correlates of opiate addition," Social Problems 17 (Fall 1969):225−33.

DENTLER, ROBERT A. and KAI T. ERIKSON. "The functions of deviance in groups," Social Problems 7 (Fall, 1959):98−102.

DOUGLAS, JACK D. *The Social Meaning of Suicide*. (Princeton, N. J.: Princeton University Press, 1967).

DURKHEIM, EMILE. *Suicide: A Study in Sociology*, trans. J. A. Spaulding and G. Simpson. (New York: Free Press, 1951).

―――. *The Division of Labor*, trans. George Simpson (New York: Free Press, 1960).

ERIKSON, KAI. *Wayward Puritans: A Study in the Sociology of Deviance* (New York: Wiley, 1966).

GLASER, DANIEL, BERNARD LANDER, and WILLIAM ABBOTT. "Opiate addiction and non-addicted siblings in a slum area," Social Problems 18 (Spring 1971):510−21.

GIBBS, JACK P. "Marital status and suicide in the United States: A special test of the status integration theory," American Journal of Sociology 74 (March 1969):521−33.

GIBBS, JACK P. and WALTER T. MARTIN. *Status Integration and Suicide: A Sociological Study* (Eugene, Ore.: University of Oregon Books, 1964).

GIBBS, JACK P. and AUSTIN L. PORTERFIELD. "Occupation prestige and social mobility of suicides in New Zealand," American Journal of Sociology 66 (Sept. 1960): 147−52.

HENRY, ANDREW F. and JAMES F. SHORT. *Suicide and Homicide: Some Economic, Sociological and Psychological Aspects of Aggression* (New York: Free Press, 1954).

LAUDERDALE, PAT. "Deviance and moral boundaries," American Sociological Review 41 (Aug. 1976):660–75.

LEMERT, EDWIN M. "Social structure, social control and deviation," in *Anomie and Deviant Behavior*, ed. Marshall B. Clinard, (New York: Free Press, 1964).

LEWIS, MICHAEL. "Structural deviance and normative conformity—the 'hustle' and the 'gang,' " in *Crime in the City*, ed. Daniel Glaser (New York: Harper & Row, 1970).

LINDESMITH, ALFRED R. and JOHN GAGNON. "Anomie and drug addiction," in *Anomie and Deviant Behavior*, ed. Marshall B. Clinard (New York: Free Press, 1964).

LISKA, ALLEN E. "Aspirations, expectations and delinquency: Stress and additive models," Sociological Quarterly 12 (Winter 1971):99–107.

MERTON, ROBERT K. "Social structure and anomie," American Sociological Review 3 (Oct. 1938):672–82.

MERTON, ROBERT. *Social Theory and Social Structure* (New York: Free Press, 1957).

MILEY, JAMES D. and MICHAEL MICKLIN. "Structural change and the Durkheimian legacy: A macro social analysis of suicide rates," American Journal of Sociology 78 (Nov. 1972):657–73.

MIZRUCHI, EPHRAIM H. and ROBERT PERRUCCI. "Prescription, proscription, and permissiveness: Aspects of norms and deviant drinking behavior," in *Approaches to Deviance*, eds. Mark Lefton, James K. Skipper, and Charles H. McCaghy (New York: Appleton-Century-Crofts, 1968).

POPE, WHITNEY. *Durkheim's Suicide: A Classic Reanalyzed* (Chicago: University of Chicago Press, 1976).

QUINNEY, RICHARD. *Analysis and Critique of Crime in America* (Boston: Little, Brown, 1975).

REISS, ALBERT J. "Settling the frontiers of a pioneer in American criminology: Henry McKay," in *Delinquency, Crime and Society*, ed. James F. Short, (Chicago: University of Chicago Press, 1976).

SCHACHTER, STANLEY. "Deviance rejection and communication," Journal of Abnormal and Social Psychology 46 (1951):190–207.

SHORT, JAMES F. "Gang delinquency and anomie," in *Anomie and Deviant Behavior*, ed. Marshall B. Clinard (New York: Free Press, 1964).

SPERGAL, IRVING. "Deviant patterns and opportunities of pre-adolescent Negro boys in three Chicago neighborhoods," in *Juvenile Gangs in Context*, ed. M. W. Klein (Englewood Cliffs, N.J.: Prentice-Hall, 1967).

———. *Racketville, Slumtown and Haulburg*. (Chicago: University of Chicago Press, 1964).

STACK, STEVEN. "Suicide: A comparative analysis," Social Forces 57 (Dec. 1978):644–53.

WINICK, CHARLES. "Physician narcotic addicts," Social Problems 9 (1961): 174–86.

tHE cHicAGo pERSpEctivE

THEORY

Contemporary American sociology emerged at the University of Chicago. The university opened its doors in 1892, and with substantial grants and endowments by the Rockefellers and others appointed the most prestigious scholars of the day. The university became an instant success and academic leader. The situation was perfect for the development of sociology as an academic department. Unlike the East, where established disciplines fathered, funded, and in some cases hampered the development of sociology, Chicago as a new university had no established departments with control over money and curricula. Sociology at Chicago encompassed a diverse set of concerns about society and human behavior. Perhaps social ecology was *the* dominant concern which pulled together much of the Chicago research, giving it shape and form.

Social Ecology

With the publication of Charles Darwin's epic works, *Origins of Species* (1859) and *Descent of Man* (1871), natural and physical scientists became increasingly concerned with the relationship between the organization of living matter and the external environment. The structure or order of living matter was thought to depend on the nature of the environment, defined as all external forces or factors to which an organism is responsive. The study of this relationship constitutes the science of ecology.

In studying this relationship, ecologists emphasize the survival and adaptation of organisms. As the properties of environments are hospitable for only some forms of life, organisms survive through adaptation; additionally, since some organisms constitute part of the environment of other organisms, they must adapt to each other. Ecologists refer to these interrelationships between organisms as the "web of life." Some organic forms are compatible; some are not. Over time only compatible forms survive. Plants, for example, require carbon dioxide from the atmosphere and give off oxygen; animals, on the other hand, need oxygen and give off carbon dioxide. Thus, a certain level of plant life is necessary to support a certain level of animal life. If plant life is restricted because of the physical properties of a region, the level of animal life will adapt. Food chains are another example of these interrelationships. For example, in North America deciduous trees support or initiate a number of food chains. Mice and squirrels feed on fruit and leaves; mice are eaten by skunks, who are eaten by red foxes, etc. A change in one part of the chain results in necessary adaptations in other parts (Hawley, 1950). These interdependencies produce biotic communities, discernible patterns of interrelationships between organisms, generally bounded by certain physical properties called natural areas. Ecologists are concerned with biotic community development or change. What happens when the physical features of an area somehow change, new forms of plant life are introduced, or new forms of animal life appear? Given the interdependencies, such changes vibrate through the biotic community. Ecologists describe this process or development in terms of invasion, competition (for resources), and succession. Generally, then, ecologists are interested in the structure and dynamics of organisms in relationship to their environment.

In a rather loose manner, the Chicago sociologists used the ecological model to conceptualize their research in the city of Chicago. They argued that the social order of the city can be understood from an ecological viewpoint as a product of various social processes, such as symbiosis, cooperation, competition, and cyclical change; they also argued, however, that humans, different from other animals, develop a culture (customs, values, norms), which restricts or limits ecological processes. Within this general framework research focused on a variety of specific topics, essentially attempting to describe and explain the spatial distribution of persistent patterns (social structure) of urban activity, such as commerce, business, industry, residence, and unconventional behavior (like delinquency, mental illness, and prostitution).

Ernest Burgess (1925) argued that the development of a city approximates a pattern of concentric circles, whereby certain activities cluster in certain spatial zones. (See Figure 3.1.) The central zone is occupied by commerce and industry. The second zone is transitional. It is in the process of being taken over by industry

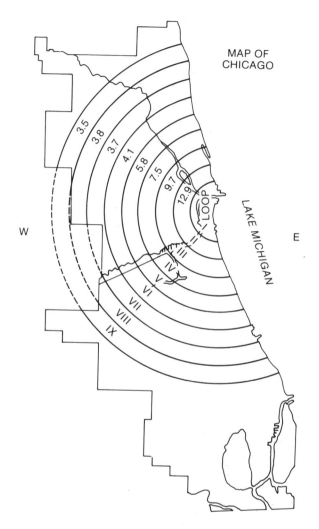

Figure 3.1. Zonal Pattern of Delinquency. This map of Chicago includes nine zones, and Burgess's hypothesis includes only five zones. On this map, Burgess's zone I is equal to zone I; his zone II is equal to zones II and III; his zone III is equal to zones IV and V; his zone IV is equal to zones VI and VII; and his zone V is equal to zones VIII and IX. The numbers refer to rates of delinquency.

and commerce, but includes areas where the poor, migrants, and immigrants reside. The third zone is a blue-collar residential district dominated by two- and three-family houses. The fourth zone is a residential zone consisting of single-family houses, a middle-class area. And the fifth zone is a commuter's residential area. Burgess did not conceive of this zonal pattern as literally describing all cities (Faris, 1967). In fact, it only generally described Chicago, as Lake Michigan cuts the pattern into a half circle. He was concerned with conceptualizing an ideal or classical pattern of city development from which actual patterns of development could be analyzed as departures.

The zonal pattern was thought to emerge through ecological processes, particularly competition. Land with the highest value is purchased and used by commerce and industry, which have the resources to afford it. Residential land adjacent to the industrial/commercial zone loses its value; consequently, it is occupied by poor and immigrant populations. Generally, the value of land increases with distance from the transitional zone, and the pattern of use and residential occupation changes accordingly. The Chicagoans also noted the development and functioning of culture within the zonal pattern. This is revealed in their studies of neighborhood and community development, particularly ethnic, racial, and unconventional communities. Louis Wirth (1928), for example, studied how Jewish culture, which developed in European ghettos, facilitated adjustment to the ecological conditions of the Chicago slums; and Franklin E. Frazier (1932) studied how the American Black culture, which developed in the rural South under slavery, affected the spatial distribution of Blacks.

Their studies, describing the order of deviant or unconventional urban worlds, drew particular attention to their theory and research, which involve three major themes: 1. describing the unconventional social order, frequently in some detail; 2. describing and analyzing the ecological conditions and processes, like competition, which give rise to this order; and 3. describing and analyzing the culture which emerges from these ecological conditions and processes, and which in turn also regulates the social order.

The work of Nels Anderson (1923) on the hobo illustrates these themes. He described the hobo social order, providing fine distinctions between types of hoboes, and between hoboes and other unconventionals, such as tramps, bums, and migrants. He examined the ecological conditions and processes, such as unemployment, seasonal work, competition, and downward mobility, through which a large number of men come to be homeless and physically isolated from the conventional community. He tried to show how the ecological problems confronting the hobo in daily life result in rules and values which in turn regulate daily life. For example, hobo culture includes rules against making fires at night in jungles (camps) subject to raids, robbing men at night who sleep in the jungles ("hijacking"), making the jungle a permanent hangout, subsisting on the leavings of meals ("buzzing"), leaving pots and utensils dirty after using, cooking without first obtaining fuel, and destroying unused equipment (Anderson, 1923:20−21). Anderson argued that these cultural rules provide social order—an unconventional order—given the ecological conditions and processes confronted by hoboes. Other similar studies were reported. Paul Cressey (1932) studied the social order and culture of the taxi-dance hall; and Frederic M. Thrasher studied the social life and culture of the delinquent gang (1927).

Given their ecological concerns, the Chicagoans also studied the patterning of deviance in physical space. Their studies of delinquency, mental illness, and suicide showed that unconventional behavior tends to center in cities, particularly in the second zone where residential and business activity intermesh. They argued that the ecological conditions which disrupt traditional social control processes are accentuated in these areas; and when social control processes weaken, unconventional and deviant behavior emerge. Various Chicagoans (Wirth, 1938; Shaw and McKay, 1931) attempted to specify exactly how an urban environment leads to deviance. Their theory of urban social disorganization can be described in two general stages. (See Figure 3.2.)

Industrialization creates a need for concentrations of unskilled labor, thereby increasing population size and density (urbanization) by migration and immigration. Both social processes, industrialization and urbanization, create various social and cultural conditions (social differentiation, value and norm conflicts, social mobility, cultural change, cultural vacuums, and a decline in primary social relationships), generally referred to as social disorganization. 1. Industrialization produces a division of labor. As people specialize in their labor, they develop different and sometimes conflicting values and norms; additionally, different ethnic groups immigrating and migrating into cities carry with them distinct and frequently conflicting cultural values and norms. 2. Compared to rural areas, horizontal and vertical social mobility in cities expose people to conflicting cultural values and norms, and make primary relationships difficult to maintain. 3. As most new urbanites have migrated and immigrated from rural areas, their cultural values and norms, relevant to the problems encountered in rural life, are not relevant to the problems encountered in urban life. In dealing with formal bureaucracies, such as with employers, police, and lawyers, for example, most new urbanites have little cultural background upon which to draw. 4. In rural communities, where friends and neighbors may also be economic associates and fellow church members, interaction with the same people over a variety of social relationships facilitates primary relationships. Industrialization and the accompanying division of labor weaken primary relationships by segmenting social relationships.

Figure 3.2. Causal Structure Underlying the Theory of Social Disorganization. Arrows describe the direction of causal effects; double-headed arrows mean that the effect flows in both directions; and a minus sign means that the effect is negative (an increase in the causal variable results in a decrease in the effect). Generally, the figure shows that industrialization and urbanization increase social disorganization, which decreases conventional social controls, which in turn increases deviant behavior.

Social disorganization (value and norm conflicts, mobility, cultural change and vacuums, decline in primary relationships) in turn reduces internal and external social control. The former refers to a process whereby people accept cultural values and norms as right and proper, and thus do not violate them; the latter refers to a process whereby people do not violate social norms because of rewards for conformity and punishments for violations. The internal process is weakened by normative conflicts, cultural change, and social mobility. People are most likely to accept cultural standards as right and proper when they are unexposed to alternatives. In a small town, characterized by a stable standard, people learn the standard as *the* standard; they accept it as the only way to do things. In urban areas, because of cultural conflicts and social mobility, people come into contact with others who accept different standards and ridicule alternate standards. External social control is also weakened by cultural conflicts and the reduction of primary social relations. For example, a young woman growing up in a small town for one reason or another may not accept the conventional standards. She may conform nonetheless because there are no unconventional groups to join and the good will of relatives and friends is important. What about a young woman growing up in a city? Since the strength of primary relationships is weak, she is less interested in the good will of others and she may be able to locate groups who approve and even practice various forms of unconventionality.

In sum the Chicagoans were impressed with ecological analyses of the biotic world. They borrowed concepts like competition, struggle for survival, symbiosis, and natural area to describe social processes and order. Also, because they realized that people are culture-bearing animals, much of their work examined the link between ecological processes and culture, and the extent to which cultural and ecological processes operate to produce social order. The Chicagoans measured behavior against what they considered to be the conventional customs and norms of society. They identified ecological processes (competition, population movements, migration, immigration, mobility) spatially distributed within urban areas as disrupting processes of social control, thereby resulting in deviant behavior.

Assuming the social control processes of urban areas to be disrupted, the Chicagoans frequently described these areas as disorganized. For the most part, however, they did not measure the disruptive processes directly, but inferred them from what they believed to be their cause (industrialization and urbanization) and their products (rates of deviance). Yet, while an area may show high rates of behavior which violate the norms of conventional society, this does not imply that the area lacks processes of social control and social order. Much of the behavior so minutely described by the Chicagoans, while deviant from the viewpoint of conventional society, may have reflected competing social orders—orders in conflict with conventional society, but orders nevertheless. In fact, social control processes may have operated to incorporate people into these orders. Accepting the conventional society may have blinded the Chicagoans to these processes. David Matza (1969), however, argues persuasively that they were far from blinded. Their research scrupulously described unconventional orders (such as Anderson's study of hoboes). However, the implications of that research did not enter their theory at the abstract level. While describing unconventional orders, they conceptualized disorder or disorganization. They were able to free themselves from their conventional middle-class values in describing their observations, but were unable to do so when conceptualizing their observations at the theoretical level.

Differential Organization: Cultural Conflict and Socialization

During the 1930s some Chicagoans began to conceptualize deviant areas as differentially organized rather than as disorganized. Rather than conceptualizing behavior in the inner city as a departure from the conventional order, some Chicagoans conceptualized it in terms of its own internal integrity, noting the conflict between the organization of the inner city and the conventional order. Thorsten Sellin (1938), examined the causes and types of cultural conflict and specified its relationship to crime and deviance. He argued that crime occurs because some cultural groups have the power to incorporate their values into laws, which other cultural groups violate. Research within the cultural conflict tradition, however, focused not on the dynamics and structure of this conflict but on social processes by which unconventional norms and values are transmitted from generation to generation; that is, on the social psychological processes by which people are socialized into a deviant culture. (The structure and dynamics of social conflict are examined in Chapter Seven.) Shaw and McKay (1931) were among the first Chicagoans to discuss this process. They argued that when social disorganization disrupts the traditional forces of social control, high rates of deviance emerge and become traditional aspects of social life. Once established, these traditions are transmitted through personal and group contacts from generation to generation.

Differential Association. Sutherland's differential association theory is probably the most influential of the cultural transmission theories of deviant socialization. The theory attempts to articulate the social psychological processes involved in deviant socialization in nine propositions (Sutherland and Cressey, 1970).

1. "Criminal (deviant) behavior is learned." It is not biologically determined, not the result of psychological characteristics which are themselves biologically caused, and not something which is invented in isolation from others. It is learned.

2. "Criminal (deviant) behavior is learned in interaction with other persons in a process of communication."

3. "The principal part of the learning of criminal (deviant) behavior occurs within intimate personal groups." The learning described in proposition two is not a result of impersonal sources, such as radio, T.V., movies, newspapers, and magazines.

4. "When criminal (deviant) behavior is learned, the learning includes

(a) techniques of committing the crime (deviance), which are sometimes very complicated, sometimes very simple; (b) the specific direction of motives, drives, rationalizations and attitudes.''

5. "The specific direction of motives and drives is learned from definitions of the legal codes as favorable or unfavorable." The mode in which people manifest general motives for wealth, social success, etc. is affected by exposure to definitions of crime (deviance) as favorable or unfavorable.

6. "A person becomes criminal (deviant) because of an excess of definitions favorable to violation of the law (conventional norms) over definitions unfavorable to violation of the law (conventional norms).''

7. "Differential association may vary in frequency, duration, priority, and intensity." Frequency refers to the number of criminal (deviant) and noncriminal (nondeviant) definitions to which a person is exposed; duration refers to the length of time for which a person is exposed; priority refers to the age of the person during exposure; and intensity refers to the level of affectivity between the person and the sources of criminal (deviant) and noncriminal (nondeviant) definitions. Differential association theory assumes that as the frequency, duration, priority (a high level refers to a young age) and intensity of deviant associations increase relative to conventional associations, the probability of deviant behavior increases relative to conventional behavior.

8. "The process of learning criminal (deviant) behavior by association with criminal (deviant) and anticriminal (antideviant) patterns involves all of the mechanisms that are involved in any other learning." The difference between criminals (deviants) and noncriminals (nondeviants) is the pattern of association, not the processes by which learning occurs.

9. "While criminal (deviant) behavior is an expression of general needs and values (material wealth or social prestige), it is not explained by those general needs and values, since noncriminal (nondeviant) behavior is an expression of the same needs and values." Some people satisfy them by noncriminal (nondeviant) behavior; others satisfy them by criminal (deviant) behavior.

Differential association theory can be succinctly conceptualized. Some of the propositions are completely or partially redundant (propositions one and two), and others criticize other theories, specifying what differential association theory is not (propositions eight and nine). For the most part, the theory is described in propositions three to seven. Generally, Sutherland argues that deviant behavior is not biologically inherited or invented; it is an expression of definitions favorable to deviant behavior learned in association with others in intimate social relations. Note that the theory does not say that deviance is a result of contact with deviant definitions. Everyone has some contact with deviant definitions; it is the ratio of deviant to nondeviant definitions that is important. The causal structure of the theory is briefly summarized in Box 3.1, Model A, where deviant behavior is conceptualized as reflecting attitudes (definitions) approving of norm violations, which are generally learned in deviant associations.

Contemporary Extensions and Revisions. The Chicago ecologists argued that certain geographical areas of the city develop cultural traditions in conflict with the conventional order. Sutherland, explicating a social psychological theory by which these cultural traditions are learned, generally conceived of social influence as operating within these areas in terms of face-to-face interaction.

Recent conceptualizations by Daniel Glaser (1956) and Walter Reckless and Simon Dinitz (1967) have emphasized non-face-to-face interaction, and subjective rather than objective dimensions of social interaction. Glaser argues that social influence is not exhausted by face-to-face interaction within geographically defined areas. The mass media, for instance, convey cultural definitions that may not be espoused in some residential areas. (When Sutherland originally developed his theory the mass media, not including television, were probably less influential than they are today.) Additionally, Glaser argues that people are influenced not only through physical associations but through subjective attachments like attraction, identification, and admiration. Some people residing in high deviance areas may be subjectively attached to nondeviants outside of the area, such as an admired teacher or a sports figure conveyed through the mass media, who may strongly influence their behavior; consequently, they may be unaffected by a high level of deviant behavior in their immediate neighborhood. On the other hand, some people residing in low deviant areas may be subjectively attached to deviants outside of the area (also conveyed by the mass media) and therefore may become involved in deviance. Reckless and Dinitz (1967) have raised similar questions about differential association theory based on studies of boys who remain nondelinquent in delinquent neighborhoods. They argue that these boys are characterized by positive and nondelinquent self-concepts, which insulate them from the influence of delinquent peers. While residing in high delinquent neighborhoods, they are unattracted to delinquent boys and avoid interaction with them; instead,

Daniel Glaser, born 1918, received his B.A. in 1939, and his M.A. in 1947 and Ph.D. in 1954 from the University of Chicago, and is currently a Professor of Sociology at the University of Southern California. He is well known for his paper "Criminal Theories and Behavior Images." (Courtesy of Daniel Glaser, reprinted by permission.)

Simon Dinitz, born 1926, received his B.A. in 1947 and his M.A. in 1949 from Vanderbilt University, and his Ph.D. in 1951 from the University of Wisconsin at Madison, and presently he is a Professor of Sociology at Ohio State University. He is best known for his work on self-concept and deviance. (Courtesy of Simon Dinitz, reprinted by permission.)

they are attracted to their parents and teachers. Even when exposed to delinquent definitions, they interpret them in a different light than do boys with negative self-concepts.

Robert L. Burgess and Ronald L. Akers (1966) make two general criticisms of differential association theory: one, its concepts (definitions of the situation) refer to mental phenomena, which are intrinsically difficult to measure; and two, the processes of learning deviant behavior are only vaguely described. Thus, they argue that the general idea encompassed by differential association theory would be on firmer theoretical and methodological ground if conceptualized in terms of behavioristic theory, a body of theory and research deemphasizing the study of mental phenomena.

Traditionally, behaviorists have argued that since mental phenomena cannot be reliably observed it cannot be part of a science. Researchers should focus their attention on what can be observed—behavior. Various behavioristic theories have developed. Operant conditioning theory, used by Robert L. Burgess and Ronald L. Akers (1966), asserts that behavior is a response to rewards and punishments. As rewards which follow a behavior increase and punishments decrease, the frequency of that behavior increases; and as rewards which follow a behavior decrease and punishments increase, the frequency of that behavior decreases. Burgess and Akers argue that deviant behavior is no different from any other behavior. It can be understood as a response to rewards and punishments. As the rewards which follow deviant behavior increase and punishments decrease, the frequency of deviant behavior increases.

Clearly, Burgess and Akers' reformulation considerably transforms Sutherland's original theory. Reflecting the concerns of sociologists at the University of Chicago, Sutherland's theory emphasizes cultural meanings or definitions; these are obscured in behavioristic reformulations where mental phenomena are de-

Ronald Akers, born 1939, received his B.S. in 1960 from Indiana State University, his M.A. in 1961 from Kent State University, and his Ph.D. in 1966 from the University of Kentucky, and is presently a Professor of Sociology at the University of Florida. He is well known for his work on learning theory and deviance, *Deviant Behavior: A Social Learning Approach,* 1977. (Courtesy of Ronald Akers, reprinted by permission.)

emphasized. Furthermore, the thrust of Sutherland's theory, that socialization takes place in primary intimate groups, is also deemphasized in Burgess and Akers' reformulation, which suggests that behavior is learned when followed by a variety of rewards (such as money and social prestige) from a variety of sources.

Rather than examining Burgess and Akers' behavioristic theory of deviant socialization as a reconceptualization of differential association theory, it may be more useful to examine it on its own terms. What does it add to our understanding of the process by which people come to engage in deviance? Differential association theory, linked with ideas of cultural conflict, focuses attention on the learning of evaluative and moral definitions. People engage in deviant acts because they learn to approve of them. Burgess and Akers, and Akers (1978) turn our attention to the role of rewards and punishments in the study of deviant behavior. While some people may commit deviant acts because they approve of them, other people may commit them because they are instrumental in increasing social status and prestige.

The ideas of Sutherland and Burgess and Akers might usefully be ''integrated'' as in Model C in Box 3.1, where deviant association results in deviant attitudes (via a socialization process), which in turn are expressed in deviant behavior, and where deviant association has a direct or immediate effect on deviant behavior (through a process of social pressure).

Summary.   Around the mid-1930s some Chicagoans began to reconceptualize urban areas from disorganized to differentially organized, that is, as characterized by various different and sometimes conflicting social orders, not always reflecting the conventional order. This conceptualization makes the concept of deviance as a norm violation problematic. What constitutes a norm violation depends on which social order or norms are assumed by sociologists. Sociologists resolved this issue by temporarily ignoring it. Rather than dealing with the question of social conflict, they implicitly or explicitly assumed the normative order of middle-class whites (the class most reflecting traditional rural American values and norms) and focused on the social psychological processes by which people become socialized into deviant social orders. A social psychological tradition of theory and research was thus initiated.

Sutherland's theory of differential association, conceptualizing the deviant socialization process in terms of symbolic learning in association with immediate intimate others, became the reference point for departure and criticism. More recently, Glaser has emphasized the role of subjective relationships; Reckless and Dinitz have emphasized the role of self-concept; and Burgess and Akers have attempted to reconceptualize the deviant socialization process in behavioristic terms. While differing as to the nature of the socialization process into deviance, Sutherland, Glaser, Reckless and Dinitz, and Burgess and Akers assume the perspective of middle-class whites from which the behavior of other groups is conceptualized as deviant, and assume that the behavior judged as deviant reflects a minority social order into which people are socialized.

RESEARCH

Social Disorganization: Delinquency

Social disorganization research consists of ecological and case history studies. Ecological studies have examined the relationship between deviance and social disorganization across areas of a city, and case history studies have attempted to show how the social disorganization of an area affects residents so as to generate a high rate of deviance.

The work of Clifford R. Shaw and Henry D. McKay set a pattern for future work. Their classic work, *Delinquency Areas* (1929), analyzed the court records of 55,998 juveniles in the city of Chicago and reported the following:

1. Spatial Distribution. Ecological areas with the highest rate of school truancy have the highest rates of delinquency and adult crime.
2. Zonal Hypothesis. Crime and delinquency rates are highest in the center of the city, decreasing progressively from the center to the suburbs.
3. Persistence. High rates of delinquency have persisted in some ecological areas, although the social and ethnic composition of the residents has changed. High rates are thus linked to the social conditions of the areas, not the ethnic composition.
4. Social Disorganization. High rate areas are characterized by population instability, high percentage of families on relief, low median income, low home ownership, high percentage of foreign born, and high percentage of nonwhites—indicators of social disorganization.

Other publications by Shaw and McKay extended this work to other cities, *Social Factors in Juvenile Delinquency* (1931), and continued the analysis of Chicago in

Juvenile Delinquency and Urban Areas (1942). With some exceptions the latter works confirm the original findings. Additionally, in such works as *The Jack-Roller* (1930), *The Natural History of a Delinquent Career* (1931) and *Brothers in Crime* (1938), Shaw, McKay, and their associates tried to show how the social conditions described in their ecological studies are experienced by individual juveniles and result in delinquency.

Other Chicago researchers studied the spatial distributions of other types of deviance, such as drug addiction, alcoholism, suicide, and mental illness. In regard to mental illness, Faris and Dunham (1939) examined the records of all first admissions to public and private hospitals in Chicago between 1922 and 1934. They reported that mental illness (especially schizophrenia) was not randomly distributed throughout the city; instead, the highest rates appeared in the most disorganized sections of the city. In accounting for these findings, they argued that mental illness is precipitated by social isolation and communication breakdowns caused by social disorganization.

Bernard Lander's (1954) research, building on Shaw and McKay, set the tone and issues for more contemporary social disorganization research on social deviance. Using 8,464 cases brought to court on delinquency petitions, he computed the delinquency rates for 155 Baltimore census tracts. High area rates are associated with overcrowding, a high percentage of nonwhites, substandard housing, a low level of owner-occupied houses, low rents, and low level of education. Lander suggests that all of these factors reflect two general underlying factors. Overcrowding, substandard housing, rental cost, and the level of education generally reflect the social class composition of an area; and the percentage of nonwhites and owner-occupied homes generally reflect the social disorganization of an area.

In what sense are the percentage of nonwhites and non-owner-occupied homes indicators of the level of social disorganization in an area? Lander reports that as the number of nonwhites increase from 0 to 50 percent, the rate of delinquency increases, but as non-whites increase from 50 percent to 100 percent the rate decreases. Thus, race itself is not the central issue; if it was, the rate of delinquency would continue to increase as the percentage of nonwhites increases beyond 50 percent. Instead, he argues that areas which are 50 percent nonwhite and 50 percent white are undergoing racial and social change, and thus are characterized by social disorganization. Lander also argues that the percentage of owner-occupied homes indicates the level of social disorganization, because renters are more transient and have less investment in a neighborhood than home owners. Lander concludes that, while the social class and disorganization levels of a neighborhood are related, it is disorganization, not social class, that causes delinquency. This work, published in 1954, became a center of controversy and provided a stimulus for work over the next fifteen years.

David J. Bordua (1959) attempted to replicate Lander's results in Detroit. While the data on the economic or social class factors (rent, housing value, and income) are consistent with Lander's, the findings for the social disorganization factors are mixed. Home ownership relates to delinquency, but percentage of nonwhites does not. As an additional indicator of area disorganization, Bordua used the ratio of unattached individuals to intact families in a neighborhood. Since the data show a relationship between this ratio and delinquency, Bordua concludes that, while his data do not exactly confirm Lander's, they generally support the disorganization thesis.

Roland J. Chilton (1964) attempts to deal with the inconsistencies between Lander's work in Baltimore and Bordua's work in Detroit, and provides the final major effort to test disorganization theory. Upon reanalyzing their data and analyzing new data on Indianapolis, he reports that home ownership relates to delinquency, but percentage of nonwhites does not. Of the various other conditions which have been used to indicate the level of social disorganization (a high proportion of unmarried men, a high proportion of working women, a high number of persons per household, and a high level of residential mobility), some link to delinquency and some do not. He thus concludes that there is no clear support for the disorganization thesis.

Chilton's research highlights the basic problem of social disorganization research: the concept of social disorganization is vaguely defined and difficult to measure. Different studies of different cities at different times use different measures. In fact, some studies use deviance itself as an indicator of social disorganization! Hence, the results are ambiguous and confusing. As these conceptual and operational problems have not been resolved, and as the social conditions which originally suggested the disorganization concept seem to have abated, this research tradition is no longer a center of attention.

Socialization: Delinquency, Drugs, Homosexuality

During the 1930s and 1940s, research on deviant socialization employing case histories and field methods began to appear. Since the mid-1950s, survey methods have been used to develop a systematic research paradigm for testing deviant socialization theories.

The work of James F. Short (1957 and 1958) in testing differential association theory is noteworthy. He argues that exposure to deviant definitions, while not directly measurable, can be indirectly measured by exposure to deviants. While exposure to deviant definitions and exposure to deviants are not equivalent (one can learn deviant definitions from conventional people and conventional definitions from deviants), the relationship is strong enough so that exposure to deviants may be used to measure exposure to deviant definitions.

Short studied delinquency and operationalized the major theoretical concepts in terms of questionnaire items. Delinquency is measured by self-reports, using the following questionnaire items:

1. Driving a car without a driver's license
2. Buying or drinking beer, wine, or liquor (including drinking at home)

James F. Short, Jr., born 1924, received his B.A. in 1947 from Denison University, and his M.A. in 1949 and Ph.D. in 1951 from the University of Chicago, and is presently the Director of the Social Research Center and Professor of Sociology at Washington State University. He is well known for his research on juvenile delinquency, for example, *Group Processes and Gang Delinquency*, 1965. (Courtesy of James F. Short, Jr., reprinted by permission.)

3. Skipping school without a legitimate excuse
4. Taking little things (less than $2) that do not belong to you
5. Purposely damaging or destroying public or private property
6. Sex relations with a person of the opposite sex
7. Taking things of medium value (worth $2 to $50)
8. Running away from home
9. Taking things of large value (worth more than $50)
10. Defying parents' authority to their faces
11. Narcotics violations.

Exposure to delinquents is measured in terms of each dimension of association and in terms of a general level of association. The following questionnaire items were used.

Frequency: Think of friends you have been associated with most often. Were (or are) any of them juvenile delinquents?

Duration: Think of the friends you have known for the longest time. Were (or are) any of them juvenile delinquents?

Priority: Think back to the first friends you can remember. Were any of them juvenile delinquents?

Intensity: Have any of your best friends been juvenile delinquents while they were your best friends?

General: Was there much crime and delinquency committed by young people in their teens or below in the community in which you grew up?

General: Have any of your friends been juvenile delinquents?

General: Are any of your present friends juvenile delinquents?

General: Do you know any adult criminals?

General: How well have you known criminals?

Short's (1957) first study used a sample of 126 boys and fifty girls (ten to seventeen years of age) from a training school. The results support the theory, showing a moderately strong relationship between exposure to delinquents and delinquent behavior. For both boys and girls, intensity and frequency are the most significant dimensions of association, and priority and duration are the least significant dimensions. While the sample is limited to juveniles confined to a training school, certainly not representative of the juvenile population, various other studies using various samples throughout the United States (Short, 1958; Voss, 1964; Reiss and Rhodes, 1964; Stanfield, 1966; and Matthews, 1968, for example) report similar results, generally supporting differential association theory.

Research has also been reported on the various extensions of differential association theory. Based on Glaser's ideas, Victor M. Matthews (1968) argues that reciprocal attachment (where two people select each other as best friends) is a measure of the intensity of a social relationship. Using measures of delinquency and exposure to delinquents similar to Short's, Matthews reports a moderate correlation between delinquency and best friend's delinquency, which is substantially increased for juveniles in reciprocal relationships. The research points to the importance of subjective emotional associations, as compared to the physical dimensions of association, like frequency and duration, in understanding delinquency.

Reckless and Dinitz (1967) have tested their theory of delinquency. To reiterate, they argue that juveniles with certain personalities or self characteristics (generally a positive self-concept) are insulated or "immune" from peer influences in high delinquent neighborhoods. To test this hypothesis, they selected 101 boys nominated by teachers as heading for trouble, "bad boys," and 125 boys nominated as avoiding trouble, "good boys," who reside in the same high delinquent neighborhoods. To determine what characterizes boys who are able to stay out of trouble in the high delinquent neighborhoods, they administered to both the "good" and "bad" boys a battery of personality tests (delinquency proneness, social responsibility, self-concept). Although differentiating the "good" from the "bad" boys, the tests include so many diverse personality dimensions that they fail to clarify what characterizes the "good" boys (Tangri and Schwartz, 1967). Whatever characterizes them, a four year follow-up study, in which 103 of the "good" boys and seventy of the "bad" boys were located, shows that the "good" boys continued to stay out of trouble, while the "bad" boys continued their troublesome behavior. (Schwartz and Tangri, 1965, show comparable results in a Detroit study.) While significant, this research leaves many questions unanswered. For example, how does a positive self-concept develop, and how or why does it insulate juveniles from peer influence?

By the mid-1960s these studies had generated considerable data, generally consistent with the thrust of the deviant socialization theories. They established a link between delinquency and association with delinquent peers modulated perhaps by self-concept and emotional attachments. They did not, however, establish the causal process underlying the link. Differential association theory suggests a socialization process whereby juveniles learn delinquent definitions and attitudes from delinquent associates. Other theories suggest other causal processes. Sheldon and Eleanor Glueck (1950), for example, suggest a social selection process whereby juveniles who engage in delinquency for whatever reason choose to associate with like peers (Box 3.1, Model D). Even sociologists accepting the causal priority of delinquent associations argue that past research does not clarify the underlying causal processes. Do juveniles emulate the behavior of peers because they have come to accept delinquent attitudes as right and proper (Box 3.1, Model A), or do they emulate the behavior of delinquent peers solely because of social pressure, while feeling that the behavior is morally wrong (Box 3.1, Model B)?

Since the late 1960s and early 1970s multivariate statistical procedures in conjunction with the logic of causal modeling have been used to address these problems. Various theoretical and research papers (Liska, 1969; Hackler, 1970; Gould, 1969; Hirschi, 1969; Jensen, 1972; Liska, 1973, and Hepburn, 1977) have attempted to assess the relative merits of the causal structures in Box 3.1 in explaining the established link between deviant associations and deviant involvement.

Box 3.1 CAUSAL STRUCTURES UNDERLYING THE LINK BETWEEN DEVIANT ASSOCIATIONS AND DEVIANT BEHAVIOR

A. Differential Association Model

Deviant Association ⟶ Deviant Attitude ⟶ Deviant Behavior

Deviant associates via processes of socialization produce deviant attitudes, which are manifested in deviant behavior.

B. Social Control Model

Deviant Associations ⟶ Deviant Behavior

Deviant associates produce deviant behavior, via pressures to conform.

C. Socialization/Social Control Model

⟶ Delinquent Attitudes ⟶
Deviant Associations ⟶ Deviant Behavior

This model includes both socialization and social pressure processes.

D. Social Selection Model

Deviant Behavior ⟶ Deviant Associations

Deviants, through social selection processes, come to associate with other deviants.

Gary F. Jensen's (1972) work provides one of the more rigorous efforts to assess these causal structures. He examines the extent to which the socialization process, as outlined in differential association theory (Box 3.1, Model A) can account for the established link between delinquent associations and delinquency.

The sample consists of 1588 nonblack high school males from Richmond, California. Delinquency involvement was measured in terms of a self-report inventory; delinquent associations were measured in terms of the number of close friends picked up by the police; and delinquent attitude was measured as approval of the police and the law. To test the socialization model, as specified by differential association theory, Jensen first computed the relationships between delinquent attitudes, associations with delinquent peers, and delinquency. Consistent with past findings, the data show moderately strong positive relationships. However, the critical test is the extent to which the relationship between delinquent associations and delinquent involvement is maintained when delinquent attitude is controlled. If delinquent attitude mediates the relationship between delinquent associations and delinquent involvement, when controlled for delinquent attitude the relationship should reduce to approximately zero. To control for the effect of delinquent attitude, Jensen computed the relationship between delinquent associations and delinquent involvement for respondents with an antidelinquent attitude, for respondents with a neutral attitude, and for respondents with a prodelinquent attitude. As these specific relationships are not too different from the overall relationship between delinquent associations and delinquent involvement, Jensen concludes that the effect of delinquent peers on delinquency is not solely a product of socialization into competing normative standards. The data appear to be most consistent with the peer socialization/social control model (Box 3.1, Model C), where delinquent associates affect delinquent behavior directly (via social pressure) and indirectly via their effect on attitudes, which in turn affect delinquency. The data also show that parental interaction (measured as supervision and emotional support) reduces delinquency. Jensen, however, does not distinguish between parental socialization, whereby high parental interaction results in nondelinquent attitudes, which reduce delinquent involvement, and parental social control, whereby parents directly reduce delinquent involvement via social pressure. Both social processes seem likely.

In sum, the research suggests that adolescents with a low level of parental interaction and a high ratio of delinquent to nondelinquent peers are most likely to be delinquent, and adolescents with a high level of parental interaction and a low ratio of delinquent to nondelinquent peers are least likely to be delinquent. Additionally, the research attempts to specify the relative effects of peers and parents and of socialization and social control processes in generating delinquency.

Some recent research on drug use among teenagers also addresses this issue. Using a sample of 1110 students from New York high schools, Denise Kandel et al. (1974) compared the effects of peers and parents on drug use (including both soft and hard drugs) among teenagers. For marijuana use, parental influence is minimal; whether or not parents used marijuana, and whether or not teenagers are emotionally attached to their parents is relatively unimportant. Peer use is the important variable. For multiple drug use (using a variety of soft and hard drugs) peer use is also the most important variable, although parental influence is more important than for marijuana use. In a follow-up study of this sample, Andrews and Kandel (1979) examined the relative effects of personal attitudes toward drug use and the use of drugs by peers, thereby comparing socialization and social pressure processes of influence. The data suggest that peer use is more important than personal attitudes. While Kandel does not explicitly compare causal structures, as Jensen does, her work seems most consistent with Model C in Box 3.1, where deviant associations affect deviant involvement directly via interpersonal social pressure and indirectly via attitude socialization. The data of Kandel and Jensen are also in agreement that peer influence is greater than parental influence.

Recent work on homosexuality has also dealt with these issues. Dank (1971) argues that defining oneself as a homosexual is significant in "coming out" or participating fully and openly in homosexuality. Prior to accepting themselves as homosexuals, people may experience guilt, anxiety, uneasiness, and self doubts about "unconventional" sexual feelings. For example, one of Dank's respondents states: "I had guilt feelings about this being attracted to men. Because I couldn't understand why all the other boys were dating, and I didn't have any real desire to date." Accepting oneself as a homosexual provides the nucleus for a cognitive organization of one's emotions, and thus facilitates homosexual behavior. Dank suggests that such cognitive reorganization and recognition takes place in a social context, generally in the company of other homosexuals, who provide the motives, vocabulary, justifications, and social support necessary for a person to redefine himself or herself as a homosexual.

Dank's research identifies three major concepts (homosexual identity, homosexual involvement, and association with homosexuals), approximating the general concepts in the deviant socialization theories. While suggesting an underlying causal structure approximating Model A in Box 3.1, his research only shows that the three concepts are related; other causal structures are also possible.

Recent work by Farrell and Nelson (1976) and Hammersmith and Weinberg (1973) addresses this question. Using questionnaire data from 148 male homosexuals, Farrell and Nelson test various causal structures underlying the relationship between homosexual involvement, homosexual identity, association with homosexuals (measured by frequency, intensity, priority, and duration), and societal reaction. They hypothesized that societal rejection stimulates a negative self-concept, which leads to association with other homosexuals (who provide the social support necessary for accepting oneself as a homosexual), which in turn leads to intense involvement in homosexuality. While data suggest the importance of homosexual associations in this sequence, the data also suggest that the effect of association is direct, not mediated through self-concept (approximating Model B in Box 3.1).

Rather than examining social support from other homosexuals, Hammersmith and Weinberg examine the role of social support from significant heterosexuals, such as parents and friends, on the psychological adjustment of homosexuals and their psychological commitment to homosexuality. Using a sample of 2497 homosexuals from the Netherlands, Denmark, and the United States, they attempted to infer the causal structure underlying relationships between social support, psychological adjustment, and homosexual commitment. Testing six causal structures, they conclude that two are most likely: social support causes commitment, which in turn causes adjustment; or commitment causes both social support and adjustment. While these studies may raise more questions than they answer about the socialization process into homosexuality, like the studies on delinquency and drug use they suggest the importance of deviant associations in the process of becoming a homosexual.

To summarize, socialization studies have been conducted on most patterns of deviance (delinquency, homosexuality, and drug use) using case study, field observation, and survey techniques. This section has focused on survey research, because it has been most critical in testing theories of deviant socialization, like differential association. Survey studies first appeared in the late 1950s with a series of papers by Short, showing that delinquency is related to delinquency of peers. Other researchers have emphasized the subjective meaning of peer associations and the role of self-concept in modulating peer influences. Since the late 1960s various researchers have closely examined the causal processes by which deviant associations and deviant involvement are linked for a variety of deviant patterns. While the data generally support the socialization process, specified by differential association theory, they also suggest the importance of social control and social selection processes.

SOCIAL POLICY

This section examines the policy implications and implementations of the two schools of the Chicago perspective, social disorganization and differential organization.

Social Disorganization: Community Building

Social disorganization theory states that social processes, like industrialization and urbanization, create disorganization in cities, which reduces social control, resulting in deviant behavior. The policy implications are reasonably clear: the chain of events leading to deviance must be arrested. Policy makers can concentrate on the more immediate causes—social control and social disorganization—or the more remote causes—industrialization and urbanization. Perhaps because of the rather unlikely prospects of altering processes of industrialization and urbanization, and the questionable desirability of doing so, the Chicagoans chose to focus on the more immediate causes. They endeavored to increase social control by building urban community organizations.

Community organization projects were initiated by Clifford R. Shaw in Chicago and came to be known as the Chicago Area Projects. Three types of projects were established. Some dealt with general community improvement, including schools, sanitation, traffic safety, physical conservation, and law enforcement. Some were designed to improve community recreational facilities for juveniles. They used community volunteers to establish conventional forms of recreation, such as summer camps, and to establish recreational space within the community through the conversion of store-fronts and unused space in churches, police stations, and homes. Other projects, specifically designed to reduce crime and delinquency in the community, emphasized helping police and juvenile courts to develop supervision plans for delinquent youths, visitations to youth training schools and reformatories, working with boys' gangs in the neighborhood, and assisting parolees in returning to the community (Kobrin, 1959).

The exact nature and content of these projects is less theoretically important than their structure and form. The Chicagoans were concerned with organizing conventional residents so as to strengthen the conventional forces of social control. They argued that such projects, whatever their specific goals, function to bring together the responsible and conventional adults of an area and to provide them with a vehicle for organization and social control.

What precisely is the role of the sociologist in the community building process? The Chicagoans were quite clear that area community development must be an area enterprise, although a catalyst is sometimes needed to stimulate development. Sociologists could play such a role, providing support and assistance, but only when needed. The Area Projects employed community residents as organizers, nominated for the position by community councils which were composed of community residents, frequently people already tied to conventional community organizations. Thus, while employed and paid to stimulate community organization, the organizers resided in the community and were ultimately responsible to the community.

What were the accomplishments of these projects? Generally, they showed that urban community organizations can be formed and can function autonomously. To some extent, they provided models for the social programs of the 1960s, such as Mobilization For Youth (see Chapter Two), and for community organization projects in developing countries (Clinard, 1966). Did they, however, reduce the level of norm-violating behavior in these areas? The answer remains unknown, as rigorous evaluation procedures were not used. The Chicagoans were more concerned with implementing the policy implications of their theory and research than in evaluating the success of their programs.

Differential Organization and Socialization

By the 1930s many Chicagoans conceptualized the inner city as differentially organized, rather than disorganized, and studied the socialization process by which unconventional forms of behavior are learned and unconventional social orders are thus perpetuated. The policy implications of socialization theory and research are less concerned with community reorganization and building than with building social relationships between unconventionals and conventionals. Specifically, differential association theory suggests that deviant behavior comes about because of deviant definitions, and research suggests that such definitions are learned in associations with deviants. Thus, to reduce deviance, policy makers must increase the ratio of nondeviant to deviant associations.

How can this be done? Conventionals surely are not going to change their life style so as to associate more with known deviants. Studies show that people released from prisons and rehabilitation centers are avoided by conventionals (Phillips, 1963; Schwartz, 1960). Even family members are troubled about reestablishing relationships with rehabilitated addicts, ex-mental patients, and exconvicts, who frequently have been a source of distress (Ray, 1961). Helping people reorganize their lives is difficult and risky work. In urbanized industrial countries, particularly Western Europe and North America, such work has evolved into occupations, such as psychiatrists, psychologists, case workers, group workers, detached workers, etc. Whatever the goals and practices of these "helping" professionals, their relationships with deviants are a source of conventional definitions. From the viewpoint of differential association theory, how useful should such programs be? It seems unlikely that a few hours a week with a representative of these agencies can make a significant difference in the ratio of deviant to nondeviant definitions. Furthermore, research suggests that affective or intense social relationships, which rarely develop between agency representatives and their clients, are crucial. Hence, the lack of success of these programs (see Box 3.2) does not disprove socialization theories; rather socialization theories suggest that these programs will be unsuccessful!

Given that conventionals are unwilling to become involved with deviants and that agencies staffed by professionals seem to be rather unsuccessful at it, what do socialization theories suggest? Self-help programs have been suggested, which bring together deviants who wish to change their lives to help each other change. Within the last decade, self-help groups composed of drug addicts, alcoholics, mental patients, etc., have sprung up throughout the United States. Some groups are constructed as communes and closed societies (Synanon), whereas others meet on a daily, weekly, or monthly basis (Alcoholics Anonymous). Theoretical

Box 3.2 BUILDING SELF-CONCEPTS

To reiterate, Walter Reckless and his associates argue that adolescents with positive self-concepts can resist the influence of delinquent peers. Hence, policy makers should build positive self-concepts in adolescents residing in high delinquent areas. To test these policy implications, Reckless and Dinitz (1967) organized a self-concept building program. Eight junior high schools in the inner city of Columbus, Ohio were selected. Teachers were asked to nominate "bad" and "good" boys; nominations were confirmed by police records. The "bad" boys were randomly divided into two groups; one was part of a self-concept building program and the other served as a control, needed so that the researchers could observe what happened to "bad" boys who were not part of the program. The self-concept building program consisted of the following. Through a summer program, teachers were trained in the techniques of building positive self-concepts in adolescents, such as providing positive feedback and presenting positive role models; and during the course of the project the teachers met regularly with the project director and with a consulting child psychiatrist. The experimental students were exposed to these specially trained teachers for three consecutive classes. Three cohorts of students were studied.

What were the results? The teachers involved were very pleased, noting marked improvement in the previously nominated "bad" boys; however, the objective data on arrests, school dropouts, school attendance, grades, school achievement scores, and even self-concept measures showed no differences between the experimental and control groups. Note the implications of this failure. The program did not use outside agencies to build self-concepts; it used school teachers who are a significant part of adolescents' everyday lives. If this program failed, how much confidence can we have in the efforts of outside agencies?

These results should also remind us of the critical attitude which must be taken toward the subjective evaluations of those who administer prevention and treatment programs. They are prone to justify their involvement. Objective data comparing those exposed to the program and those not exposed is needed for an adequate evaluation (Lundman et al., 1976).

justifications for such groups are varied and abundant. From the viewpoint of socialization theories, they constitute deviants who provide nondeviant definitions to each other, and should be effective resocialization agents to the extent to which they become a significant part of peoples' lives, extensively affecting the frequency, duration, and intensity of social relationships. Thus, communes should be more effective than groups which meet only once a week or once every two weeks for an evening (see Box 3.3). It should also be noted that, while self-help groups are frequently organized consistent with the policy implications of socialization theories, they are limited to deviants who wish to change their lives (many do not) and to deviants who are willing and able to undergo the problems and traumas which frequently accompany membership in self-help groups.

Box 3.3 SYNANON

Synanon, organized in 1958 by former drug addicts to help each other stay off drugs, was studied by Rita Volkman and Donald R. Cressey (1963). Volkman (a nonaddict) obtained permission to visit Synanon on weekdays and live in on weekends; after about one year of this, she obtained permission to reside at the Synanon House. Cressey (a nonaddict) visited the organization about once a week for one year. This discussion is based on their report.

They examine the organization of Synanon in terms of differential association theory. 1. The admission policy is very selective. Addicts are only admitted after the group is convinced that they are sincerely interested in changing their lives, rather than just recuperating or reducing their level of drug tolerance. Hence, individuals who may espouse pro-drug definitions are not allowed into the program. 2. The group is organized to emphasize no drug use (nonalcohol and anticrime definitions as well). A new member is thus exposed to an atmosphere where antidrug definitions are espoused and drug use and drug talk are banned. Additionally, a new member must participate in indoctrination sessions where he or she is asked to explain his or her past and present behavior. Old members drill the new member, defining his or her reasons and motives for using drugs as excuses and rationalizations. 3. Synanon is also organized to maximize attraction between members; they eat together, work together, play together, and generally live together. In differential association terms, this should increase the intensity of association, and thus increase the level of group influence. Generally, Volkman and Cressey report that Synanon is a commune organized to maximize social influence over its members.

What are the results? The members are, of course, convinced of Synanon's effectiveness. Based on Synanon's records and their own observations, Volkman and Cressey report that of the 372 enrollees, 29 percent were off drugs. More importantly, of the 215 members who resided at Synanon for one month, 48 percent were off drugs; of the 143 who resided at Synanon for three months, 66 percent were off drugs; and of the 87 who resided at Synanon for seven months, 86 percent were off drugs. Clearly, the longer the stay at Synanon, the higher the rate of success. Herein lies the problem. Because of the severe demands of the program, it draws few applicants; of those who seek admission not all are allowed to join; and of those who do join, very few remain for more than three months. Over a three-year period, 263 were admitted to the program of which 72 percent dropped out against the advice of the older members and leaders. Ninety percent of the drops occurred within the first three months. Hence, while the program may be very successful for those who stay, few enrollees stay more than three months.

In conclusion, it should be noted that some recent reports suggest that the organization of Synanon has changed, and that it no longer functions as described by Volkman and Cressey.

In sum, both social disorganization and socialization theories suggest social policies. The former suggests building conventional organizations to exercise social control, exemplified by the Chicago Area Projects. In terms of reducing deviance, the results of these and similar projects are ambiguous; they do, however, show the feasibility of community organization in the inner city, at least on a limited scale. The socialization theories of deviance shift policy from community building to building relationships between deviants and the existing conventional community. Such programs have also been of limited success. Either the relationships are so weak (detached worker programs) that they have little or no effect on a deviant's interaction patterns, or they are so encompassing (Synanon) that most deviants avoid involvement.

CRITIQUE

Social Disorganization

Contemporary Applications. Rates of industrialization, urbanization, and immigration and migration have lessened in American Society. Laws have reduced the level of immigration to insignificance; rural-urban migration has substantially decreased; and industrialization is now a way of life. Hence, the social disorganization theory may be less applicable to contemporary America than to a bygone era. It may, however, be very applicable to deviance in developing nations where industrialization and urbanization processes are just beginning (Clinard and Abbott, 1973).

Middle-Class Rural Bias. The Chicagoans' own research questions whether the theory of social disorganization was ever applicable to the United States for any prolonged period of time. While they abstractly conceptualized social disorganization, they studied organizational diversity, describing in some detail the cultural and social order of the inner city. David Matza (1966) refers to this discrepancy between concept and research as the central dilemma of the early Chicagoans. C. Wright Mills (1943) argues that the Chicagoans' conceptualization of the inner city, even the city itself, as disorganized reflects their rural, Protestant, middle-class backgrounds. As the city, particularly the inner city, did not reflect the cultural and social order of rural America, the Chicagoans conceptualized it as lacking order. In effect, the Chicagoans' values blinded them to the order revealed in their own research.

Operationalizing Social Disorganization. While the Chicagoans conceptualized social disorganization as a social state, which results in high rates of deviance, they sometimes used the latter as an index of the former. When disorganization is so operationalized, the proposition that social disorganization causes deviance is not subject to empirical verification; its operational form is tautological. Social disorganization will always be present when deviance is present and will always be absent when deviance is absent (a perfect relationship), because both conditions are measured by the presence of deviance. For the above proposition to be subject to empirical research and verification, the presence of social disorganization must be measured independently of the presence of deviance. In more recent research (Lander, 1954; Bordua, 1959; Chilton, 1964), disorganization is operationalized independently of social deviance; yet its conceptual ambiguity continues to plague research. Whether an area is designated as disorganized or not depends on what research study is considered. Some studies use percentage of nonwhites, some use home ownership, some use detached individuals, and some use still other indexes. The underlying problem lies in the ambiguity of the concept itself.

Accomplishments. Most critics of the early Chicago school also acknowledge their major accomplishments, and there were many. For example, the research findings did much to counter the eugenics movement based on the growing prestige of the biological sciences. Eugenics proponents argued that the high crime and deviance rate associated with urban slums is a result of generations of selective breeding of defectives. Many suggested changing reproductive patterns, including sterilization. The Chicago researchers showed that the high deviance and crime rate is associated with the slum, not the inhabitants who reside there. It is linked to sites and situations, to the ecological and social situations confronted by the people who reside there. As successions of ethnic groups (Poles, Italians, Germans, Irish) moved out of the slum their rates of deviance decreased (Faris, 1967).

Differential Organization

Theory of Society. While many Chicagoans rejected the social disorganization conceptualization by the mid-1930s, they only incipiently formulated a differential organization conceptualization. For example, does differential organization mean conflict? If so, what are the dimensions of conflict (cultural, economic, and political)? What is the role of the state in social conflict? Why are the norms of some groups but not others translated into laws? For the most part these questions were ignored. With the exception of Sellin (1938) and a few others, it was not until 1958 that Vold's monograph on crime and social conflict appeared; even this work included only a few chapters on social conflict and crime. (More will be said in Chapter Seven.) Instead, the Chicagoans developed a social psychology of deviance, focusing on the process by which people are socialized and operate in social worlds which conflict with the conventional order.

Range of Application. Socialization theories are most applicable to deviance that is subcultural, describing the process by which deviant definitions are learned. Yet not all deviance is subculturally supported. Certain acts lack subcultural support (child molesting and suicide) in the United States in the sense that no groups actively encourage involvement; and many acts are not actively supported, although subcultural norms may indirectly contribute to their occurrence (rape and homicide). Acknowledging the limitations of socialization theories of deviance may sharpen their usefulness in directing research and social policy.

Social Policy. Socialization theories have recently been criticized (Wilson, 1975) because they focus on conditions that are not tractable to policy implementation. Manipulating social definitions is difficult compared, for example, to manipulating the penalties for law violations. Yet studies of Synanon, Narcotics Anonymous, Alcoholics Anonymous, Overeaters Anonymous, and various other self-help groups suggest that it is possible. Policy makers might concern themselves with fostering and facilitating such groups.

REFERENCES

AKERS, RONALD L. *Deviant Behavior* (Belmont, Calif.: Wadsworth Publishing, 1978).

ANDERSON, NELS. *The Hobo* (Chicago: University of Chicago Press, 1923).

ANDREWS, PAUL and DENISE B. KANDEL. "Attitude and behavior: a specification of the contingent consistency hypothesis," American Sociological Review 44 (April 1979):297–307.

BORDUA, DAVID J. "Juvenile delinquency and anomie: An attempt at replication," Social Problems 6 (Winter 1959):230–38.

BURGESS, ERNEST. "The growth of a city," in Robert E. Park and Ernest Burgess (eds.) *The City (Chicago: University of Chicago Press, 1925).*

BURGESS, ROBERT L. and RONALD L. AKERS. "A differential association-reinforcement theory of criminal behavior," Social Problems 14 (Fall 1966): 128–47.

CHILTON, ROLAND J. "Continuity in delinquency area research: A comparison of studies for Baltimore, Detroit and Indianapolis," American Sociological Review 29 (Feb. 1964):71–83.

CLINARD, MARSHALL B. "Rural criminal offenders," American Journal of Sociology 50 (July 1944):38–45.

———. Slums and Community Development (New York: Free Press, 1966).

CLINARD, MARSHALL B. and D. J. ABBOTT. *Crime in Developing Countries (New York: Wiley, 1973).*

CRESSEY, PAUL. *The Taxi-Dance Hall* (Chicago: University of Chicago Press, 1932).

DANK, BARRY M. "Coming out in the gay world," Psychiatry 34 (1971): 180–97.

DARWIN, CHARLES. *Descent of Man and Selection in Relation to Sex.* (New York: D. Appleton Co., 1871).

———. *Origins of Species by Means of Natural Selection* (London: John Murray, 1859).

DEFLEUR, M. L. and R. QUINNEY. "A reformulation of Sutherland's differential association theory and a strategy for empirical verification," Journal of Research in Crime and Delinquency 3 (Jan. 1966):1−22.

FARIS, ROBERT E. L. *Chicago Sociology, 1920−1932* (San Francisco: Chandler Publishing Co., 1967).

FARIS, ROBERT E. L. and H. WARREN DUNHAM. *Mental Disorders in Urban Areas* (Chicago: University of Chicago Press, 1939).

FARRELL, RONALD A. and JAMES F. NELSON. "A causal model of secondary deviance: the case of homosexuality," The Sociological Quarterly 17 (Winter 1976):109−20.

FRAZIER, E. FRANKLIN. *The Negro Family in Chicago* (Chicago: University of Chicago, 1932).

GANS, HERBERT. *The Urban Villages* (New York: Free Press, 1962).

GLASER, DANIEL. "Criminality theories and behavioral images," American Journal of Sociology 61 (March 1956):433−44.

GLUECK, SHELDON and ELEANOR GLUECK. *Unraveling Juvenile Delinquency* (New York: Commonwealth Fund, 1950).

GOULD, LEROY C. "Juvenile entrepreneurs," American Journal of Sociology 74 (May 1969):710−20.

HACKLER, JAMES C. "Testing a causal model of delinquency," Sociological Quarterly 11 (Fall 1970):511−23.

HAMMERSMITH, SUE KIEFER and MARTIN S. WEINBERG. "Homosexual identity: commitment, adjustment and significant others," Sociometry 36 (March 1973):56−79.

HAWLEY, AMOS H. *Human Ecology: A Theory of Community Structure* (New York: Ronald Press, 1950).

HEPBURN, JOHN R. "Testing alternative models of delinquency causation," Journal of Criminal Law and Criminology 67 (1977):450−60.

HIRSCHI, TRAVIS. *Causes of Delinquency* (Los Angeles: University of California Press, 1969).

JENSEN, GARY F. "Parents, peers and delinquency action: A test of the differential association perspective," American Journal of Sociology 78 (Nov. 1972): 562−75.

KANDEL, DENISE, DONALD TREIMAN, RICHARD FAUST and ERIC SINGLE. "Adolescent involvement in legal and illegal drug use: A multiple classification analysis," Social Forces 55 (Dec. 1974):438−58.

KOBRIN, SOLOMON. "The Chicago Area Projects—A twenty-five year assessment," The Annals of the American Academy of Political and Social Sciences 322 (March 1959):20−29.

LANDER, BERNARD. *Towards an Understanding of Juvenile Delinquency* (New York: Columbia University Press, 1954).

LISKA, ALLEN E. "Interpreting the causal structure of differential association theory," Social Problems 16 (Spring, 1969):485−93.

————. "Causal structures underlying the relationship between delinquent involvement and delinquent peers," Sociology and Social Research 58 (Oct. 1973):23−26.

LUNDMAN, RICHARD J., PAUL T. MCFARLANCE, and FRANK R. SCARPETTI. "Delinquency prevention: A description and assessment of projects reported in the professional literature," Crime and Delinquency 22 (July 1976):297−308.

MATTHEWS, VICTOR M. "Differential identification: An empirical note," Social Problems 15 (Winter 1968):376−83.

MATZA, DAVID. Becoming Deviant (Englewood Cliffs, N.J.: Prentice-Hall, Inc., 1966).

MILLS, C. WRIGHT. "The professional ideology of social pathologists," American Journal of Sociology 69 (Sept. 1943):1965−80.

PHILLIPS, DEREK L. "Rejection: A possible consequence of seeking help for mental disorders," American Sociological Review 28 (1963):963−72.

RAY, MARSH B. "Abstinence cycles and heroin addicts," Social problems 9 (Fall 1961):132−40.

RECKLESS, WALTER and SIMON DINITZ. "Pioneering with self-concept as a vulnerability factor in delinquency," Journal of Criminal Law, Criminology and Police Science 58 (1967):515−23.

REISS, ALBERT and LEWIS RHODES. "An empirical test of differential association theory," Journal of Research in Crime and Delinquency 1 (Jan. 1964): 5−18.

SCHWARTZ, MICHAEL and SANDRA S. TANGRI. "A note on self-concept as an insulator against delinquency," American Sociological Review 30 (Dec. 1965):922−26.

SELLIN, THORSTEN. Cultural Conflict and Crime (New York: Social Science Research Council, 1938).

SHAW, CLIFFORD R. The Jack-Roller; A Delinquent Boy's Own Story (Chicago: University of Chicago Press, 1930).

―――. The Natural History of a Delinquent Career (Chicago: University of Chicago Press, 1931).

SHAW, CLIFFORD R. and HENRY D. MCKAY. Social Factors in Juvenile Delinquency (Washington, D.C.: U.S. Government Printing Office, 1931).

―――. Juvenile Delinquency and Urban Areas (Chicago: University of Chicago Press, 1942).

SHAW, CLIFFORD R., HENRY D. MCKAY, and JAMES F. MCDONALD. Brothers in Crime (Chicago: University of Chicago Press, 1938).

SHAW, CLIFFORD R., FREDERICK M. ZORBAUGH, HENRY D. MCKAY, and LEONARD S. COTTRELL. Delinquency Areas (Chicago: University of Chicago Press, 1929).

SHORT, JAMES F. "Differential association and delinquency," Social Problems 4 (Jan. 1957):233−39.

―――. "Differential associations with delinquent friends and delinquent behavior," Pacific Sociological Review 1 (Spring 1958):20−25.

STANFIELD, ROBERT. "The interaction of family variables and gang variables in the aetiology of delinquency," Social Problems 13 (Spring 1966):411–17.

SUTHERLAND, EDWIN. *Criminology* (Philadelphia: J. B. Lippincott, 1924).

———. *Criminology* (Philadelphia: J. B. Lippincott, 1939).

SUTHERLAND, EDWIN and DONALD CRESSEY. *Principles of Criminology* (New York: J. B. Lippincott, 1970).

SYKES, GRESHAM M. and DAVID MATZA. "Techniques of neutralization: A theory of delinquency," American Sociological Review (Dec. 1957):664–70.

TANGRI, SANDRA and MICHAEL SCHWARTZ. "Delinquency research and the self-concept variable," The Journal of Criminology and Police Science 58 (1967):182:90.

THRASHER, FREDERIC M. *The Gang* (Chicago: University of Chicago Press, 1927).

TRICE, HARRISON M. *Alcoholism in America* (New York: McGraw-Hill, 1966).

VOLD, GEORGE B. *Theoretical Criminology* (New York: Oxford University Press, 1958).

VOLKMAN, RITA and DONALD R. CRESSEY. "Differential association and the rehabilitation of drug addicts," American Journal of Sociology 69 (Sept. 1963):129–42.

VOSS, HARWIN. "Differential association and delinquent behavior," Social Problems 12 (Summer 1964):78–85.

WILSON, JAMES Q. *Thinking About Crime* (New York: Basic Books, 1975).

WIRTH, LOUIS. *The Ghetto* (Chicago: University of Chicago Press, 1928).

———. "Urbanism as a way of life," American Journal of Sociology 40 (July 1938).

tHE sociAl coNTROl/dETERRENCE pERSpECTiVE

THEORY

Like the structural/functional and Chicago theories, social control theory defines norm violations as the proper subject of study, assumes that a conventional order can be identified, making norm violations relatively simple to define, and is concerned with explaining why some people violate norms while others do not. Social control theory, however, sharply differs from both the structural/functional and Chicago theories concerning the role of deviant motivation in deviant behavior. Both theories assume that deviants differ from conformists in terms of deviant motivation, and examine how some people, but not others, come to acquire these motivational dispositions. Structural/functionalism assumes that as a consequence of certain structural conditions some people experience stress, which motivates or "pushes" them into norm violations. The Chicago socialization theory assumes that as a consequence of involvement in minority subcultures some people learn attitudes and values which motivate or "push" them into norm violations. Social control theory, to the contrary, assumes that norm violations are generally so attractive, exciting, and profitable that most people are motivated to violate norms. Thus, it is not necessary to explain deviant motivation; rather, it is necessary to explain why so few people act upon their deviant motives and violate norms. Social control theorists focus this issue by examining what controls (Hirschi, 1969) or contains (Reckless, 1967) most people from acting upon their deviant motives. Rather than assuming a high level of conformist motivation and asking why some people violate norms, they assume a high level of deviant motivation and ask why most people conform!

To some extent, contemporary social control theory can be viewed as a social psychological extension of the Chicago disorganization school. The Chicagoans examined the ecological and social conditions (industrialization and urbanization) that generate an urban environment (social change, reduction in primary group relationships, and normative conflict) in which social controls deteriorate. Contemporary social control theorists examine the dynamics or processes by which a deterioration of social controls leads to norm violations.

They distinguish two types of social control: inner and outer. The former refers to those societal rules or norms which people internalize as their own. Internalized rules control behavior because people experience self-righteousness and satisfaction when behaving consistently with them, and guilt, self reproach, and self-condemnation upon behaving inconsistently with them. Again note a distinction between social control and socialization theories of deviance. The latter conceptualize deviance as an outcome of socialization into a subculture conflicting with the conventional order. Deviants are moral animals marching to the beat of a different drummer. To the contrary, social control theories conceptualize deviance as an outcome of a lack of moral socialization.

Equally if not more important than inner controls are outer controls—the social rewards foregone and social punishments experienced upon being socially identified as a norm violator. While various punishments associated with being identified as a norm violator are well known, social control theorists remind us that rewards in different sectors of life are tied to maintaining an acceptable public identity. People identified as deviants may lose their jobs and the respect of their family and friends (social rewards foregone), as well as being fined and imprisoned (punishments). It is the prospect of these rewards foregone that inhibits the expression of deviant motivations. For example, which of the following men would be more likely to visit a prostitute: a man who is unemployed and unmarried or one who is employed and married? From the viewpont of social control theory, while both men may find such an encounter equally attractive, the former is more likely to visit a prostitute. Upon being publicly identified as a ''john'' he has little to lose. The married employed man is committed to conformity by virtue of his link to society. Being publicly identified as a ''john'' may adversely affect his career and marriage.

According to social control theory, then, people conform, not because of a lack of deviant motivation, but because of inner and outer social controls. The theory predicts the highest level of deviance for those who lack both inner and outer controls, and, conversely, the lowest level of deviance for those who experience both inner and outer controls. Various specific social control theories have emerged. Some have focused on inner controls (Sykes and Matza, 1957), and some have focused on a combination of inner and outer controls (Hirschi, 1969). Of those focusing on outer controls, some have focused on institutional controls, like the family and school, whereas others have focused on governmental controls (deterrence theory).

Social Bonds

Travis Hirschi (1969) focuses on the bond between people and conventional society. He assumes a common or at least a dominant normative system and that norm violations result from a lack of bond to the conventional society. The bond consists of four elements: belief, attachment, commitment, and involvement. Belief refers to the extent to which the conventional norms are internalized; it is thus another term for inner controls. Hirschi argues that the more people internalize conventional norms the lower their probability of violating them. Commitment refers to the extent to which people's social rewards are tied to conformity. Hirschi argues that the more people have to lose upon being socially identified as norm violators, the lower their probability of violating social norms. Attachment refers to people's sensitivity to the opinions of others. People unconcerned with the respect and status afforded them by others are not very subject to outer controls; the respect and status associated with conformity are only sources of social control for people sensitive to the feelings and opinions of others. Hence, Hirschi argues that the more people are socially attached, the lower their probability of violating norms. Involvement refers to the amount of time people devote to conventional

Travis W. Hirschi, born 1935, received his B.A. in 1957 and his M.A. in 1958 from the University of Utah, and his Ph.D. in 1968 from the University of California at Berkeley, and is presently a Professor of Criminal Justice at the State University of New York at Albany. He is well known for his book *Causes of Delinquency*, 1969. (Courtesy of Travis W. Hirschi, reprinted by permission.)

activities. People involved in conventional activities simply have little time available for deviant activities. For example, an adolescent's day occupied with school activities, sports, adult-sponsored recreation, and homework leaves little time for delinquency. Hirschi thus argues that the higher people's level of social involvement, the lower their probability of violating norms.

Hirschi delineates the links between people and society. Bond indirectly refers

---

Box 4.1 SOCIAL CONTROL RESEARCH

Hirschi (1969) has tested his theory, using a sample of approximately 1300 sixth to twelfth grade white males from a West Coast county. The major concepts of the theory are measured by questionnaire as follows:

Delinquency: measured as self-report, including items on theft and vandalism.

Attachment: measured as attraction to parents, school, and peers; for example, "Would you like to be the kind of person your father is?"

Commitment: measured as the importance placed upon good grades.

Involvement: measured as the amount of time devoted to school activities (such as studying).

Belief: measured as adherence to conventional beliefs, such as respect for the police and the law.

For the most part, the data support Hirschi's theory, showing that a strong bond (a high level of attachment, commitment, involvement, and belief) relates to a low level of delinquency. For example, of the juveniles who "would like to be like their father in every way," 64 percent show a low level of delinquency, whereas of those who do not wish to be like their father only 41 percent show a low level of delinquency.

Hindelang (1973) has attempted to replicate Hirschi's results, using a predominantly rural sample from the East Coast. The sample characteristics and measures of delinquency and societal bond are similar to Hirschi's; and with some exceptions the data are remarkably similar to Hirschi's. For example, of the juveniles who "would like to be like their father in every way," 61 percent show a low level of delinquency, whereas of those who do not wish to be like their father only 36 percent show a low level of delinquency. There is one major exception to Hirschi's findings. While Hirschi finds that a high level of peer attachment relates to a low level of delinquency (consistent with his theory), Hindelang finds the opposite. Other studies report findings more consistent with Hindelang's findings than Hirschi's. Consistent with socialization theory (Chapter Three), Hindelang's findings suggest that peers are not necessarily a source of conventional social control; rather they may be a source of unconventional social control.

While most of Hirschi's and Hindelang's findings are consistent with social control theory, their data do not establish the temporal order of the variables. They assume that a weak societal bond causes delinquency; yet the latter may cause a weak social bond. Delinquency may fracture attachments with parents, weaken commitment to school, and decrease available time for conventional activities.

to inner and outer social controls. Belief refers to inner control; and attachment, commitment, and involvement refer to outer control. Conventional beliefs increase inner controls (personal satisfaction following from conformity and personal dissatisfaction following from norm violations); and attachment, commitment, and involvement increase outer control (social rewards following from conformity and punishments following from norm violations).

Neutralization

Sykes and Matza (1957; Matza, 1964) formulated a situational social control theory. They argue that conventional norms are more flexible and loose than frequently portrayed by sociologists. Various justifications are accepted by society for an occasional violation of social norms. Even some law violations can be legally justified, for example, in terms of drunkenness, self-defense, insanity, and lack of criminal intent. They argue that violators do not have different values than nonviolators; rather, while accepting conventional values, they extend society's acceptable justifications for the violation of social values, norms, and laws. Norm violations, then, are based on justifications viewed as valid by violators but not by the legal system or society at large. Psychologically, these justifications function to neutralize internalized moral rules, thereby allowing people to violate social norms and laws without a sense of guilt and shame. In effect, they neutralize inner controls.

Sykes and Matza enumerate five such justifications, called techniques of neutralization: denial of responsibility, denial of injury, denial of a victim, condemnation of the condemners, and appeal to high loyalties. Deviants frequently deny responsibility for their acts by viewing themselves as a product of their social environment. They refer to social forces beyond their control (their home situation, poverty) which act upon them and force them into situations and delinquent actions. Deviants frequently deny that their actions cause any real harm to anybody. Vandalism is frequently justified as mischief; auto theft is frequently justified as "borrowing"; and gang fighting is frequently justified as a private quarrel. Deviants sometimes deny the existence of a victim, psychologically transforming the victim into someone who deserves injury. Homosexuals, alcoholics, addicts, or minority groups may be defined as people who deserve injury, and school vandalism may be justified as revenge against unfair teachers. Condemning the condemners is a psychological technique which shifts attention to the wrongdoings of others, the pillars of society. If "everybody's doing it" one's own transgressions are less significant.

In sum, Sykes and Matza argue that deviance does not reflect attitudes and values which conflict with the attitudes and values of conventional society; instead, deviance comes about because of learned justifications, which temporarily and situationally neutralize internalized conventional attitudes and values as inner controls.

Deterrence Theory

Deterrence theory, as a special case of social control theory, assumes that people are motivated to violate norms but are constrained by social controls. It ignores inner controls and emphasizes punishment as *the* means of social (outer) control, particularly state-administered punishment. Consequently, its focus is on law violations rather than norm violations in general. The idea of state-administered punishment as a deterrent of law violation is not new. Philosophers have discussed the idea for hundreds of years; in fact, the idea was reasonably systematized over one hundred years ago (Bentham, 1843). After being ignored by social researchers for decades, deterrence theory has recently been rejuvenated. In fact, it is now the most popular approach to the study of social control.

For the most part, deterrence theory assumes that people are rational and that crime is the result of rationally calculating the costs and benefits of law violations. Therefore, the theory assumes that the higher the costs of crime, the lower the level of crime. As punishment is a significant cost of crime, it follows that the higher the level of punishment, the lower the level of crime.

Two types of deterrence processes have been discussed: general and specific. The former refers to a process by which the punishment of some law violators provides information about the costs of crime to those unpunished (the general public), thereby reducing their law violations. The latter refers to a process by which punishment reduces the law violations of those punished. In addition to providing information about the costs of crime, punishment is assumed to sensitize those punished to the realities of punishment. Upon being punished people become aware that it can happen to them. Punishment is not just an abstract event which can happen to others; it is a concrete reality.

Specific concern focuses on three dimensions of punishment: severity, certainty, and celerity. Severity refers to the harshness or degree of punishment, such as the length of incarceration or the amount of a fine. Deterrence theory generally assumes that the more severe the punishment, the lower the level of law violations. When the effect of severity of punishment on law violation is studied, only law violations subject to the same form of punishment can be compared. Law violations subject to incarceration can be ordered in terms of severity of punishment, and law violations subject to fines can be ordered in terms of the severity of punishment; however, it is difficult to order the former and the latter relative to each other. How many days or years in prison is the equivalent of a $10,000 fine?

Certainty of punishment refers to the probability of experiencing punishment. For some crimes the probability of apprehension, arrest, prosecution, and incarceration is much higher than for others. Even for a specific law violation (such as auto theft), the probability of apprehension, arrest, prosecution, and incarceration differs, sometimes quite drastically, from jurisdiction to jurisdiction. In one jurisdiction, 80 percent of the crimes committed may be reported, 70 percent may result in an apprehension, 60 percent in an arrest, 50 percent in a prosecution, and

40 percent in incarceration; yet for another jurisdiction these figures might be 60, 50, 40, 30, and 20 percent. Deterrence theory assumes that the more certain the punishment, the lower the level of law violations.

Celerity of punishment refers to the swiftness of punishment, the interval of time between committing a law violation and experiencing a punishment. In some jurisdictions the average crime may result in an arrest in six months, a prosecution in one year, and an incarceration in two years, whereas in another jurisdiction the respective time intervals may be one, three, and five years. Deterrence theory assumes that the more immediate the punishment, the lower the level of law violations. While the theoretical logic underlying this assumption is less than clear, it is sometimes argued that more immediate punishments are subjectively more ''real'' to people.

In sum, state punishment can be described in terms of severity, certainty, and celerity (see Figure 4.1). Deterrence theory predicts that law violations are highest when severity, certainty, and celerity are lowest. While seemingly straightforward, there are ambiguities in the theory concerning the relative effects of these three dimensions, the shape or form of each effect, and the combined effects of the three dimensions.

One, the theory does not specify the relative effects of the dimensions. Which dimension has the strongest effect and which has the weakest effect? In social policy terms, would it be more effective to increase severity (length of prison sentence) or certainty (probability of a prison sentence) by 15 percent?

Two, the shape of the effect of each dimension is assumed to be generally linear; the higher the level of punishment, the lower the level of law violations. Yet the effect may be nonlinear; each dimension may have no effect until a certain level of punishment is reached. For example, an increase in the arrest clearance rate from a 10 percent clearance rate to a 25 percent clearance rate may produce no corresponding decrease in the level of law violations; but a further increase to a 40 percent clearance rate may produce a substantial decrease in the level of law violations (Tittle and Rowe, 1974). People may not think about punishment probabilities in fine, quantitative terms (10, 20, 30 percent); they may think more qualitatively. Low probabilities of 1 to 20 percent, for example, may be perceived

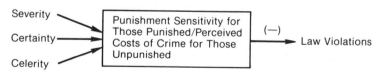

Figure 4.1. Causal Structure of Deterrence Theory. The figure shows that severity, certainty, and celerity of punishment positively affect the punishment sensitivity of those punished and the perceived costs of crime for those unpunished (the general public), which in turn negatively affect the level of law violations. Therefore, a high level of punishment should result in a low level of law violations.

as ''no probability of being caught'' or as ''improbable of being caught.'' Perhaps a 25 or 30 percent objective level of certainty is needed before people think that being punished is a viable possibility. The effects of severity and celerity may also be nonlinear.

Three, considerable debate has occurred as to whether each punishment dimension has an independent effect on law violations. Jack P. Gibbs (1975) suggests that the effect of severity of punishment may depend on certainty of punishment. That is, the level of severity may not enter into people's decision making when the certainty of punishment is low. Relatively high levels of certainty may be necessary before people seriously consider the severity of punishment. Perhaps the higher the level of certainty the greater the effect of severity on the level of law violations. The effect of certainty may also depend on severity. If this argument is correct, then the total deterrence effect of all three dimensions cannot be estimated by adding the independent effects of each dimension. (See Box 4.2.)

To summarize, social control theories assume that norm- and law-violating behavior is sufficiently rewarding to induce deviant motivation. Hence, it is not necessary to explain why some people develop deviant motives; most people do. Instead, we have to explain why so few people act on their deviant motives. Control theorists argue that people generally do not act on these motives because of

---

Box 4.2 ADDITIVE AND INTERACTIVE MODELS FOR ESTIMATING THE COMBINED EFFECTS OF SEVERITY AND CERTAINTY

		SEVERITY	
		High	Low
Certainty	High	(0)0	(10)5
	Low	(10)5	(10)10

The table shows a hypothetical crime rate (the number of crimes per one hundred population) for two levels of severity and certainty. The figures outside of the parentheses show that at a low level of both severity and certainty (lower-right corner) the crime rate is high (10); a high level of either severity or certainty reduces the crime rate by 50 percent (5); and a high level of both severity and certainty reduces it by 100 percent (0). These figures are said to illustrate an additive model, because the effects of severity (50 percent crime reduction) and certainty (50 percent crime reduction) can be added together to estimate the combined effects of severity and certainty (100 percent crime reduction). The figures inside the parentheses illustrate an interactive model. When both severity and certainty are low, the crime rate is high (10), like the additive model. However, contrary to the additive model, the figures show that an increase in either the level of severity or certainty has no effect on the crime rate. It remains high (10). Severity and certainty have no effect independent of each other; both must be high before the crime rate decreases (upper-left corner).

inner and outer controls, which make deviant behavior costly. Differences in the strength of these controls explains differences in deviant behavior among people. Hirschi discusses the bonds between people and conventional institutions and Sykes and Matza discuss psychological techniques by which people neutralize inner controls. Other specific theories have been formulated by Nye, 1958; Stinchcombe, 1964; Reiss, 1951; and Reckless, 1967. Deterrence theory is a special case of social control, emphasizing state punishment as the major cost of law violations, and people's rationality in estimating the net rewards and costs of law violations.

RESEARCH

In recent years most research in the social control/deterrence perspective has focused on deterrence. Reflecting this trend, this section concentrates on deterrence research, particularly that which directly bears on the model in Figure 4.1.

Specific Deterrence: Crime

Specific deterrence research concerns the effect of state-administered punishment on those punished. Depending on the values and concerns of the researcher this work is labeled either recidivism or rehabilitation research.

In what is generally acknowledged to be the most extensive recidivism study in the United States, Daniel Glaser (1964) reports that approximately one-third of those released from prison are subsequently reincarcerated. (This figure does not include those who commit subsequent crimes but are not reincarcerated.) Although this figure is quite high and, consequently, seems to disprove the specific deterrence thesis, the figure is not relevant to the thesis, as we do not know the

---

Box 4.3 DETERRENCE AND INCAPACITATION EFFECTS

In addition to deterrence processes, some researchers (Wilson, 1975) have emphasized incapacitation as a "process" by which state punishment affects law violations. Incapacitation simply refers to the obvious fact that various forms of punishment incapacitate people from committing future crimes (capital punishment, incarceration). Because a high proportion of crimes are committed by recidivists, it is assumed that, if somehow those people could be incapacitated, the general crime rate would drop substantially. While incapacitation is not normally considered part of deterrence theory, its effects can be confused with deterrence effects. For example, if certainty and severity of punishment are high, a relatively high proportion of law violators will be incarcerated for a relatively long interval of time. Hence, a high level of punishment could produce a low level of law violations, because of either a deterrence or an incapacitation effect, or both.

percentage of unpunished law violators who commit subsequent law violations and are incarcerated. A crucial test of the specific deterrence thesis requires a comparison of the subsequent law violations of those who have committed law violations and have gone unpunished and those who have committed law violations and have been punished.

As systematic records are not kept on people who commit crimes but are not punished, studies tend to compare the subsequent violations of people who have experienced different degrees of punishment (probation and length of incarceration). These studies, too, appear to contradict the specific deterrence thesis. They suggest that as the severity of punishment (generally, length of sentence) increases, recidivism increases (Gibbs, 1975) rather than decreases! The findings, however, may be a result of punishment selection. People with the worst prior records and who commit the most serious crimes generally receive the most severe punishments. Upon release they are likely to continue their life of crime. Also, as they are likely to be under police surveillance, their law violations are likely to be detected. Hence, while severe punishments may reduce law violations, the effect may not be observable by simply comparing those who have experienced different levels of punishment.

Some researchers have tried to deal with this problem by comparing the recidivism of people with the same or similar prior records who have been committed or have been charged with committing the same type of offense. The prospects for future law violations are thus equalized. In a study of adolescents, Martin Gold and Jay R. Williams (1969) used a self-report questionnaire to estimate past level of delinquency (seriousness and frequency of offenses). They were able to identify thirty-five apprehended juveniles who could be matched by level of past delinquency with another thirty-five adolescents who had not been apprehended. Thus, each of the thirty-five pairs was similar in respect to offense history. Gold and Williams then examined the delinquency level of each member of each pair after being apprehended. The findings are, again, contrary to deterrence theory. For twenty of the pairs the apprehended adolescent showed the highest level of delinquency; for ten of the pairs the apprehended adolescent showed the lowest level of delinquency; and for the remaining five pairs both adolescents showed similar levels of delinquency. In sum, when the effects of prior offense and severity of present offense are controlled, there is little consistent evidence showing that punishment decreases future law violation (Mahoney, 1974; Gibbs, 1975).

In fact, an equally good case may be made for the opposite conclusion: punishment increases future law violations. Various causal processes may generate this effect. According to deviant socialization theory and research (Chapter Three), it seems reasonable to argue that as the length of time in prison increases, exposure to criminal values and attitudes increases, which in turn may increase the level of criminal behavior upon release. Also, incarceration is socially stigmatizing. Upon release it may decrease involvement in conventional groups and economic opportunities, which in turn may increase law violations (Chapter Two). Hence, while incarceration may increase sensitivity to punishment, which may decrease future law violations, it may also increase criminal socialization and social stigma, which may increase future law violations. (See Figure 4.2.)

The net result of imprisonment then, may be a function of the relative strengths of these different causal processes (Tittle, 1975). If criminal socialization and social stigma processes are stronger than the punishment sensitivity process, the net effect of imprisonment should increase the future level of law violations; if on the other hand criminal socialization and social stigma processes are weaker than the punishment sensitivity process, the net effect of imprisonment should decrease future law violations. The strengths of these causal processes may depend on various conditions (Tittle, 1975), such as the characteristics of the prison and the social environment to which exconvicts return. To establish the effect of imprisonment on those imprisoned, future research must study these causal processes and their relative strengths. Simply comparing the subsequent law violations of those imprisoned for varying lengths of time, while controlling for prior record and offense seriousness, cannot resolve the issue.

General Deterrence: Objective Indicators

General deterrence refers to a process by which the punishment of some people reduces the law violations of those not punished, the general public. Relevant research is extensive, variable in methodological rigor, and very difficult to synthesize. This discussion focuses on research which directly bears on the model in Figure 4.1. Two methodological designs are employed: comparative and time series. The former compares the crime rates of jurisdictions with different levels of punishment at one point in time; and the latter compares the crime rate of a jurisdiction before and after a change in the level of punishment.

Comparative. Most studies deal with three basic concepts: crime rate, severity of punishment, and certainty of punishment. (Celerity of punishment has been ignored.) Although varying somewhat from study to study and from design to design, these concepts are operationalized as follows. Crime rate is operation-

Figure 4.2. Causal Processes Mediating the Effect of Imprisonment on Future Law Violations. The figure shows that imprisonment affects criminal socialization, deterrence, and social stigma, which in turn affect law violations. Thus, the size and direction of the effect of imprisonment on law violations is a function of the relative strengths of at least six causal effects (paths in the diagram).

alized as the ratio of reported crimes to the population in a jurisdiction. Severity of punishment is operationalized as the mean or medium length of sentence (time served in prison) in a jurisdiction. Certainty of punishment is operationalized as the ratio of the number of arrests or prison admissions to the number of crimes reported in a jurisdiction; note that this ratio expresses the probability of being arrested or incarcerated upon committing a crime. According to deterrence theory, as the average length of sentence increases and as the ratio of arrests or prison admissions to reported crimes increases, the crime rate should decrease.

Using states as jurisdictional units, Jack P. Gibbs (1968) and Charles R. Tittle (1969) report supportive findings. Gibbs reports that homicide is negatively related to the severity and certainty of punishment. Extending Gibbs' analysis to the seven major FBI offense categories, Tittle reports that the negative effect of severity is limited to homicide, but that the negative effect of certainty extends to other offenses. For most offenses high levels of certainty are associated with low crime rates. Various reanalyses of Gibbs' data (Gray and Martin, 1969), Tittle's data (Bailey, Martin, and Gray, 1974), and more recent studies (see Gibbs, 1975) confirm their original conclusions: evidence for a severity effect exists only for homicide but evidence for a certainty effect exists for all seven major offenses.

Extending these findings, Charles H. Logan (1972) reports that states with high severity have low certainty, and suggests that when punishment is very severe, judges and juries are reluctant to find people guilty and to incarcerate them. This may explain why most previous studies have not reported a negative severity effect, except for homicide. The effect of certainty may overshadow and obscure the effect of severity. Upon controlling for the effect of certainty, Logan reports a small negative effect of severity, consistent with deterrence theory. He also suggests that the level of severity alters the effect of certainty: it is strongest when the level of severity is highest.

Jack P. Gibbs, born 1927, received his B.A. in 1950 and his M.S. in 1952 from Texas Christian University, and his Ph.D. in 1957 from the University of Oregon, and is presently a Professor of Sociology at Vanderbilt University. He has published a variety of papers and books on deviance and most recently is known for his work on deterrence, *Crime, Punishment and Deterrence*, 1975. (Courtesy of Jack P. Gibbs, reprinted by permission.)

Recent research has focused on the certainty effect. Two questions in particular have been asked. One, is the effect linear or nonlinear? Some theorists have argued that variation at the low end of the certainty continuum is meaningless; a high level of certainty must be obtained before a substantial decrease in the crime rate will occur—the "tipping" effect. Charles R. Tittle and Allan R. Rowe (1974) report data that bear on this question. Although limited to Florida cities and counties, their data show that certainty of arrest only makes a substantial difference in crime rates after a 30 percent clearance level is reached (30 percent of reported crimes are cleared by arrest). For both cities and counties variation in certainty below 30 percent has little effect on crime rates; variation above that level has a substantial negative effect. However, recent data on California cities and counties suggest that the tipping effect is limited to small cities (Brown, 1978).

A second issue involves the causal process that accounts for the consistently observed negative relationship between certainty and the crime rate. Does certainty affect the crime rate as suggested by deterrence theory, or does the crime rate affect certainty? Concerning the latter, when the crime rate is low police can devote considerable time to each case, increasing the probability of arrest and conviction and thereby increasing the level of certainty; on the other hand, when the crime rate is high police can devote little time to each case, decreasing the probability of arrest and conviction and thereby decreasing the level of certainty (overload hypothesis). The overload hypothesis assumes that the level of police resources is a constant; therefore, as the level of crime decreases, the same level of police resources can more effectively solve each case, thereby increasing the certainty of punishment. Tittle and Rowe report, however, that as the crime rate decreases, so do police resources.

In an attempt to further explicate the general deterrence thesis, Michael R. Geerken and Walter R. Gove (1977) argue that deterrence effects should be expected only for crimes which occur in situations where people have the time and motivation to accurately calculate the profits (rewards and costs) of behavior alternatives. They classified the seven FBI index crimes into economic crimes (robbery, burglary, larceny, and auto theft), which tend to be committed in circumstances where rewards and costs are calculable, and crimes of violence (assault and homicide), which tend to be committed while in emotional states and involve less thoughtful assessments of consequences. Rape falls somewhere in between economic and emotional crimes, as it is a crime of violence which is frequently planned. They examined the correlation between certainty of punishment (measured as arrest clearance rate) and crime rates for all metropolitan areas over 500,000 population in the United States for 1971, 1972, and 1973. The data support their hypothesis. For the four economic crimes the correlations are substantial and negative (an average correlation of $-.42$); for rape it is $-.26$; and for the two emotional crimes the correlations are insignificant and positive (an average correlation of $+.09$).

Time Series. Gibbs (1975) argues that, while an extensive number of time series studies have been reported, few are methodologically sophisticated and the results are frequently subject to various interpretations. Among the many methodological problems described by Gibbs, perhaps the regression problem is the most serious. This problem occurs because crime rates are cyclical, and because an increase in crime rates frequently motivates legislative bodies to increase the level of punishment. A typical time series study compares the crime rate before and after the legislative action, and frequently attributes any subsequent decrease to the legislation; yet the decrease may be nothing more than the normal downswing in the crime rate cycle. (See Figure 4.3.)

Tittle and Logan (1973), in a review of the literature, report that the most rigorous methodological time series studies provide little evidence of a severity effect but suggest a certainty effect. For example, Barry Schwartz's (1968) analysis of rape in Philadelphia before and after an increase in punishment severity for rape reveals no evidence of a severity effect; but the analysis by H. Lawrence Ross et al. (1970) of the level of traffic casualties before and after the enactment of a breath analyzer law in England reveals considerable evidence of a certainty

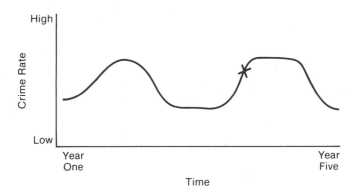

Figure 4.3. Cyclical Pattern of Crime Rates. The figure shows the cyclical nature of crime rates. They rise and fall within limits. The "x" marks the point of the cycle at which the punishment level is increased. To show a deterrence effect, research must show that the subsequent decrease in the crime rate is greater than the decrease expected as a normal part of the downward swing of the crime cycle.

effect. In 1967 England passed a breath analyzer law allowing police to test automobile drivers for drunkenness at the point of arrest. If convicted in court, the law mandated a standard penalty. In effect, the breath analyzer law increased the certainty of punishment, particularly as perceived by the public. Controlling for regression effects, Ross et al. report a considerable reduction of traffic casualties following the enactment of the law.

To summarize, the comparative and time series studies of general deterrence suggest similar conclusions. One, there is little consistent evidence for a severity effect, although some data suggest that an effect may be present when the certainty level is high. Severity of punishment may not be important to people unless they feel that the chances of getting caught and punished are high. Two, there is consistent evidence of a certainty effect, although the shape and size of the effect remain unclear.

General Deterrence: Individual Perception

General deterrence studies are frequently criticized for assuming that people are able to accurately perceive objective severity and certainty punishment levels. A California study suggests considerable perceptual inaccuracy (Social Psychiatry Research Associates, 1968). For rape, drunken driving, robbery with bodily injury, burglary with bodily injury, and marijuana possession only 16, 39, 20, 16, and 36 percent of the population, respectively, were able to demonstrate accurate knowledge of recently increased penalties. These penalty increases, therefore, could not enter into the decision making of the majority of the population. If people's perceptions of the severity and certainty of punishment are unrelated to objective levels of punishments, then by the logic of deterrence theory objective levels of punishment should not relate to crime rates.

Given the distinct possibility of a weak relationship between objective levels and subjective perceptions of severity and certainty, it may be useful to examine the relationship between the perception of punishment and law violation. Deterrence theory suggests that law violators perceive the levels of severity and certainty to be lower than do nonviolators. Reviewing the literature, Gibbs (1975) reports that there are few significant differences between the perceptions of law violators and nonviolators, although the former tend to have more accurate perceptions of the certainty and severity of punishment. Gibbs suggests that the more accurate perceptions of known violators may be less a cause of their law violations than a consequence of their arrest, prosecution, and imprisonment experience. Violators come to learn that the probability of punishment is much less than they originally perceived.

To circumvent this problem, some studies examine the relationship between the level of self-reported crime and perceptions of punishment severity and certainty of people with no legal experience. Gary F. Jensen (1969) and Gordon P. Waldo and Theodore G. Chiricos (1972) report that the level of perceived certainty is negatively related to the level of self-reported crime. More recent studies, also reporting a negative relationship (Jenson, et al. 1978; Tittle, 1977; and Silberman, 1976), try to specify it by the type of crime and isolate it from the effect of informal social controls.

A study by Gary F. Jenson, Maynard L. Erickson, and Jack Gibbs (1978) addresses both of these questions. Using a sample of 5000 Tucson high school students, they examined the relationship between self-reported crime, perceived certainty of official punishment, and informal social controls for fifteen different crimes (such as homicide, assault, and marijuana use). Perceived certainty, for example, is measured by the following question. "Of the last one hundred cases of homicide (car theft, rape, etc.) committed by a juvenile (adult) here in Tucson, what is your guess as to the number that resulted in an arrest of a suspect?" They report a negative relationship between perceived certainty and self-reported crime for each of the fifteen offenses, and that the strength of the relationship depends on the seriousness of the offense. For example, the relationship is strongest for grand theft, robbery, and burglary, and lowest for drinking, truancy and defiance, smoking, and marijuana use. Concerning the second issue, some researchers argue that the relationship between perceived certainty of official punishment and the level of law violation is noncausal and dependent on the level of informal social disapproval or condemnation. A high level of informal social condemnation may cause both a high level of perceived certainty of punishment and a low level of crime. Erickson et al. find no support for this argument, reporting that the relationship between perceived certainty and criminal involvement is independent of informal social disapproval, as measured by personal disapproval and involvement with deviant others. Yet Silberman (1976) and Tittle (1977) report that personal approval (attitudes) and informal social approval (peers and associates) have a stronger effect on involvement in various deviant and criminal activities than does perceived certainty of official punishment.

While specifying the relationship between perceived certainty of official punishment and law violations by type of offense, and while showing that the relationship exists independently of the effect of informal social disapproval, research has still not clarified the time order between perceived certainty and law violations. Deterrence theorists assume that the level of perceived certainty affects the level of violations; however, it seems equally reasonable to argue that the level of law violations affects the level of perceived certainty. Violating the law, generally without apprehension, probably lowers perceived certainty. Future research must partition the negative relationship between perceived certainty of punishment and law violations into the effect of perceived certainty on law violations and the effect of law violations on perceived certainty.

Box 4.5 OBJECTIVE AND PERCEIVED CERTAINTY AND THE CRIME RATE

Considerable research has been reported on the relationship between objective certainty and the crime rate for political units, and between perceived certainty and law violations for individuals; however, little research has examined the extent to which objective certainty affects crime rates because it affects perceived certainty—as suggested by deterrence theory. Recently, Maynard L. Erickson and Jack P. Gibbs (1978) examined this proposition. While most deterrence research examines the relationship between objective certainty and crime rates among states or counties, Erickson and Gibbs examine the relationship among ten different crimes in the same jurisdiction —Tucson, Arizona. For each crime, the crime rate and objective certainty were computed from official statistics, and perceived certainty was measured in an interview of a random sample of 1200 Tucson residents. For the ten crimes, the correlations between the above concepts are as follows:

objective certainty and crime rate	$r = -.67$
perceived certainty and crime rate	$r = -.49$
objective certainty and perceived certainty	$r = .55$

The signs of the correlations are consistent with deterrence theory; however, the relative size of the correlations is not. Deterrence theory suggests that the correlation between perceived certainty and the crime rate should be stronger than the correlation between objective certainty and the crime rate. The opposite is true. Furthermore, deterrence theory suggests that, upon controlling for the effect of perceived certainty on the crime rate, the correlation between objective certainty and the crime rate should reduce to zero; the data showed that it only reduces from $-.67$ to $-.54$. Hence, for the most part, the relationship between objective certainty and the crime rate is not mediated through perceived certainty. Perhaps it is accounted for by the effects of the crime rate on objective certainty—the overload hypothesis.

Summary

In terms of the general model illustrated in Figure 4.1, where do we stand? Two deterrence processes have been discussed: specific and general. Specific deterrence assumes that being punished decreases the future level of law violations of those punished through punishment sensitivity. However, recidivism studies of the severity of punishment provide little supportive evidence. While imprisonment may increase the level of punishment sensitivity, thereby decreasing future law violations, it may also increase criminal socialization and social stigma, thereby increasing future law violations. The net effect may be negligible. Future research must attempt to partition the net relationship between the severity of punishment and future law violations into these component effects. General deterrence assumes that punishment decreases the level of law violations of those unpunished. Three types of studies have been examined: comparative studies of crime rates across jurisdictions; time series studies of the crime rates in one jurisdiction; and perceptual studies. While the results are varied, certain commonalities can be identified. Most studies do not suggest a severity effect, but consistently suggest a certainty effect. Some suggest that it is nonlinear (the "tipping" effect), some that it is dependent on the level of severity, and others that it is less significant than the effect of informal social controls. Future research must expand this work, isolating the effects of certainty on law violations from the effects of law violations on certainty, and examining the link between objective and perceptive certainty.

SOCIAL POLICY

Reflecting the major thrust of the research section, this section focuses on the policy implications and implementations of deterrence theory, as a special case of social control theory. The policy implications of deterrence theory are straightforward: increase the severity, certainty, and celerity of state punishments for law violations. However, the policy implications of deterrence research are anything but straightforward. Celerity of punishment, for the most part, has not been the subject of research; and research on the severity of punishment has been inconsistent with deterrence theory. Only research on the certainty of punishment has been consistent with deterrence theory, and even the policy implications of these findings are ambiguous. While deterrence theorists assume that the observed negative relationship comes about through the effects of certainty of punishment on law violations, it may also come about through the effects of law violations on certainty of punishment (overload hypothesis). Also, while research on general deterrence suggests that increasing the certainty of punishment may decrease the law violations of those not punished, some research on specific deterrence suggests that increasing the certainty of punishment (increasing the proportion of law violators who are punished) may increase the probability of these violators committing second and third offenses.

Empirical research questioning the validity of deterrence theory has not arrested the call for policy implementation. In fact, cries for increasing legal punishments have escalated in the last five to ten years (Wilson, 1975, Van den Haag, 1969 and 1975). As argued in the Introductory Chapter, the implementation of policy frequently depends more on feasibility, social values, and social power than on supporting research.

Consider first celerity and certainty. Is it possible to increase them? If so, at what cost? To increase either substantially would probably involve a major restructuring of the criminal justice system. Other than being prohibitively expensive, this would disrupt, and in some cases dismantle, the careers of many criminal justice employees. As those responsible for criminal justice policy and planning also participate in administering the present system or have a vested interest in it, it is unlikely that any major reorganization will occur. The more likely response by those involved is to expand the present system, increasing personnel and capital expenditures. In fact, starting with the war on crime program, initiated by the Johnson and Nixon administrations, billions of dollars have been funneled into the criminal justice system. Jeffery I. Chapman et al. (1975) report that all levels of government spent about $3.3 billion on crime control in 1960, but by 1973 this figure had risen to $13 billion. This is not just a matter of inflation. Statistics show that a higher proportion of the gross national product is being allocated to crime control. The Center for Research on Criminal Justice (1975) reports that the proportion of the GNP spent on the criminal justice system has increased from one-half of one percent in 1955 to one full percent in 1971. This is reflected in local and municipal police budgets. David Lewin and John H. Keith (1976) report that in 1965 American cities employed 1.9 police officers per 1,000 population; by 1972 this figure rose to 2.4; and the 1975 statistics show that the figure has further increased to 2.5. This trend is further accentuated for cities over 250,000 population. For 1965, 1972, and 1975 the figures are 2.6, 3.3, and 3.6, respectively. This expansion, of course, has greatly increased the career opportunities and power of criminal justice personnel, with no documented increase in the certainty and celerity of punishment.

Increasing severity (generally, the length of incarceration) meets with little resistance, probably because it is much less expensive than increasing certainty and celerity. It only requires changing the law, increasing minimum and maximum penalties. For example, a California study (Zimring and Hawkins, 1973:57) reports that when prison space is available the cost of one extra year of imprisonment is $620 per adult prisoner. The California adult prison population is about 30,000; thus, the extra cost for adding one year to each person's sentence would be $18,600,000, certainly expensive, but cheap in comparison with the cost of restructuring the criminal justice system. Additionally, increasing the length of sentence seems to be consistent with public sentiment, and is not disruptive of the careers of criminal justice personnel!

Since empirical studies show little support for a deterrent effect of severity,

Wilson (1975) and others have justified increased prison sentences in terms of an incapacitation effect. Their argument is simple: Criminals cannot commit crimes if they are imprisoned. True, or at least they cannot commit them against people not also imprisoned; the crimes of prisoners against other prisoners are apparently of little concern. (See Box 4.3.)

Various researchers have attempted to calculate the probable reduction in crime which would occur from different incapacitation policies. Using national data, David E. Greenberg (1975) argues that the present incarceration policy (average sentence of two years), as against a policy of no incarceration, has reduced the level of index crime by about 8 percent. The upper limit of an incapacitation effect would be achieved by a "throw away the key" policy, a policy of life imprisonment for all offenders. Greenberg reports that about 33 percent of all new prisoners and parolees for any one year have a prior record; thus, he estimates that a "throw away the key" policy would reduce recorded law violations by approximately 33 percent. Note that as the recidivism rate for the most serious crimes (homicide) is much lower, a "throw away the key" policy would produce a much lower rate of reduction for these crimes. Also, fewer juveniles than adults have prior records. Using the same logic, Greenberg estimates that a "throw away the key" policy would reduce juvenile crimes by only 15 to 25 percent.

These figures, of course, are projections. They are built on the assumption that the cause of crime resides in people; if present law violators are incarcerated, law violations will decrease. This ignores theory and research suggesting that crime rates are affected by the pattern and shape of the social structure; therefore, shifting people within that structure will not change the general level of crime, only the people who are the law violators. For example, some research suggests that the level of illegitimate opportunities (availability of unlocked cars, unlocked houses) affects the level of law violations. Incarcerating those who used these illegitimate opportunities may not reduce the general level of law violations; it may only make them available to others!

While considerable research and controversy have emerged over the extent to which different incapacitation policies would reduce the level of law violations, few researchers have examined other consequences of incapacitation. One, the economic cost of long-term incarceration (of just a small percent of the criminal population) may be staggering—in many cases far more than the cost of their crimes. At the very least it would require a massive prison construction program. Two, as female crime is generally much lower than male crime, a long-term incapacitation policy would produce an imbalance in the male/female sex ratio—accentuated for the lower class and minority groups. Three, just about all those incarcerated will someday be released; if incarceration increases recidivism (as some studies suggest), then incapacitation may generate a body of adult career law violators.

Considering the ambiguity as to the projected reduction in crime, the economic costs, the long-range social effects, and the possibility of increased recidivism, incapacitation as a social policy should be considered cautiously.

To summarize, while the policy implications of deterrence theory are reasonably clear, the supporting research suggests caution. For the most part little research has been reported on the celerity of punishment thesis; research has not supported the severity of punishment thesis; and while research appears to be consistent with the certainty of punishment thesis, many questions remain. This, however, has not arrested efforts at implementing the policy implications of deterrence theory. As to the certainty and celerity of punishment, efforts have been expended to increase the size of the criminal justice system with no noticeable increase in the level of certainty and celerity. And as research has not been very supportive of the severity thesis, incarceration has been rationalized in terms of incapacitation effects without seriously considering its long-range consequences.

CRITIQUE/SUMMARY

Theory

Instrumental and Expressive Crimes. Instrumental refers to crimes (generally economic crimes) which involve rational calculation of benefits and costs (such as tax evasion) and are committed in an atmosphere in which weighing alternatives is feasible (corporate decision to violate restraint of trade laws). Expressive refers to crimes less subject to rational calculation, and which tend to be committed in an atmosphere in which the weighing of alternatives is difficult (crimes of passion). Many assaults, rapes, and homicides occur in an emotional social and psychological atmosphere in which decisions must be made quickly, if not instantaneously. In a barroom altercation or a lovers' bedroom quarrel there is little time to calculate the costs and benefits of behavioral alternatives. Actions occur quickly in response to a rapidly changing situation. While the distinction between instrumental and expressive crimes has been discussed (Chambliss, 1967) and has been the subject of some research (Geerken and Gove, 1977), there has been little concerted effort to systematically incorporate this distinction into deterrence theory. Theoretical attention should be directed toward the social and psychological conditions under which rational calculation occurs; such conditions could then be employed to classify violations by the extent to which they are applicable to the logic of deterrence theory.

Perceptive and Objective Levels of Punishment. Deterrence theory emphasizes subjective perceptions of punishment; yet much research examines objective levels of punishment. If the relationship between subjective perceptions and objective punishment is weak, according to the logic of deterrence theory the relationship between objective punishment and the crime rate should be weak. Unfortunately, the relationship between objective and perceptive punishment levels has been vaguely assumed, rather than the subject of theoretical discussion and research. The relationship may be stronger for some types of crimes and persons than others, and may be shaped by the mass media. In some cities the mass media may publicize reported crimes without publicizing the level of enforcement, creating an image of low punishment certainty; and in other cities it may do the opposite, creating an image of high certainty.

Interactive Model. Deterrence theory does not seriously deal with issues in estimating the combined effects of certainty and severity. It simply treats the effects independently. Yet some research suggests that the severity effect may depend on the level of certainty and that the certainty effect may depend on the level of severity. Research should examine the conditions under which the effects are additive and interactive. Also, the combined effects of celerity and severity, and celerity and certainty, may be interactive. If punishment is perceived to be remote, perhaps the certainty and severity of punishment are ignored. (See Box 4.2.)

Research

Temporal Order. Research on both specific and general deterrence frequently leaves the temporal order of the critical variables equivocal. For example, various cross-sectional or comparative studies show that the certainty of punishment is negatively correlated with the crime rate, suggesting that high certainty causes a low crime rate. Yet it also seems reasonable to argue that a low crime rate may produce a high level of punishment certainty. As the crime rate decreases, the level of police resources devoted to each crime increases, which increases the probability of solving each crime, thereby increasing the level of punishment certainty. The observed negative correlation between certainty of punishment and the crime rate probably reflects both the negative effect of certainty on the crime rate and the negative effect of the crime rate on the certainty of punishment. A similar problem may exist in estimating the effect of severity of punishment. While high severity of punishment may reduce the crime rate (producing a negative relationship), a high crime rate may stimulate legislators into increasing the severity of punishment (producing a positive relationship). These two effects, difficult to disentangle in cross-sectional research designs, may produce the often observed negligible relationship. For the most part, little research has gone into partitioning the observed relationships between certainty and severity of punishment, and crime rates into the underlying causal effects.

Controlling for the Effect of Other Social Conditions. As various social conditions correlate with the level of punishment, their effect on the crime rate may obscure the effect of punishment on the crime rate. In states and cities in which a particular act (such as rape) violates the common moral conscience, official punishments are probably very severe and processes of socialization and informal social control are probably intense and rigorous. A corresponding low crime rate may then be a function of the high level of official punishment and the rigorous socialization and informal social control processes. With some exceptions, research has not attempted to isolate the effect of official punishment from the effects of socialization and informal social control processes.

Social Policy

While deterrence theory is frequently praised for its clear policy implications, deterrence research suggests considerable caution. Of the three punishment dimensions, research is only consistent with the certainty of punishment thesis, and even the observed negative relationship between certainty and the crime rate may be explained by other causal processes.

Wilson (1975) has argued for more deterrence research because the variables are tractable to social policy manipulation while the variables of other theoretical perspectives are not. He argues that we cannot manipulate social cohesion, illegitimate opportunities, social attitudes, and family ties. Agreed, these social and psychological conditions are not easy to change, but it is not easy to change the level of punishment either. Significant changes in the celerity and certainty of punishment would require nothing less than a reorganization of the criminal justice system. The cost and difficulties involved have already been noted. Minor changes, such as increasing police expenditures and deployment patterns, have produced ambiguous results (Wilson, 1975). Only the severity of punishment is simple to change—by legislative fiat; yet there is little research support for severity as a deterrent.

Aside from these problems, what is most disturbing about state punishment as a social policy (justified according to deterrence or incapacitation) is its political nature. It is considered an appropriate social response only to predominantly lower-class crimes (murder, assault, rape, burglary, robbery, auto theft). Either by omission or commission, it is rarely discussed or studied as a social response to middle- and upper-class crimes, such as fee splitting between doctors, plagiarism of professors, embezzlement, false advertising, and restraint of trade. The president of a major corporation can be stopped from violating pollution laws by incapacitation just as easily as a lower-class youth can be stopped from stealing automobiles by incapacitation. In terms of deterrence theory it may even be more logical to use state punishments to control corporate economic offenses than lower-class economic offenses, as the former are probably more subject to rational calculation than are the latter.

REFERENCES

BAILEY, WILLIAM, J. DAVID MARTIN, and LOUIS GRAY. "Crime and deterrence: A correlational analysis," Journal of Research in Crime and Delinquency 11 (July 1974):124—43.

BENTHAM, JEREMY. "An introduction to the principles of morals and legislation," Works 1 (1843).

BONJEAN, C. M. and R. McGEE. "Scholastic dishonesty among undergraduates in different systems of social control," Sociology of Education 38 (1965):127—37.

BOWERS, W. I. and R. G. SALEM. "Severity of formal sanctions as a repressive response to deviant behavior," Law and Society Review 6 (1972):427−41.

BRIAR, SCOTT and IRVING PILIAVIN. "Delinquency, situational inducements and commitments to conformity," Social Problems 13 (1965):35−45.

BROWN, DON W. "Arrest rates and crime rates: When does a tipping effect occur?" Social Forces 57 (Dec. 1978):671−82.

Center for Research on Criminal Justice. *The Iron Fist and the Velvet Glove: An Analysis of the U.S. Police* (Berkeley, Calif.: Berkeley Center for Research on Criminal Justice, 1975).

CHAMBLISS, W. T. "Types of deviance and the effectiveness of legal sanctions," Wisconsin Law Review (Summer 1967):703−19.

CHAPMAN, JEFFREY I., WERNER HIRSCH, and SIDNEY SONENBLUM. "Crime prevention, the police production function and budgeting," Public Finance 30 (1975):197−215.

CHIRICOS, THEODORE G. and GORDON P. WALDO. "Punishment and crime: An examination of some empirical evidence," Social Problems 18 (Fall 1970): 200−17.

ERICKSON, MAYNARD L. and JACK P. GIBBS. "Objective and perceptual properties of legal punishment and the deterrence doctrine," Social Problems 25 (Feb. 1978):253−64.

GEERKEN, MICHAEL R. and WALTER R. GOVE. "Deterrence, overload, and incapacitation: An empirical evaluation," Social Forces 56 (Dec. 1977): 424−47.

GIBBS, JACK P. *Crime, Punishment and Deterrence* (New York: Elsmere, 1975).

———. "Crime, punishment, and deterrence," Social Science Quarterly 48 (March 1968):515−30.

GLASER, DANIEL. *The Effectiveness of a Prison and Parole System* (Indianapolis: Bobbs-Merrill, 1964).

GOLD, MARTIN and JAY R. WILLIAMS. "National study of the aftermath of apprehension," Prospectus 3 (1969).

GRAY, LOUIS N. and J. DAVID MARTIN. "Punishment and deterrence: Another analysis," Social Science Quarterly 50 (Sept. 1969):389−95.

GREENBERG, DAVID E. "The incapacitative effect of imprisonment: Some estimates," Law and Society Review 9 (Summer 1975):541−80.

HINDELANG, MICHAEL J. "Causes of delinquency: A partial replication and extension," Social Problems 20 (Spring 1973):471−78.

HIRSCHI, TRAVIS. *Causes of Delinquency* (Los Angeles: University of California Press, 1969).

JENSEN, GARY F. "Crime doesn't pay: Correlates of shared misunderstanding," Social Problems 17 (Fall 1969):189−201.

JENSEN, GARY F., MAYNARD L. ERICKSON, and JACK GIBBS. "Perceived risk of punishment and self-reported delinquency,'' Social Forces 57 (Sept. 1978): 57−58.

LEMERT, EDWIN. *Human Deviance, Social Problems, and Social Control* (Englewood Cliffs, N. J.: Prentice-Hall, Inc., 1967).

LEWIN, DAVID and JOHN H. KEITH. "Managerial responses to perceived labor shortages,'' Criminology 14 (May 1976):65−93.

LOGAN, CHARLES H. "General deterrence effects of imprisonment,'' Social Forces 51 (Sept. 1972):63−72.

MAHONEY, ANNE RANKEN. "The effect of labelling upon the juvenile justice system: A review of the evidence,'' Law and Society Review 9 (Summer 1974):583−614.

MATZA, DAVID. *Delinquency and Drift* (New York: Wiley, 1964).

NYE, F. IVAN. *Family Relationships and Delinquent Behavior* (New York: Wiley, 1958).

RECKLESS, WALTER C. *The Crime Problem (4th ed.)* (Englewood Cliffs, N.J.: Prentice-Hall, Inc., 1967).

REISS, ALBERT J. "Delinquency as the failure of personal and social controls,'' American Sociological Review 16 (1951):196−207.

ROSS, H. LAWRENCE, DONALD T. CAMPBELL, and GENE V. GLASS. "Determining the social effect of a legal reform: The British breath analyser crackdown of 1967,'' American Behavioral Scientist 13 (1970):493−509.

SALEM, R. G. and W. J. BOWERS. "Severity of formal sanctions as a deterrent to deviant behavior,'' Law and Society Review 5 (Aug. 1970):21−40.

SCHWARTZ, BARRY. "The effect in Philadelphia of Pennsylvania's increased penalties for rape,'' Journal of Criminal Law, Criminology and Police Science 59 (Dec. 1968):509−15.

SILBERMAN, MATTHEW. "Toward a theory of criminal deterrence,'' American Sociological Review 41 (June 1976):442−61.

Social Psychiatry Research Associates, Public Knowledge of Criminal Penalties: A Research Report. 1968.

STINCHCOMBE, ARTHUR L. *Rebellion in a High School* (Chicago: Quadrangle, 1964).

SYKES, GRESHAM and DAVID MATZA. "Techniques of neutralization: A theory of delinquency,'' American Sociological Review 22 (Dec. 1957):664−70.

TITTLE, CHARLES R. "Crime rates and legal sanctions,'' Social Problems 16 (Spring 1969):408−23.

———. "Deterrents or Labeling?'' Social Forces 53 (March 1975):399−410.

———. "Sanction, fear and the maintenance of social order,'' Social Forces 55 (March 1977):579−96.

TITTLE, CHARLES R. and CHARLES H. LOGAN. "Sanctions and deviance: Evidence and remaining questions,'' Law and Society Review 7 (Spring 1973): 371−92.

TITTLE, CHARLES R. and ALLAN R. ROWE. "Certainty of arrest and crime rates: A further test of the deterrence hypothesis," Social Forces 52 (June 1974): 455–62.

VAN DEN HAAG, ERNEST. "On deterrence and the death penalty," Journal of Criminal Law, Criminology and Police Science 60 (June 1969):141–47.

———. *Punishing Criminals: Concerning a Very Old and Painful Question* (New York: Basic Books, 1975).

WALDO, GORDON P. and THEODORE G. CHIRICOS. "Perceived penal sanction and self-reported criminology: A neglected approach to deterrence research," Social Problems 19 (Spring 1972):522–40.

WILSON, JAMES Q. *Thinking About Crime* (New York: Basic Books, 1975).

ZIMRING, FRANKLIN E. and GORDON J. HAWKINS. *Deterrence* (Chicago: University of Chicago Press, 1973).

cHApTER fiVE

THE lAbEliNq pERSpECTiVE

THEORY

The traditional norm violation approach to deviance assumes normative stability and consensus, which constitute a reference point from which behavior is judged as deviant or nondeviant. When the norms of different segments of society conflict (lower versus middle class; black versus white; young versus old), the norms of the more powerful segments tend to be accepted as reference points. Even the Chicago socialization researchers implicitly assume a dominant culture of meanings and focus on the processes by which people are socialized into deviant subcultures.

During the 1960s, numerous sociologists (Gouldner, 1970) questioned the assumptions of normative consensus and stability, and thus by implication the viability of theoretical perspectives built upon them. Instead, they emphasized the emerging, changing, and conflicting character of social norms, thereby stimulating a reconceptualization of the subject matter of the sociology of deviance. Without clear and stable reference points for judging behavior, normative violations are definitionally problematic. Hence, since the 1960s many sociologists have defined deviance as a social definition which some groups and people use to describe the behavior of others. Theory and research have focused on two general questions: What is defined as deviance? Who is defined as deviant?

The first question has directed theory and research toward the emergence of social norms and social categories for labeling people as deviant. Some sociologists have focused on the historical emergence of general societal norms of behavior. They ask such questions as, why are the norms of alcohol consumption in Russia different from the United States, and why are the norms of sexual behavior in Mexico different from the United States? Other sociologists (ethnomethodologists) have directed their attention to studying how social norms, and consequently what is defined as deviance, depend on specific social situations. They argue that general societal norms of behavior are frequently very ambiguous as behavioral directives in specific situations. For example, the norms which govern alcohol consumption vary, not only from country to country and from region to region within a country, but from situation to situation. The norms of proper drinking depend on the day (weekend or weekday), the time (morning or evening), and even the duration of time which has elapsed at a party. Greater freedom is frequently permitted as a party goes on.

Sociologists have also examined the emergence of the social labels or categories used to describe and define norm violations and violators. This is not a question of semantics, but involves the issue of how norm violations and violators are socially treated.

The category of mental illness is an instructive example. Today people who experience emotional problems and cognitive distortions are treated in many ways like people with a physical illness (Scheff, 1966). They are treated by experts trained in medicine (psychiatrists) and are frequently treated in hospitals. This type of social treatment has not always been the case in the United States and is not now the case in all parts of the world. In the United States at one time or another such people have been labeled as evil, lazy, and as witches and, accordingly, have experienced a very different societal treatment. Why? How can we explain the emergence of mental illness as a social category? Generally, then, the question, "what is defined as deviance?" refers to the study of the emergence of social norms and social categories for describing norm violations and violators.

The study of legal norms (laws) and the categories used to describe law violations and violators is a special case of the above question. Why are some norms transformed into laws, thus making some norm violators law violators (Quinney, 1970; and Turk, 1969)? For example, marijuana smoking is illegal, but cigarette smoking and alcohol use are not. Why? Prostitution is illegal in most but not all states and cities. Why? It is also important to study the emergence of categories for describing law violations and violators. Juvenile norm violators, for example, are treated differently not only by the public but by legal authorities. They constitute a formal legal category in the United States; and consequently are treated under a specific set of legal procedures (juvenile court) and are subject to a specific set of court dispositions. Why? How can the emergence of this legal category for describing and treating law violators be explained?

The second major question (who is defined as deviant?) refers to the study of the process by which existing categories for describing norm violators and violations are applied in specific situations (Lemert, 1967). Of all individuals who violate norms only some are socially identified and labeled by family, friends, colleagues, the public, and authorities. Others somehow escape the social label. Their norm violations remain socially unnoticed. Why? On the other hand some non norm violators are falsely identified as norm violators. Why? Under what circumstances are people identified (correctly or incorrectly) as norm violators (drug addicts, witches, mentally ill)? These concerns are important, because of the psychological and social consequences of being publicly identified—correctly or falsely—as a norm violator. Sociologists have studied the extent to which being publicly labeled as a norm violator affects social relationships, such as family relations, friendship patterns, and economic opportunities, and the extent to which these changes in turn influence future norm violations.

As a special case of this question, some sociologists have examined how legal categories are applied to individuals and the consequences of such applications. Like norm violators, only some law violators are publicly identified. Of those who violate laws only some are arrested; of those arrested only some are prosecuted; and of those prosecuted only some are sentenced. What affects the degree to which law violators become involved in the legal process and what are the consequences of different levels of involvement? To what extent does imprisonment or just prosecution affect psychological dispositions and social relationships, and to what extent do the latter in turn affect future law violations?

Generally, the study of deviance as a social definition focuses on the following questions:

1. What is defined as deviance?
   a. What are the general and situational social norms and how have they emerged?
   b. What are the social categories and labels for describing norm violators and norm violations, and how have they emerged?
   c. As a special case of the above, what are the legal norms (laws) and legal categories for describing law violators and violations, and how have they emerged?
2. Who is defined as deviant?
   a. Who is socially labeled a norm violator?
   b. What are the consequences of being labeled a norm violator?
   c. As a special case of the above, who is labeled a law violator, and what are the consequences of being so labeled?

These questions are of primary concern in the labeling perspective (the subject of this chapter), the ethnomethodology perspective (the subject of Chapter Six), and the conflict perspective (the subject of Chapter Seven). Each perspective, because of its general assumptions about society and people, focuses on different facets of the above questions.

Labeling theory is identified with the work of sociologists concerned with the study of social process rather than structure, and with the study of micro (social psychology) rather than macro sociology. These concerns have focused attention on the second question, who is defined or labeled a deviant. As the first part of this question (the application of labels) is also dealt with by the ethnomethodology and conflict perspectives, it is discussed in Chapters Six and Seven. This chapter examines the consequences of social labeling. Edwin M. Lemert's work provides the general theoretical orientation.

Deviance as a Social Label (Edwin M. Lemert)

Lemert (1951 and 1967) assumes a pluralistic society. Norms and laws are conceived as temporary and emergent products of a social process whereby different interest groups compete and struggle for social power and dominance. In this continuing process some groups' norms become defined as society's norms and some as society's laws; consequently, some people become defined as norm violators (deviants) and some as law violators (criminals). While noting the fluid nature of society, Lemert assumes that at any point in time some standards prevail over others and that behavior can be judged by these standards. He does not, however, assume any necessary relationship between the violation of these standards and being labeled as a deviant or criminal. This is a subject for research.

The terms "primary" and "secondary" deviance are central to Lemert's theory. Primary is defined as deviance (norm violations) which does not affect an individual's psychological structure and performance of social roles. It is transitory and caused by a variety of conditions.

> Primary deviance is assumed to arise in a wide variety of social, cultural and psychological contexts and at best has only marginal implications for the psychic structure of the individual; it does not lead to symbolic reorganization at the level of self-regarding attitudes and social roles (Lemert, 1967:17). Primary deviation, as contrasted with secondary, is polygenetic, arising out of a variety of social, cultural, psychological and physiological factors, either in adventitious or recurring combinations (Lemert, 1967:40).

Secondary deviance is defined as deviance (norm violations) which is a response to the problems or conditions caused by the societal reaction to primary deviance. It is generally prolonged and affects psychological structure and the performance of social roles.

> Secondary deviation is deviant behavior or social roles based upon it which becomes a means of social defense, attack or adaptation to the overt and covert problems created by the societal reaction to primary deviance (Lemert, 1967:17). Secondary deviation refers to a special class of socially defined responses which people make to problems created by the societal reaction to their deviance (Lemert, 1967:40). When a person begins to employ his deviant behavior or role based upon it as a means of defense, attack or adjustment to the overt and covert problems created by the consequent societal reaction to him, his deviation is secondary (Lemert, 1951:76).

Lemert is concerned with deviance which is prolonged and which affects psychological structure and the performance of social roles, secondary deviance. He argues that primary deviance does not necessarily lead to secondary deviance; instead, secondary deviance is a response to the problems created by the reaction to primary deviance. He suggests that being publicly labeled a deviant is socially stigmatizing, adversely affecting social relationships and opportunities. It alters informal social relationships, for conventionals are not prone to associate with known deviants; and it decreases job opportunities, as employers are not prone to hire known deviants. Hence, if a reduction in economic opportunities and conventional social relationships increases the probability of involvement in deviance (see Chapters Two and Three), being publicly labeled a deviant should increase the probability of deviance. Also, he argues that people tend to see themselves as others see them, and that people tend to act on self definitions. Hence, if people are socially labeled as deviant, they come to see themselves as deviant and behave accordingly. In sum, Lemert argues that societal reaction to primary deviance initiates social and psychological processes which sustain deviance and make it more central in people's lives. In studying secondary deviance, we must focus on these processes, rather than on the conditions which cause primary deviance.

Lemert's theory may be succinctly conceptualized as asserting that primary deviance and "other" factors frequently lead to societal reaction, which in turn leads to secondary deviance. The term "other factors" is used here to summarize a variety of situational contingencies (such as demeanor) and social statuses (race and sex), which in combination with or without primary deviance lead to being labeled a deviant. (These factors will be discussed in the next two chapters.) The term reflects Lemert's thesis that labeling is affected by a variety of factors and considerations other than primary deviance.

Lemert's work, deriving from role theory and symbolic interaction, provided a stimulus and general orientation in the formulation of labeling theory. Recent formulations emphasize two related themes: deviance as a social status and deviance as a self-concept.

Deviance as a Social Status (Howard Becker)

Concerned with deviance as a social definition, Becker (1963:9) states:

> From this point of view, deviance is not a quality of the act the person commits, but rather a consequence of the application by others of the rules and sanctions to an "offender." The deviant is one to whom that label has successfully been applied; deviant behavior is behavior that people so label.

Becker emphasizes that a deviant label or definition operates like a social status and that the process by which labeling produces systematic deviance is comparable to that which underlies a conventional career.

Social statuses refer to positions in the social order linked to structural patterns of social interaction (female, black, physician). They affect the course and pattern

Howard S. Becker, born 1927, received his B.A. in 1946, his M.A. in 1949, and his Ph.D. in 1951 from the University of Chicago, and presently is a Professor of Sociology at Northwestern University. He is well known for his work on labeling theory, *Outsiders*, 1967. (Courtesy of Howard S. Becker, reprinted by permission.)

of social interaction to which a person is exposed. In analyzing social statuses, the concepts "master status" and "career" have proven useful (Hughes, 1958). Master statuses are those statuses which generally override other statuses in affecting the course and pattern of interaction. Race, for example, is a master status. Blacks in the United States experience discrimination somewhat independent of income, education, occupation, and age. Career refers to a set of statuses occupied in an orderly sequence. In the occupational world, for example, people frequently occupy an orderly sequence of statuses (apprentice, journeyman, master, retiree).

Becker argues that a public identity as a deviant operates similarly to a social status in that it structures the course of social interaction. For example, people who acquire the label of drug addict, alcoholic, or mentally ill because of their behavior or because they have been confined to a rehabilitation or mental institution may experience difficulty in employment and in maintaining conventional social relationships. A public deviant identity may function as a master status in that it may override other statuses in affecting social interaction. An alcoholic physician and an alcoholic carpenter, for example, may be extremely different in all respects, including the manner in which they imbibe; yet because of their identity as an alcoholic, they may be treated very similarly in social interaction. Additionally, some types of deviance seem to follow the pattern of a career. For example, James H. Bryan (1965) has analyzed prostitution in terms of an orderly sequence of statuses: young girl apprentice (learning the trade), part-time prostitute, regular full-time prostitute, and madam; and Erving Goffman (1961) has analyzed the process of becoming a mental patient in terms of a sequence of stages: prepatient, patient, and postpatient. Becker argues that, as in the study of conventional careers, sociologists should study the contingencies by which people move from one stage to the next, and that being publicly labeled is the major contingency affecting the movement through a deviant career.

120

Box 5.1 PROCESSUAL THEORIES OF DEVIANCE

Becker (1963) distinguishes between processual (sequential) and simultaneous theories of norm violations. He argues that most theories of norm violations assume that the factors which explain initial involvement are the factors which explain continued and systematic involvement. The structural/functionalism, Chicago, and social control perspectives implicitly, if not explicitly, make this assumption. For example, Robert Merton's theory assumes that ends-means discrepancies caused by structural dysfunctionalism explain equally well why some people initially become involved and why some people continue involvement over a lifetime; and Sutherland's differential association theory assumes that association with deviants explains equally well why some people initially become involved and why some people continue their involvement over a lifetime. Becker refers to these as simultaneous theories, because they assume that all causal factors operate simultaneously over the course of a deviant career.

Sequential refers to theories in which the factors which explain initial involvement are not necessarily the factors which explain continued involvement or systematic involvement. The original causal factors may cease to operate, but the initial involvement brings into being new environments, which facilitate a deviant career. Labeling theories are clearly sequential, asserting that the factors which cause initial norm violations (primary deviance) are not the factors which explain continued involvement, which is explained by the societal reaction to primary deviance. Although the original causal factors may cease to exist, continued deviance is sustained by the social label.

Becker's conceptualization of deviance as a social definition emphasizes the orderliness and stability in the process by which labeling transforms someone into a systematic norm violator. While deviance may not always function as a master status and may not always take on the appearance of an orderly career, the analogy sensitizes us to certain social processes by which public labeling affects the course and pattern of deviance.

Deviance As A Self-Concept

Whereas some sociologists, such as Becker, have examined the orderly aspects of the labeling process, emphasizing the external restrictions and patterning of opportunities for interaction, other sociologists (Schur, 1971; Matza, 1969) have viewed the labeling process as less orderly, emphasizing its emergent and negotiated character, and the importance of self-concepts or definitions. Edwin M. Schur (1971) argues that people are not automatically labeled as deviant because of what they have done (norm violations) or because of who they are (minority group member), and that the process of becoming a secondary deviant does not necessarily take on the character of an orderly career. It is more like a protracted meandering negotiation. Some people are accused and are stigmatized, while

Edwin M. Schur, born 1930, received his B.A. in 1952 from Williams College, his LL.B. in 1955 from Yale Law School, his M.A. in 1957 from the New School for Social Research, and his Ph.D. in 1959 from the London School of Economics, and he is presently a Professor of Sociology at New York University. He is well known for his work on labeling theory, *Labelling Deviant Behavior*, 1971. (Courtesy of Edwin M. Schur, reprinted by permission.)

others may successfully negotiate a nonstigmatized social label; others accused may successfully defend themselves and even successfully label the original accusers, as in some mental commitment proceedings; and still others may label themselves without any community initiation. Warren and Johnston (1972), for example, report that most people who engage in prolonged homosexual behavior are never publicly labeled as homosexuals, but nonetheless may come to view themselves as homosexuals. Hence, rather than emphasizing public identities and the limits which they impose on social interaction, Schur emphasizes self labels or self-concepts, and self-imposed limits on social interaction. He argues that secondary deviance is less a function of imposed external restrictions on inter-action accompanying a public label than an expression of a deviant self-concept or identity.

To summarize, labeling theory implicitly assumes some minimal level of social consensus as a reference point for defining norm violations. However, the thrust of the theory is not directed toward the study of norm violations, but toward the study of deviance as a social definition. The theory asks: why are some people publicly labeled as deviants whereas others are not, and what are the consequences of being labeled, particularly in respect to the level and patterning of future norm viola-tions? Lemert was one of the first sociologists to examine deviance as a social definition, and his work provides a general orientation for research. Within this general orientation, some sociologists (Becker, 1963) have emphasized the order-ly aspects of the process by which labeling affects secondary deviance, noting external restrictions on social interaction imposed by a public label. Other sociolo-gists have emphasized the negotiated character of the process by which labeling affects secondary deviance, noting the importance of self-labels and identities. These are not distinct schools, however. Becker discusses self-concept, and Schur discusses external restrictions on interaction; both examine deviance as a social definition and are concerned with the process by which labeling leads to secondary deviance. Rather than two schools, they constitute two different thrusts in labeling theory.

Mental Illness

The medical model of physical illness assumes that physical states of the body can be defined and classified as healthy or ill, that illness or disease can be correctly diagnosed by observations of the body (temperature, appetite, etc.), that effective treatments are available, and that if not treated illness tends to worsen. Most traditional theories of mental illness assume that the mind functions in much the same manner, that is, that mental or psychic states can be defined and classified as healthy or ill, that mental illness can be diagnosed by observable mental states (nervousness, delusions, etc.), that effective treatments are available, and that if not treated mental illness tends to worsen. Some theories assume the cause of mental illness to be biological (genetic defects); some assume the cause to be psychological (defective ego); and some assume the cause to be social (a demanding social environment).

Since the early 1960s, labeling theorists (Szasz, 1960; Goffman, 1961; Scheff, 1966) have rigorously criticized this model. One, they argue that, unlike physical states, mental states cannot easily be defined and classified into those that are healthy and those that are diseased. Practitioners (psychiatrists and clinical psychologists) frequently disagree as to the criteria to be used in deciding what constitutes mental illness. That which constitutes illness to one psychiatrist may constitute health to another. Moral judgments and cultural values affect these decisions. This is generally not the case for physical illness. There is considerable consensus among practitioners as to what states of the body are healthy and what states are diseased. Two, labeling theorists argue that, unlike physical disease, diagnosing mental disease is generally difficult. Mental health practitioners frequently disagree as to the observable mental states which should be used to infer types of mental abnormalities (schizophrenia, neurosis). While physicians may disagree from time to time over what observations should be used to infer particular diseases, there is considerable agreement as to what observations are necessary and sufficient to infer the presence of a large number of diseases like cancer or pneumonia. Disagreement exists within a general context of consensus. Three, labeling theorists argue that, unlike physical medicine, effective treatments for mental diseases do not exist; people treated do not necessarily recover significantly faster than those not treated. Four, labeling theorists argue that, unlike physical diseases, mental states diagnosed as abnormal do not always worsen when not treated; they frequently improve.

Note the similarity between this critique of traditional approaches to mental illness and the general critique of traditional approaches to social deviance. Labeling theorists argue that because of a low level of social consensus, norm violations are frequently difficult to define and that norm violations from the perspective of one group are frequently acts of conformity from the perspective of another group. Essentially the same argument is made about mental illness. Because of a low level of consensus about mental health, even among psychiatrists, mental illness is difficult to define and mental illness from the viewpoint of one social group or one psychiatrist is mental health from the viewpoint of another social group or psychiatrist. Thus, like social deviance in general, mental illness may be fruitfully studied as a social definition or label which is applied by some people to the behavior of others. Labeling theorists thus focus our attention on two specific questions: who is labeled mentally ill and what are the psychological and social consequences of being so labeled? Of the many labeling theories which have been constructed, Thomas Scheff's (1966) theory is probably the most significant and well known. It is composed of nine propositions.

Proposition 1: "Residual deviance arises from fundamentally diverse sources." Scheff argues that most norm violations are named or socially categorized: crime, delinquency, drunkenness, drug addiction, bad manners, etc. When these categories are exhausted, there remains a residue of norm violations for which no clear names or social categories exist. For example, while carrying on a conversation, people are expected to face their conversational partner rather than look away; gaze toward his or her eyes rather than elsewhere; and stand at a proper distance, neither two inches apart nor across the room. How do we categorize someone who violates these norms? How do we define or categorize someone who regularly watches the sun between 1:00 P.M. and 3:00 P.M., someone who is socially noninvolved, someone who claims to walk on water, or someone who believes that the world is persecuting him or her? There are no specific terms to categorize and describe these people although they are frequently thought of as strange, unusual, bizarre, perhaps even frightening. Scheff argues that when people appear strange or irrational and are not clearly understood in terms of typical or standard cultural meanings, they tend to be labeled mentally ill.

Proposition 2: "Relative to the rate of treated residual deviance (mental illness), the rate of unrecorded residual deviance is extremely high." Scheff cites various surveys which suggest that the psychological and behavioral characteristics used to label people as mentally ill (hearing voices, seeing visions, social withdrawal) are quite prevalent in American society. Depending on the study and the specific definition of mental illness, estimates of the rate of mental illness vary from 1 to 33 percent of the population (and even higher).

Proposition 3: "Most residual deviance is denied and is transitory." Scheff argues that most people are not labeled by themselves, friends, or professionals as mentally ill on the basis of the above behaviors. Generally, the behaviors are normalized or explained away as a transitory response to an unusual or temporary situation (being a soldier at the front or experiencing the loss of a job or a loved one). When the situation changes the behaviors generally disappear. What, then, accounts for the small percentage of residual deviants who go on to have deviant careers? Scheff argues that residual deviance stabilizes if it is socially defined as evidence of mental illness and the person is thereby treated as mentally ill. Like secondary deviance (Lemert's term), stabilized residual deviance is a response to the problems created by being defined and treated as mentally ill. Labeling produces a social environment which encourages residual deviance through processes of social control and socialization (see propositions six, seven, and eight).

Propositions 4 and 5: "Stereotyped imagery of mental disorders are learned in early childhood" and " . . . are continually reaffirmed, inadvertently, in ordinary social interaction." Scheff argues that the behaviors used to infer mental illness (stereotypes of mental illness and insanity) are cultural constructs. They differ from culture to culture and like other culture concepts are learned starting in childhood through social interaction and the mass media.

Propositions 6 and 7: "Labelled deviants may be rewarded for playing the stereotype mental illness role" and ". . . punished for attempting to return to conventional roles." Psychiatrists and hospital personnel frequently encourage and reward patients whose behavior fits their diagnosis. Patients who accept their illness are frequently thought of as manifesting insight into their problems, and patients who show the "right" signs may get more attention from hospital personnel, who find it is easier and more pleasing to treat people who fit into standard disease patterns than people who do not. Additionally, patients frequently find it difficult to return to conventional social roles. Their jobs may have been filled and their spouses may have found another life. By comparison the role of mental patient may be relatively rewarding.

Proposition 8: "In the crisis occurring when a primary deviant is publicly labelled the deviant is highly suggestible and may accept the preferred role of the insane as the only alternative." Scheff states that definitions of self are highly influenced by social definitions, especially in times of crisis. Upon being defined as mentally ill, people come to accept themselves as mentally ill, and thus make less effort to control their behavior to conform to social norms, particularly in stress situations. A person may ask: "Why try? After all, I am mentally ill." Furthermore, the mental illness role offers an acceptable social role from which to deal with others after other social roles have been destroyed.

Proposition 9: "Among residual deviants, labelling is the single most important cause of careers in residual deviance."

Commonalities

Some commonalities in the work of Lemert, Becker, Schur, and Scheff should be noted.

1. All four are unconcerned with unorganized, casual, occasional, or sporadic norm violations. Lemert uses the term primary deviance and Scheff uses the term transitory deviance to describe them.

2. All four focus on organized or systematic deviance prolonged over a period of time. Lemert refers to secondary deviance; Becker refers to career deviance; Schur refers to role engulfment; and Scheff refers to stabilized deviance.
3. All four are concerned with processual or sequential theories, which emphasize the role of social definitions or labeling in transforming primary deviance into secondary deviance.

The general thrust of their work, as represented in the causal diagram in Figure 5.1, suggests that the effect of societal reaction on secondary deviance is mediated by interpersonal networks, self-concept, and structural opportunities.

As to structured opportunities, it seems reasonable to argue that being labeled a deviant (criminal) reduces legitimate economic opportunities. Employers may be very cautious about hiring known exdeviants (excriminals). On the other hand, being labeled a criminal and being imprisoned may increase illegitimate opportunities. Novice inmates may learn from seasoned criminals how to be more technically proficient, and thus how to be more successful in committing future crimes. Hence, if official labeling (especially incarceration) decreases legitimate opportunities and increases illegitimate opportunities, according to the logic of Cloward and Ohlin's theory (Chapter Two), it should increase future deviance. As to mental illness, the reduction of legitimate opportunities (conventional economic roles) may well increase psychological stress and the relative value of the mental illness role.

Labeling may also alter interpersonal relationships. Conventionals may not wish to associate with publicly known deviants, fearing that the social stigma may rub off; thus, labeled deviants may seek out each other for assistance or companionship. In terms of socialization theory and research (Chapter Three), association with deviants facilitates learning deviant attitudes and values, and reinforces previously held deviant attitudes and values. Hence, if labeling decreases interaction with conventionals and increases interaction with nonconventionals, according to the logic of socialization theory it should increase future deviance. Concerning mental illness, labeling may produce social isolation, which may increase psychological strain and stress, thereby stabilizing residual deviance.

Labeling also affects self-definitions. People who are socially labeled as deviants may come to view themselves in these terms. If people tend to act consistently with their self-concepts, labeling people as deviant should increase their level of future deviance.

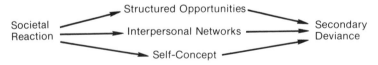

Figure 5.1. Causal Processes Underlying the Effect of Societal Reaction on Secondary Deviance. The diagram shows that societal reaction (labeling) affects structured opportunities, interpersonal networks, and self-concept, which in turn affect secondary deviance.

Opportunity structure, interaction networks, and self-concept are not the only conditions and processes mediating the effect of labeling or secondary deviance. Clearly, there are many mediating processes; each specific type of norm violation may entail a unique combination of processes. Yet opportunity structure, interpersonal networks, and self-concept seem to be central and illustrate the continuity between the study of primary and secondary deviance.

RESEARCH

Secondary Deviance: Delinquency and Crime

Labeling research on crime and delinquency addresses two questions: who is labeled and what are the consequences of the label? Following the theory section, this section focuses on the latter question. The organization of the section closely follows the causal diagram in Figure 5.1. The first set of studies examines the link between labeling and the mediators (interpersonal networks, self-concept, and structural opportunities), and the second set examines the link between labeling and secondary deviance.

Labeling and the Mediators. Richard D. Schwartz and Jerome H. Skolnick (1962) used a rather clever field experiment to study the link between being labeled a deviant and future economic opportunities. Four sets of employment credentials were prepared. In all sets the applicant was described as thirty-two years old, single, male, high school trained in a trade with a record of successful employment in unskilled jobs, the normal characteristics of applicants for the specific job. The four sets of credentials differed only in the following respect: one indicated that the applicant had been sentenced for assault; one indicated that the applicant had been tried for assault but acquitted; one indicated that the applicant had been tried for assault and acquitted and included a letter by the presiding judge affirming the applicant's innocence; and one did not mention anything about a criminal record. A sample of one hundred employers was selected. The employers were not told that they were participating in a field experiment. Each employer was presented with only one of the four sets of employment credentials, so that each of the four sets was presented to twenty-five employers. Representing themselves as agents of an employment agency, the researchers simply asked each employer if they could use the person in question, and categorized their response as positive and negative. Table 5.1 shows the relationship between the level of involvement in the criminal justice system (degree of labeling) and the level of employment. For those with no record, 36 percent of the employers gave a positive response (the base mark); for those acquitted with a letter, 24 percent gave a positive response; for those acquitted with no letter, 12 percent gave a positive response; and for those convicted, only 4 percent gave a positive response. Note the relatively low rate of positive response (12 percent) for those accused and acquitted. Being found

Table 5.1. CONSEQUENCES OF LABELING

SCHWARTZ AND SKOLNICK STUDY

	No Record	Acquitted With Letter	Acquitted	Convicted	Total
	(N=25)	(N=25)	(N=25)	(N=25)	(N=100)
Positive	36%	24%	12%	4%	19%
Negative	64%	76%	88%	96%	81%
	100%	100%	100%	100%	100%

BUIKHUISEN AND DIJKSTERHUIS STUDY

	No Record	Convicted Theft	Convicted Drunken Driving	Total
	(N=50)	(N=50)	(N=50)	(N=150)
Positive	52%	32%	26%	37%
Negative	48%	68%	74%	63%
	100%	100%	100%	100%

innocent does not appear to deter the social consequences of being accused and prosecuted. At least to the employers in this study a person is not "innocent until proven guilty."

Wouter Buikhuisen and P. H. Dijksterhuis (1971) have reported a similar study conducted in the Netherlands. They constructed three sets of credentials: one included a conviction for theft; a second included the temporary loss of a driver's license for drunken driving; and a third made no mention of a criminal record. Employment applications were sent to seventy-five large companies. As in Schwartz and Skolnick's study, the companies did not know that they were participating in a field experiment and their responses were simply categorized as positive or negative. The results, given in Table 5.1, show that 52 percent of the applicants with no record received a positive response, while only 32 percent and 26 percent of those with records of theft and drunken driving, respectively, received a positive response. Although more research is certainly needed, these two studies suggest a strong link between criminal labeling and subsequent economic opportunities.

Labeling theory also asserts that being labeled a deviant affects interpersonal networks and attitudes. Various studies have examined different segments of this process. For example, Jack D. Foster et al. (1972) have examined juveniles' subjective impressions of how their involvement with police and courts influenced their relationships with peers, teachers, and parents. They interviewed 196 boys whose behavior had brought them into contact with the police and courts; the interviews occurred no later than twenty days after the final disposition. The vast majority did not feel any stigma or change in their relationships with their parents, peers, and teachers. Only 27 percent, for example, thought that their parents' attitudes toward them had changed as a result of their involvement with legal authorities. On the other hand, they did feel that their involvement with the law would affect their future economic opportunities. Of those incarcerated, 73 percent felt that future employers would hold that against them.

Labeling may have a more severe effect on interpersonal networks for certain types of deviance. Marsh B. Ray (1961) interviewed addicts at various stages of the cure and relapse cycle. He reports that after a period of addiction many addicts enter a hospital, either voluntarily or involuntarily, to be cured. Upon being physiologically cured and released, many try to become involved in conventional associations and groups but are frequently rejected. Family members and old friends (addicts and nonaddicts) tend to think of them in terms of old and established social identities and are very skeptical of their "cure." In the words of one person:

> My relatives were always saying things to me like "Have you really quit using that drug now?" and things like that. And I know that they were doing a lot of talking behind my back because when I came around they would stop talking but I overheard them. It used to burn my ass.

As a consequence of rejection, Ray argues, physiologically cured addicts turn to their old drug-using friends, who are willing to accept them, and with time again become involved with drugs. The cycle of addiction, cure, and relapse begins anew.

Labeling theory also suggests that people who are labeled deviants come to view themselves as deviants, consequently lowering their self esteem. Gary F. Jensen (1972) has examined this relationship, using a large sample of juveniles from eleven junior and senior high schools in California. The survey collected information on officially recorded delinquency, self-reported delinquency, perception of self as a delinquent, and self-esteem. He reports a moderate to strong relationship between having an official record and viewing oneself as a delinquent, which is accentuated for whites. Jensen argues that being labeled a delinquent is more meaningful for whites than blacks. Blacks occupy a negative social status irrespective of their social behavior and official reactions to it. As outsiders they may be insensitive to official reactions. In fact, for some blacks, middle-class norms may constitute negative reference points. Whites, on the other hand, are more tied to conventional institutions; thus, their self-concepts more directly reflect official actions. Suzanne Ageton and Delbert Elliot (1974) also deal with this issue. They studied a large sample of adolescents from eight California secondary schools. The students were interviewed annually from ninth to twelfth grade and law violation information was taken from local police records. Over the four-year period, whites with police contact showed a decrease in self-esteem compared to whites with no police contact; for nonwhites, however, there was no relationship between police contact and self-esteem. Anthony R. Harris (1975) has reported data also suggesting that whites are more sensitive than blacks to involvement in the criminal justice system. He measured the expected value of criminal and conventional careers for 129 blacks and 105 whites incarcerated in the New Jersey correctional system. Each person was asked to judge the value of having a successful criminal career and a successful conventional career, and to estimate their probability of actually being successful in a criminal career and a conventional career. Labeling theory predicts that since imprisonment exposes one to a criminal subculture, the longer one is imprisoned the lower one's expected value of a conventional career and the higher one's expected value of a criminal career. After the initial six months, Harris found such an effect, accentuated for whites.

To summarize, concerning the link between labeling and the causal mediators, certain relationships seem to emerge. Studies suggest that being labeled a criminal or delinquent reduces economic opportunities, affects self-concept particularly for whites, and appears to affect interpersonal networks for certain types of deviance (such as drug addiction).

Effects of Labeling on Future Deviance. If labeling decreases economic opportunities, conventional associations, and self-esteem, then it follows that labeling should increase the level of future deviance. Note that this proposition is contrary to deterrence theory (Chapter Four), which asserts that state punishment (a special case of labeling) should decrease the future level of law violations of those punished (labeled). As there is little research on the effects of labeling by friends and parents, this section will examine the state punishment studies from the viewpoint of labeling theory.

The student should note a major methodological problem with much of this research. It may be argued that those who are most severely labeled have probably committed the most numerous and serious violations; hence, if they show a high level of future law violations, this may be an effect of labeling or just a continuation of prior behavior. To answer this question, research must examine the future violations of people who are differentially labeled for the same law violations and who have committed the same prior violations. Three such studies will be examined.

Martin Gold and Jay R. Williams (1969) interviewed a national sample of youths thirteen to sixteen years of age. Of the youths who had committed four or more illegal acts, some were apprehended and some were not. Gold and Williams matched thirty-five apprehended and unapprehended youths by sex, race, and age, and then examined their future level of delinquency. For twenty of the pairs the apprehended youths committed the most offenses; for ten the unapprehended youths committed the most offenses; and for five the apprehended and unapprehended committed an equal number of crimes. While the study suggests that labeling (apprehension) increases delinquency, it should be noted that the pairs were not matched by seriousness of past offenses and the sample is small.

A. W. McEachern (1968) examined the effect of differential probationary practices on future delinquency. He studied 2290 California youths exposed to different practices; youths not made a ward of the court and received no treatment; youths not made a ward of the court and received treatment; youths made a ward of the court and received no treatment; and youths made a ward of the court and received treatment. Although not clearly defined, treatment appears to mean some type of contact between the probation officer and the youth. It seems reasonable to assume that the youths who are made a ward of the court and received treatment are the ones most severely labeled and thus in terms of labeling theory should show the highest level of future delinquency. McEachern compared the level of delinquency for each of the above categories before and after labeling. The results are ambiguous, showing that the youths made a ward of the court committed fewer future delinquent acts than those not made a ward (not supporting labeling theory), and that the youths treated committed more delinquent acts than those not treated (supporting labeling theory).

Terrence P. Thornberry's (1973) work is based on data collected on all boys born in 1945 who lived in Philadelphia between the ages of ten and seventeen. Their police records were examined and classified into four official dispositions: remedial arrest (the boy is released by the police with no further action); adjustment (the boy is referred to the probation department and warned to stay out of trouble); probation (the boy is given a court hearing and placed under supervision); and institutionalization (the boy is incarcerated). Thornberry examined both the number and seriousness of future offenses. The results are complex and few clear patterns can be discerned. Consistent with labeling theory, as involvement in the juvenile justice system increased (up to institutionalization) the volume of future delinquency increased, but only for whites, upper-social-class youths, and boys apprehended for less serious crimes; however, contrary to labeling theory, the

---

Box 5.2   SOCIAL REJECTION AND SECONDARY HOMOSEXUALITY

In a recent study, Ronald A. Farrell and James F. Nelson (1976) have examined the extent to which self-concept and interpersonal networks mediate the relationship between social rejection and secondary homosexuality. Using a sample of 148 male homosexuals located in homosexual bars, social clubs, and organizations, they measured the following concepts by questionnaire: perceived rejection, stereotypic self-concept, homosexual associations, and secondary homosexuality. Perceived rejection refers to the degree to which homosexuals perceive rejection by conventionals; stereotypic self-concept refers to the extent to which homosexuals accept cultural stereotypes of themselves; homosexual associations refers to the level of homosexual associations compared to conventional associations; and secondary homosexuality refers to the extent to which homosexuals take on the subcultural homosexual role.

Consistent with labeling theory, they tested the following model: Perceived rejection causes both homosexual associations and stereotypic self-concept, which influence each other, and in turn cause secondary homosexuality. The data suggest that stereotypic self-concept does not mediate the effect of perceived rejection on secondary homosexuality; while stereotypic self-concept strongly relates to perceived social rejection, it does not affect secondary homosexuality. Instead, the data point to the importance of homosexual association as a mediator through which social rejection affects secondary homosexuality.

institutionalized youths showed fewer future offenses and less serious offenses upon release than did the noninstitutionalized youths.

Where do we go from here? As stated in Chapter Four, research on the effects of punishment on those punished is ambiguous and subject to various interpretations. Findings are frequently inconsistent from study to study. One interesting observation, however, seems to recur. Whites appear more sensitive to official labeling than do blacks in respect to self-concept (Jensen, Ageton and Elliott), the expected value of a criminal career, (Harris), and the effects of labeling on future delinquency (Thornberry). It seems reasonable to hypothesize that, since blacks occupy a negative social status and are not well integrated into society, they are not very sensitive to official reactions of society. Labeling may have its maximum effect on people well integrated into society; hence, the effects of labeling should be maximal for first offenders, the middle-class, and whites, and minimal for prior offenders, the lower class, and blacks.

Residual Deviance: Mental Illness

Research focuses on two questions: who is labeled mentally ill and what are the consequences of being so labeled? Like the previous section, this section examines only the latter question. Following the diagram in Figure 5.1, studies are reviewed which examine the effect of labeling on the mediating conditions and on mental illness (career residual deviance) directly.

Labeling and the Mediators. In Scheff's theory social stigma is an important concept. He argues that it makes conventional roles inaccessible, thereby highlighting the relative rewards of the mental illness role, and it generates stress, thereby increasing susceptibility to social influence (Scheff's proposition eight) and producing psychological discomfort.

Derek Phillips (1963) developed an interesting design for studying the relative effects of psychological behavior symptoms and involvement with mental illness practitioners on social rejection (social stigma). He constructed case abstracts describing a paranoid schizophrenic, a simple schizophrenic, a depressed-neurotic, a phobic-compulsive, and a normal individual. The following is a description of a normal individual.

> Here is a description of a man. Imagine that he is a respectable person living in your neighborhood. He is happy and cheerful, has a good enough job and is fairly well satisfied with it. He is always busy and has quite a few friends who think he is easy to get along with most of the time. Within the next few months he plans to marry a nice young woman he is engaged to.

Five versions of each case were constructed, differing only by the level of involvement with mental illness practitioners. For example, in one version of the paranoid schizophrenic case the phrase was added, "He has been in a mental hospital because of the way he was getting along." In a second version the person was said to be seeing a psychiatrist; in a third the person was said to be seeing a physician; in a fourth the person was said to be seeing a clergyman; and in a fifth there was no mention of professional help. Through this procedure twenty-five case studies were generated, five illnesses times five sources of professional help. (See Table 5.2.)

During an interview each of 300 respondents from a small New England town was presented with five of the twenty-five cases. Combinations of five were selected so that each respondent was presented only once with each set of symptoms (illness) and each help source. The following questions (social distance scale) were asked:

Would you discourage your children from marrying someone like this?

If you had a room to rent in your home, would you be willing to rent it to someone like this?

Would you be willing to work on a job with someone like this?

Would you be willing to have someone like this join a favorite club organization of yours?

Would you object to having a person like this as a neighbor?

Scoring the answers as either rejection (1) or acceptance (0), scores range from zero (no items indicate rejection) to five (all items indicate rejection).

Each cell in Table 5.2 shows the mean rejection score for all respondents responding to that case. For example, the depressed-neurotic seeking no help shows a mean rejection score of 1.45 and the simple schizophrenic seeing a psychiatrist shows a mean rejection score of 2.85. Generally, rejection scores increase as the severity of symptoms increases, and as the level of involvement with the help source increases. Hence, the highest level of rejection is received by the hospitalized paranoid schizophrenic (4.33) and lowest by the normal involved with no help source (.02).

Although both the level of symptoms and the help source make a difference, which is more important? The mean effect of the help source can be estimated by comparing the mean rejection scores for each type of help source (given at the bottom of each column). For those seeking no help the mean rejection score is 1.35 and for those hospitalized the mean rejection score is 3.04, a difference of 1.69. In

Table 5.2. REJECTION SCORES FOR EACH HELP-SOURCE AND EACH SET OF BEHAVIOR SYMPTOMS

Behavior	HELP-SOURCE UTILIZED					
	No Help	Clergy-man	Physi-cian	Psychia-trist	Mental Hospital	Total
Paranoid schizophrenic	3.65	3.33	3.77	4.12	4.33	3.84
Simple schizophrenic	1.10	1.57	1.83	2.85	3.68	2.21
Depressed-neurotic	1.45	1.62	2.07	2.70	3.28	2.22
Phobic-compulsive	.53	1.12	1.18	1.87	2.27	1.39
Normal individual	.02	.22	.50	1.25	1.63	.72
Total	1.35	1.57	1.87	2.56	3.04	—

Scores refer to the mean number of items rejected on the Social Distance Scale.

terms of symptoms, the mean rejection score is 0.72 for normal individuals and 3.84 for paranoid schizophrenics, a difference of 3.12. Clearly, symptoms are more important than help source; yet this is to be expected. Phillips' work is significant because it shows that the help source is also very important. Consistent with labeling theory, the data suggest that in part people learn who is mentally ill (thus, who may be unpredictable and dangerous) by who is seeking professional help.

Phillips' work has led to a variety of studies using the same or a similar research design. Rather than confirming Phillips' findings, they have raised complex issues. Studies by Richard Bord (1971) and Stuart Kirk (1974) suggest that, relative to behavioral symptoms, the level of professional help has little effect on social rejection. In fact, Bord suggests that for paranoids, depressed-neurotics, and phobic-compulsives, not seeking professional help produces the highest level of social rejection. Recently, L. Anthony Loman and William Larkin (1976) have given a different twist to Phillips' methodology. Arguing that verbal descriptions of cases are somewhat artificial, they used video tapes of people in natural situations. One situation involves a female college student discussing with a counselor her poor academic record. In one tape the girl calmly explains her problem. In a second tape, she accuses her teachers of actively disregarding the quality of her academic work and accuses her counselor of being antagonistic toward her. Two versions of each tape were presented. In one the girl is labeled by the experimenter as normal, although experiencing some difficulties; and in the other she is described as having past academic and psychiatric problems with paranoid tendencies. These conditions (two levels of psychiatric symptoms and two levels of professional labeling) were systematically varied to approximate Phillips' general design. We might expect the highest level of social rejection for the girl who manifests psychological symptoms and is labeled paranoid. However, the data show that only the label makes a difference.

What can be concluded from this series of studies as to the relative effects of behavioral symptoms and professional labels on social stigma and rejection? Except for the video study, all of the studies show that behavioral symptoms play a major role in social rejection; however, inconsistency exists among the studies concerning the effect of labeling. Some suggest a strong effect (Phillips, 1963; Loman and Larkin, 1976) and some do not (Bord, 1971; Kirk, 1974). Clearly, more research is needed.

Rather than examining verbal responses to hypothetical situations (either verbally described or video scenarios), some research has studied the effects of labeling by examining the subjective feelings of people who have been hospitalized. The results are also inconsistent. For example, Joel Kotin and J. Michael Schur (1969) report that about two-thirds of former hospitalized patients describe their experience as helpful, but John and Elaine Cumming (1965) report that 41 percent feel stigmatized. Contrary to labeling theory, Walter Gove and Terry Fain (1973) report that the level of employment slightly increases after hospitalization, relative to the period prior to hospitalization. Harold Sampson et al. (1961) suggest that hospitalization is frequently helpful in alleviating tense and conflictive family situations; families frequently attribute the interpersonal conflict to the "disease" and pull together to help the hospitalized member.

To summarize, studies of the relationship between labeling and social stigma in terms of hypothetical situations and the subjective feelings of people hospitalized for mental illness provide only marginal support for labeling theory.

Effects of Labeling on Mental Illness. Various studies have examined the relationship between hospitalization and the subsequent level of mental illness. Studies reported in the 1960s (Goffman, 1961; Wing, 1962) suggest that the level of mental symptoms is positively related to the duration of hospitalization. J. K. Wing (1962), for example, reported that the longer the duration of hospitalization, the less people wish to leave the hospital, the less realistic their future plans, and the higher their levels of social withdrawal and socially inappropriate behavior, such as muteness, inaccessibility, and laughing or talking to oneself. Wing argued that these psychological states and behaviors are a response to the social environment of the hospital, although frequently confused by patients and hospital personnel alike as signs of disease deterioration. The major problem with these studies is that they compare patients hospitalized for different periods of time rather than examining a sample of patients over time. Hence, it is not clear whether the length of hospitalization relates to the severity of symptoms because of the psychological effects of hospitalization or because those with severe symptoms are simply hospitalized for a long period of time.

More recent studies, reported in the late 1960s and 1970s, have not clearly confirmed even this relationship. While some studies show a relationship between the level of symptoms and the length of hospitalization, others do not (see Townsend, 1976). Additionally, Gove (1975) notes that the patients studied by Wing had been hospitalized for many years. Today this is the exception. In 1971, for example, the median length of stay was forty-one days. In addition, today many people are admitted on an outpatient basis, and to regular purpose hospitals. Hence, Gove argues that, while the effects described by Wing are quite possible and may have been quite prevalent in the past, today they are the exception. Most people simply do not stay long enough for institutionalization effects to occur.

Granted that the extreme effects described by Erving Goffman and J. K. Wing may not be the case today, to what extent are patients today affected at all by their hospital experience? Lee Robins (1966) reports a follow-up study of children labeled by parents and teachers as having psychological problems. Some were sent to psychiatric clinics and some were not. Thirty years later psychological tests revealed no significant differences between those treated and those not treated. A study by William Eaton (1974) suggests similar conclusions. Rather than examining psychological symptoms, he examined rates of hospitalization and rehospitalization. Labeling theory suggests that hospitalization, because it accentuates psychological problems, should increase the probability of rehospitalization over the probability of initial hospitalization. The data, however, suggest that hospitalization has little effect on the probability of rehospitalization.

To summarize, various studies have examined the effects of being labeled mentally ill. Studies have examined the relative effects of labeling on social rejection in hypothetical situations, the subjective experience of hospitalized patients, and the social relationships of hospitalized patients, and the effect of treatment (hospitalization) on future behavior, as measured by psychological symptoms and future hospitalization. Clearly, simple conclusions are difficult to draw. Some studies are consistent with labeling theory (Phillips, 1963; Loman and Larkin, 1976; Wing, 1962) and some are not (Gove and Fain, 1973; Eaton, 1974). While much work remains to be done, it seems reasonable to conclude that labeling theorists have overstated their case. Labeling certainly can be debilitating, but it need not be. Hospitalization, the most visible indicator of being labeled mentally ill, can be restorative (Sampson, 1961), and frequently may have no effect at all (Eaton, 1974). On the other hand, research showing that treatment has no effect is equally critical of the medical model, which suggests that treatment should be beneficial, reducing psychological symptoms and the probability of future hospitalization. In this sense labeling theory has been very useful; for, while all that labeling theory asserts about mental illness may not be true, it has forced us to take a more critical look at the medical model.

SOCIAL POLICY

In regard to crime and delinquency and mental illness, the implications of labeling theory for social policy are reasonably clear: reduce labeling or the social stigma attached to it.

Deinstitutionalization: Crime and Delinquency

While the theoretical implications for social policy in respect to crime and delinquency may be clear, the research implications are not. Most recent studies do not show a clear and simple link between societal reaction and social stigma, and between societal reaction and recidivism. Some studies suggest linkages while some do not; and still others suggest linkages for some segments of the population but not for others. First offenders, for example, may be more sensitive to official societal reaction than are third and fourth offenders, who have already gone through the stigmatizing process and are already secondary deviants. Also, whites may be more sensitive to official societal reaction than are blacks. Because blacks constitute a negatively labeled minority group, deviant labels may be less significant socially and psychologically than they are for whites. Hence, a decrease in societal reaction may be more effective in reducing secondary deviance for first offenders and whites than for prior offenders and blacks. Continued analysis might identify various social categories (race, class, sex, ethnicity, age) for whom a reduction in societal reaction may be effective in reducing secondary deviance.

What does this mean? If research shows that those social categories most subject to social discrimination and stigma are the least sensitive to the additional stigma attached to societal reaction, are we to implement a social policy which results in further discrimination? Should social reaction for white first offenders be reduced because research suggests that it might benefit them, but be maintained for black first offenders because as a result of past discrimination they are less sensitive to it? While this is a potential ethical and policy issue, present research is too weak to support any policy derived from labeling theory, least of all one which is discriminatory.

The scarcity of supporting research has in no way dimmed the fervor of labeling theorists for social policies which reduce or change the present pattern of societal reaction to norm violations. The Presidential Commission on Law Enforcement and Administration of Justice (1967) has strongly advocated consideration of and concern for "diverting" youth from the stigmatizing effect of involvement in the criminal justice system. In fact the term "diversion" has recently come into vogue, although the exact meaning of the term remains vague.

To radical labeling theorists, diversion means social tolerance (Schur, 1973). They advocate tolerance of norm violators, thereby diverting them from the justice system. Granted, for example, that the marijuana smoker and perhaps even the juvenile who has committed a minor theft for the first time should be diverted from the justice system, but what about the first offender who commits a serious offense, such as homicide, or the perennial offender?

On the other hand, those involved in the "treatment" industry have interpreted diversion to mean social and psychological treatment and therapy. For the most part this is what diversion has come to mean in practice (Lundman, 1976). In effect, youths are diverted from the formal justice bureaucracies to the formal treatment bureaucracies, generally administered by probationary officers or social welfare workers.

Exactly how these programs reduce social stigma is not clear. In fact, to many youths it may be more stigmatizing to be labeled sick and in need of professional help than to be labeled a criminal. Additionally, Richard Lundman (1976) and Malcolm Klein (1976) argue that such programs may widen the net of juveniles who are officially labeled and brought under state supervision. In the past, by necessity, diversion was regularly practiced at different stages of the juvenile justice system. While police may have had the choice of referral for prosecution or dismissal, because of the high ratio of cases to processing facilities most youths simply had to be dismissed. Now police have an additional option, which allows them to avoid both the overcrowded prosecution process and outright dismissal. They can refer youths for treatment. If this type of social reaction, whether labeled punishment or treatment, is socially stigmatizing and if social stigma leads to secondary deviance, diversionary programs may have the effect of increasing the number of secondary delinquents!

Program selection is a major problem in evaluating the success of these programs. Frequently, those in charge of assigning youths to diversionary programs select for diversion those youths whom they feel will benefit most from the program and will fit into the program, generally youths least involved in law violations. Hence, differences in postrelease delinquency between youths assigned and youths not assigned to diversionary programs may not be a result of the

---

Box 5.3 TWO DIVERSION STUDIES

Delbert S. Elliott and Fletcher Blanchard (1975) evaluated two diversion projects. One was conducted in a Northwestern city and the other in an Eastern city. Both projects, sponsored by the Department of Health, Education and Welfare, involved youths referred by police and probation departments to a counseling (diversion) program which was designed to decrease feelings of social stigma, to increase perceived access to legitimate social roles, and to decrease delinquency. Elliott and Blanchard studied the first fifty youths referred to each project and matched them with fifty youths on regular probation by age, sex, and ethnicity. Based on interviews after four and twelve months, the findings show few differences between the diverted and nondiverted youths. While the diverted youths showed a somewhat lower level of perceived stigma, both groups showed the same level of self-reported delinquency.

Malcolm Klein (1976) attempted to solve the problem of comparable groups by randomized assignment. Using a sample from a West Coast city, the research design called for the random assignment of 800 youths to the following four conditions: a group counseled and released, a group which received a nondetention petition, a group referred to a community agency with the purchase of social services, and a group referred to a community agency without the purchase of social services. However, the final study ended up with only 306 youths partially randomized, for the police frequently assigned youths to the condition they thought would be best for them, thus making the groups noncomparable. (The real world is not like a laboratory where researchers have control over events. In field studies researchers must deal with agencies that have their own ideas about how things should be done.) After six months Klein sent questionnaires to the youths' parents asking about the youths' behavior, obtained self-reports of delinquency from the youths themselves, and examined police statistics. For the most part, the four groups showed few differences on any of the three delinquency measures.

These two studies are indicative of the literature. It is difficult for researchers to construct comparable groups either by matching or randomization, sample attrition rates are very high, and differences in future delinquency among those assigned to different programs, whether labeled detention, treatment, or diversion, are minor.

program, but just a continuation of past law violation differences between those assigned and those not assigned. To adequately evaluate these programs, youths assigned to them must be similar to youths not assigned. Various recent studies have endeavored to deal with this problem, either by matching the youths assigned and not assigned on such characteristics as prior record and seriousness of present offense, or by randomizing the assignment. (See Box 5.3.) Reviews of this literature by Don C. Gibbons and Gerald F. Blake (1976) and Richard Lundman (1976) conclude that frequently the samples are very small. the matching of those diverted and those not diverted is less than perfect, the observation of postrelease delinquency is limited to a short time interval, and the results reveal little difference in postrelease delinquency between youths diverted and youths not diverted.

In evaluating diversion as a societal response to crime and delinquency, one should remember that, while the data may be ambiguous as to the net effects of diversionary programs, such programs are generally more humane and less expensive than most incarceration programs. For example, R. Baron et al. (1973) estimate that the cost of diversion is one-tenth the cost of most regular programs, and R. Gemignani (1973) estimates that $1.5 billion could be saved by a national program of diversion.

Deinstitutionalization: Mental Illness

Labeling theorists have emphasized two general alternatives to hospitalization, assumed to be a central component in the stigmatizing process. Radical labeling theorists have advocated a policy of social tolerance (Szasz, 1960), whereas others have advocated various forms of nonhospital treatment, such as outpatient care, community psychiatry, drug therapy, and home care. For evaluating the success of these alternatives to hospitalization, David Mechanic (1969) suggests the following three criteria: psychological symptoms of the patients, performance in normal social roles, and economic and social costs.

One of the more comprehensive efforts to compare hospitalization and various alternatives is a study by Benjamin F. Pasamanick et al. (1967). One hundred and fifty-two schizophrenics referred to a state hospital were randomized into three groups: a hospital group, a home-care drug group, and a home-care placebo group. Those receiving home care were seen frequently by a nurse and infrequently by a psychologist, a social worker, and a psychiatrist; they were further divided into those treated with drugs and those led to believe they were treated with drugs but were not (a placebo group). Patients were involved in the study from six to thirty months.

Economic costs were estimated in terms of the number of hospital days saved by home care. Over the duration of the study, 77 percent of the home-care drug group required no hospitalization; home care resulted in a savings of 4800 hospital days for the drug group and 1150 for the placebo group. This savings must be balanced by the problems the patients presented to their families, although after six months of home care such problems abated. For example, in terms of causing trouble with neighbors, producing strain on others, and requiring excessive amount of attention, the families of 16 percent of the hospital group, 57 percent of the home-care drug group and 55 percent of the home-care placebo group reported initial problems, but after six months only 2, 19, and 29 percent, respectively, reported such problems. In terms of psychological symptoms and role functioning, all three groups were evaluated after six, eighteen, and twenty-four months. All three groups improved after the first six months, but did not improve much after that; more significantly, there was little difference in improvement between the home-care and hospitalized groups. Also, the level of rehospitalization required of the hospitalized group was actually higher than the level of initial hospitalization required of the patients treated at home. Generally, the data suggest that home care is significantly less costly than hospitalization, and that it is as effective as hospitalization in improving psychological symptoms and role functioning and in reducing future hospitalization.

Five years later, Davis, Dinitz, and Pasamanick (1972) located and studied 92 percent of the original sample. They interviewed the patients and their significant others, and surveyed clinic and hospital records over the five years to identify patients receiving hospital and clinical care. They found few statistically significant differences between the three groups in terms of hospitalization, psychological symptoms, and social adjustment. For example, during the five-year period 61 percent of the previously hospitalized and the home-care drug patients and 57 percent of the home-care placebo patients were hospitalized and approximately 27 percent of all three groups were employed. Generally, while the follow-up study shows that without any care at all patients diagnosed as schizophrenic deteriorate, it also shows that hospitalization is no more effective than home care coupled with community services.

Since the 1960s numerous studies have compared the relative effects of alternatives to hospitalization on a variety of criteria (see Townsend, 1976 for a review). Generally, the studies show:

1. Except for long-term hospitalization, mental hospitals do not show the debilitating effects suggested by labeling theory.
2. On the other hand, evidence supporting the short-term benefits of hospitalization compared to alternative responses is equivocal. Findings are generally consistent with the data of Pasamanick et al.: benefits for the patient over the short term are no greater from hospitalization than from a variety of alternatives (Huey, 1976).

Given these findings, it seems reasonable to advocate the social policy that is least costly and most humane to those concerned. Mechanic (1969) suggests that the optimal social policy is either home care with maximal services to reduce the strain on the family during the first six months, or a short period of hospitalization mainly for the benefit of the family, followed by home care.

In sum, the policy implications of labeling theory are relatively clear: reduce the level of negative social labeling. Reduce involvement in the criminal justice system for those accused or convicted of law violations and reduce hospitalization for those showing signs of mental illness. Social policies vary from radical nonintervention (community tolerance) to various forms of nonincarceration, such as diversion programs, and nonhospitalized treatment such as community and home-care programs. Because of program selection and attrition, evaluation of these programs is difficult. Generally, the data seem to suggest that, while labeling theorists have rightly alerted us to the negative consequences of various forms of societal reaction, they have overstated their case. For crime and delinquency there is little evidence showing that present diversionary programs are more successful at reducing future violations than are traditional forms of societal reaction; and for mental illness there is little evidence showing that alternatives to hospitalization are more effective than short-term hospitalization. (Problems associated with long-term hospitalization have been more clearly documented.) On the other hand, if research does not show major differences in effectiveness between forms of societal reaction, then a good case may still be made for the policies advocated by labeling theorists, as they are economically less costly and are more humane to those involved.

CRITIQUE

Labeling theory has been a center of attention since the mid-1960s. As well as generating considerable research, it has generated considerable controversy. This section reviews some of the prominent critiques.

Theory

Primary Deviance. By focusing on secondary deviance, labeling theory neglects the study of primary deviance and the deviance of the powerful. Lemert, Becker, and Scheff argue that primary deviance is episodic and is engaged in by a large variety and number of people; therefore, it is of minimal importance for the deviant and society. To the contrary, primary deviance may frequently be of considerable importance to both the deviant and society. What about suicide, assault, rape, murder, and child molesting (to mention only a few)? Are these actions unimportant when committed by primary deviants? Additionally, the emphasis on secondary deviance unobtrusively directs research away from the deviance of the powerful who possess the resources to actively resist societal reaction. As they frequently commit norm and law violations without prosecution and frequently even without detection, their violations tend to be ignored by labeling theorists. The powerless, lacking the resources to avoid labeling, become the objects of social labeling, and thus the objects of study.

Labeling and Secondary Deviance. Recently, some sociologists have questioned the role of labeling in explaining secondary deviance. Milton Mankoff

(1971) makes an interesting distinction between necessary and sufficient causal conditions. The former refers to those conditions which must be present before deviance occurs, and the latter refers to those conditions which always produce deviance. Mankoff argues that labeling is neither necessary nor sufficient to produce secondary deviance. As to the latter, he cites various studies showing that secondary deviance does not automatically follow from labeling; sometimes labeling even functions as a deterrent (see Chapter Four). Concerning the necessity of labeling, he argues that many people involved in a lifetime of deviance may have never been formally or informally labeled. They become career deviants because of persistent exposure to social situations which cause deviance. For example, secondary deviance may be a persistent response to a persistent lack of legitimate opportunities or a persistent political effort to change society as specified in Merton's theory.

Delimiting the Application of Labeling Theory. Labeling theory, like most theories of behavior, may be limited in its scope of application. For the most part labeling theorists and researchers have not taken this issue seriously. They have rather indiscriminately applied labeling theory to all patterns of norm violations and people. Yet labeling theory may be more useful, for example, in explaining the secondary deviance of those well integrated into conventional society than those marginal to it.

Research

Selection. People are not randomly labeled. Those who most frequently commit the most serious violations are most likely to be labeled. Thus, a higher level of future violations by those labeled than those not labeled may simply reflect behavioral continuity over time, not social labeling. While researchers have tried to deal with this problem, their efforts have not been very successful. Some researchers have attempted to randomize the labeling process; hence, those labeled are no different socially and psychologically from those not labeled except for chance differences, which can be statistically estimated. Such studies generally involve the cooperation of official agencies legally charged with the responsibility for processing people accused of norm and law violations. The agencies are not always cooperative. They may agree to randomize, but in practice may assign people to the program they believe to be most helpful for them.

Critical Tests of Mediators. Most research has examined the relationship between labeling and future norm violations. Yet research on the hypothesized mediating conditions, such as structured opportunities, interpersonal relationships, and self-concept, may be more useful in understanding why labeling is found to increase future norm violations in some studies, decrease it in others, and have no effect in still others.

Social Policy

The social policy implications and implementations of labeling theory can be divided into two broad categories: radical nonintervention and treatment programs. Most efforts to implement labeling theory involve some form of treatment. For crime and delinquency these programs have been termed diversionary and for mental illness they have been called community and home care. The problem with these programs is that those involved are frequently still labeled by agents of the programs and by acquaintances. In fact, many diversionary programs are not too different from traditional probationary programs. Although diversionary programs may be somewhat more flexible and entail somewhat less supervision, the accused norm violator is still under some form of agency supervision. Can this be avoided? It is difficult for people (as agents of social control bureaucracies or as friends) to suspend their moral judgments when dealing with norm violators; some form of labeling may be inevitable. It is the role of social researchers to discover how primary deviance can be responded to, in some cases even deterred, without increasing secondary deviance.

REFERENCES

AGETON, SUZANNE and DELBERT S. ELLIOTT. "The effects of legal processing on self-concept," Social Problems 22 (Oct. 1974): 87–100.

BARON, R., F. FEENEY, and W. THORNTON. "Preventing delinquency through diversion: The Sacramento County 601 Diversion Project," Federal Probation 37 (March 1973):13–19.

BECKER, HOWARD. Outsider (New York: Free Press, 1963).

BORD, RICHARD. "Rejection of the mentally ill: continuities and further developments," Social Problems 18 (Spring 1971):469–509.

BRYAN, JAMES H. "Apprenticeships in prostitution," Social Problems 12 (Winter 1965):287–97.

BUIKHUISEN, WOUTER and P. H. DIJKSTERHUIS. "Delinquency and stigmatization," British Journal of Criminology 11 (April 1971):186.

CUMMING, JOHN and ELAINE CUMMING. "On the stigma of mental illness," Community Mental Health Journal 1 (Summer 1965):135–43.

DAVIS, ANNE E., SIMON DINITZ, and BENJAMIN PASAMANICK. "The prevention of hospitalization in schizophrenia; Five years after an experimental program," American Journal of Orthopsychiatry 12 (April 1972):375–88.

EATON, WILLIAM. "Mental hospitalization or a reinforcement process," American Sociological Review 39 (April 1974):252–60.

ELLIOTT, DELBERT S. and FLETCHER BLANCHARD. "An import study of two diversion projects," American Psychological Association Meetings, 1975.

FARRELL, RONALD A. and JAMES F. NELSON. "A causal model of secondary deviance: The cause of homosexuality," Sociological Quarterly 17 (Winter 1976):109−20.

FOSTER, JACK D., SIMON DINITZ, and WALTER C. RECKLESS. "Perceptions of stigma following public intervention for delinquent behavior," Social Problems 20 (1972):202−09.

GEMIGNANI, R. "Diversion of juvenile offenders from the juvenile justice system," in P. Lejins (ed.), *Criminal Justice Monograph: New Approaches to Diversion and Treatment of Juvenile Offenders.* (Washington, D.C.:U.S. Government Printing Office, 1973).

GIBBONS, DON C. and GERALD F. BLAKE. "Evaluating the impact of juvenile diversion programs," Crime and Delinquency 22 (Oct. 1976):411−20.

GIBBS, JACK P. "Conceptions of deviant behavior: The old and the new," Pacific Sociological Review 9 (1966):9−14.

GOFFMAN, ERVING. *Asylums: Essays on the Social Situation of Mental Patients and Other Inmates.* (Garden City, N.Y.: Doubleday, 1961).

GOLD, MARTIN and JAY R. WILLIAMS. "The effect of getting caught: Apprehension of the juvenile offender as a cause of subsequent delinquencies," Prospectus 3 (Dec. 1969): 1−12.

GOLDMAN, NATHAN. *The Differential Selection of Juvenile Offenders for Court Appearance* (New York:National Council on Crime and Delinquency, 1963).

GOVE, WALTER R. "Labelling and mental illness, a critique," in Walter R. Gove (ed.), *The Labelling of Deviance* (New York: Halsted, 1975).

GOVE, WALTER and TERRY FAIN. "The stigma of mental hospitalization: An attempt to evaluate its consequences," Archives of General Psychiatry 28 (April 1973):494−500.

GOULDNER, ALVIN W. *The Coming Crises of Western Sociology* (New York: Basic Books, 1970).

HARRIS ANTHONY R. "Imprisonment and expected value of criminal choice, a specification and tests of aspects of the labelling perspective," American Sociological Review 40 (Feb. 1975):71−87.

HUEY, KAREN. "Alternatives to mental hospital treatment," Hospital and Community Psychiatry 27 (March 1976):186−92.

HUGHES, EVERETT C. *Men and Their Work* (New York: Free Press, 1958).

JENSEN, GARY F. "Delinquency and adolescent self-conceptions: A study of the personal relevance of infraction," Social Problems 20 (1972):84−102.

KIRK, STUART. "The impact of labelling on rejection of the mentally ill: an experimental study," Journal of Health and Social Behavior 15 (June 1974): 108−17.

KLEIN, MALCOLM W. "Issues and realities in police diversion programs," Crime and Delinquency 22 (Oct 1976):421−27.

KOTIN, JOEL and J. MICHAEL SCHUR. "Attitudes of discharged mental patients toward their hospital experiences," Journal of Nervous and Mental Disease 149 (1969):408−14.

LEMERT, EDWIN M. *Social Pathology* (New York: McGraw-Hill, 1951).

———. *Human Deviance, Social Problems and Social Control* (Englewood Cliffs, N.J.:Prentice-Hall, Inc., 1967).

LIAZOS, ALEXANDER. "The poverty of the sociology of deviance: nuts, sluts, and perverts," Social Problems 17 (Summer 1972):103−20.

LOMAN, L. ANTHONY and WILLIAM LARKIN. "Rejection of the mentally ill: An experiment in labelling," Sociological Quarterly 17 (Autumn 1976): 555−60.

LUNDMAN, RICHARD J. "Will diversion reduce recidivism?" Crime and Delinquency 22 (Oct. 1976):428−37.

MCEACHERN, A. W. "The juvenile probation system," American Behavioral Scientist 11 (1968):1−10.

MAHONEY, ANNE RANKIN. "The effect of labelling upon youths in the juvenile justice system: A review of the evidence," Law and Society Review 4 (Summer 1974):583−611.

MANKOFF, MILTON. "Societal reaction and career deviance: A critical analysis," The Sociological Quarterly 12 (Spring 1971):204−18.

MATZA, DAVID. *Becoming Deviant* (Englewood Cliffs, N.J.: Prentice-Hall, Inc., 1969).

MECHANIC, DAVID. *Mental Health and Social Policy* (Englewood Cliffs, N.J.: Prentice-Hall, Inc., 1969).

PASAMANICK, BENJAMIN, FRANK R. SCARPETTI, and SIMON DINITZ. *Schizophrenics in the Community: An Experimental Study in the Prevention of Hospitalization* (New York: Meredith, 1967).

PHILLIPS, DEREK. "Rejection: A possible consequence of seeking help for mental disorders," American Sociological Review 28 (Dec. 1963):963−72.

QUINNEY, RICHARD. *The Social Reality of Crime* (Boston: Little, Brown, 1970).

RAY, MARSH B. "Abstinence cycles and heroin addicts," Social Problems 9 (Fall 1961):132−40.

REISS, ALBERT J., JR. "The integration of queers and peers," Social Problems 9 (Fall 1961):102−20.

ROBINS, LEE. *Deviant Children Grown Up.* (Baltimore: Williams and Wilkins, 1966).

SAMPSON, HAROLD, SHELDON MESSINGER, and ROBERT TOWNE. "The mental hospital and marital family ties," Social Problems 9 (Fall 1961):141−55.

SCHEFF, THOMAS. *Being Mentally Ill* (Chicago: Aldine, 1966).

SCHUR, EDWIN M. *Radical Non-Intervention: Rethinking the Delinquency Problem* (Englewood Cliffs, N.J.: Prentice-Hall, Inc., 1973).

————. *Labelling Deviant Behavior* (New York: Harper & Row, 1971).

SCHWARTZ, RICHARD D. and JEROME H. SKOLNICK. "Two studies of legal stigma," Social Problems 10 (1962):133—43.

SZASZ, THOMAS S. "The myth of mental illness," American Psychologist 15 (Feb. 1960):113—18.

TAYLOR, IAN, PAUL WALTON, and JOCK YOUNG. *The New Criminology* (New York: Basic Books, 1973).

THORNBERRY, TERRANCE P. "Race, socio-economic status and sentencing in the juvenile justice system," The Journal of Criminal Law, Criminology and Police Science 64 (March 1973):90—98.

TOWNSEND, J. MARSHALL. "Self-concept and the institutionalization of mental patients: an overview and critique," Journal of Health and Social Behavior 17 (Sept. 1976):263—71.

TURK, AUSTIN. *Criminality and Legal Order* (Chicago: Rand McNally, 1969).

WARREN, CAROL A. B. and JOHN M. JOHNSTON. "A critique of labelling theory from the phenomenological perspective," in Robert A. Scott and Jack D. Douglas (eds.), *Theoretical Perspectives on Deviance* (New York: Basic Books, 1972).

WING, J. K. "Institutionalism in mental hospitals," British Journal of Social and Clinical Psychology 1 (1962):38—51.

YARROW, MARIAN RADKE. "The psychological meaning of mental illness in the family," Journal of Social Issues 11 (1955): 12—24.

CHAPTER SIX

THE ETHNOMETHOdOLOGY PERSPECTIVE

THEORY

Ethnomethodology is philosophically linked to phenomenology, which emphasizes two themes: "back to the phenomenon" and "show how the phenomenon is built up." "Phenomenon" refers to perceptions, cognitions, and consciousness. Hence, phenomenology ignores the objective world and is concerned with describing people's subjective perceptions and interpretations of the world, and the processes by which people "build up" or construct their worlds. To explain action, phenomenologists argue that we must come to know people's constructions. Theories of action must capture people's constructions or at least be consistent with them. Alfred J. Schutz (1966) argues that people construct their realities using a set of cognitive rules or principles, and that it is the role of phenomenologists to discover these rules.

Ethnomethodology and Sociology

Much of phenomenology is quite divorced from the traditional concerns of sociology. Ethnomethodologists endeavor to link the concerns of phenomenology and sociology. Some use the insights of phenomenology to bear on the traditional problems of sociology (Garfinkel, 1967), whereas others use the social context to further develop phenomenology. This chapter examines the former.

Symbolic interactionists are concerned with subjective meanings and their role in the emergence of joint action, and emphasize the importance of such social psychological and social processes as role-taking, empathy, and negotiation in constructing social reality and in the emergence of joint action. Borrowing from phenomenology, ethnomethodologists extend this work.

Sociologists are concerned with formal organizations—structures, processes, and products. Ethnomethodologists (Cicourel, 1968) examine these as emergent manifestations of situational interactions, which are understandable in terms of people's subjective constructions of reality and their methods of constructing reality (typifications and common sense theories). Furthermore, as structures of organizational activity are reflected in organizational statistics, ethnomethodologists (Cicourel, 1968; Douglas, 1967 and 1971) argue that organizational statistics are also understandable in terms of people's constructions of reality and their methods of constructing reality. For example, Cicourel (1964) argues that student grades are less a description of students than an outcome of teachers' and administrators' typifications (abstract concepts) and common sense theories of education. Teachers' typifications about children affect their interaction with them. If teachers believe that minority children are less capable than majority children, they may challenge and encourage them less than majority children, and may interpret their comments and examinations differently than those of majority children. (A wrong answer on a mathematics test may be interpreted as a sign of either inability or creativity.)

Many sociologists define the study of social order as the master problem of sociology. Ethnomethodologists (Garfinkel, 1967) argue that social order can be understood as a manifestation of microsituational interactions, which reflect commonalities in people's constructions of reality, which in turn reflect commonalities in language and assumptions about reality.

In summary, borrowing from phenomenology, ethnomethodologists examine the methods people use in constructing reality and attempt to show how this knowledge is useful in approaching some of the traditional issues of sociology, such as situational joint action; organizational structures, processes, and products; and social order.

Ethnomethodology and Deviance

From the perspective of ethnomethodology, deviance is a social construction of people, organizations, and societies. Ethnomethodologists are concerned with such constructions (what is defined as deviant in what social situations?), with the specific application of such constructions (who is defined as deviant in what specific social situations?), and with the methods people and organizations use in constructing and applying definitions of deviance.

Box 6.1 LABELING AND ETHNOMETHODOLOGY PERSPECTIVES

Before proceeding it may be useful here to compare the ethnomethodology and labeling perspectives. As stated in Chapter Five, both define deviance as a social definition and are similar in many other respects. In fact, in the work of some sociologists (Schur, 1971) the perspectives tend to merge. Yet, because the perspectives make somewhat different assumptions about reality, they lead to different theoretical and research questions. Labeling theory takes a more or less pluralistic view of society, assuming that social norms are in flux and constantly emerging. Deviance, as norm violations, can be defined at any one point in time relative to the dominant norms; however, as norms are conceptualized as shifting and emerging, deviance, as norm violations, is viewed as more relative, situationally contingent, and difficult to identify than in the traditional perspectives. Some labeling theorists thus use societal reaction (labeling) to define deviance. Like ethnomethodologists, they view deviance as a social definition or construction; but unlike ethnomethodologists, they do not suspend or ignore reality. In discussing social labels and labeling processes, they use terms like "discrimination" and "bias," and ask, why are only some norm violators and some nonviolators labeled, and what are the consequences of labeling in structuring and patterning future norm violations. These are nonsensical issues, if reality is suspended. The use of words like "discrimination" and the posing of questions about norm violations assume some underlying reality as a reference point. In suspending reality ethnomethodologists ignore these questions and examine the processes and methods by which deviance is constructed and people are constructed as deviants. Constructions are not described as "right" or "wrong" or even as "correct" or "incorrect." Hence, in Chapter Five the labeling perspective is used to examine the extent to which being labeled a deviant affects future levels of norm and law violations; and in this chapter the ethnomethodology perspective is used to examine the processes by which some behavior is defined as deviant and some people are defined as deviant.

Images of Deviance. General categories are a necessary and natural outcome of people's inability to cognitively process the intricate and detailed complexities of the environment; they simplify the environment, thereby making it stable and understandable. Traditionally, sociologists (Lippman, 1922) have been concerned with the extent to which general categories and images (particularly ethnic and racial images) are accurate and unbiased reflections of the world. Upon suspending or ignoring reality, ethnomethodologists, of course, suspend this type of question and focus on the role of such images in perceiving and processing information—in constructing reality. Thus, rather than using the traditional term "stereotype," ethnomethodologists use such terms as "typification" and "ideal type" to refer to such general categories and images.

The general images of deviance which prevail in a society are simply a special case of general cognitive categories (typifications) which people use to describe and order the world. Images of deviance do not exist in isolation, but are embodied and only meaningful within general common sense theories of deviance. Popular theories have traditionally conceptualized deviance in moralistic and legalistic terms, thereby viewing the deviant as responsible for his or her behavior and implying punishment as the appropriate societal response. More recently popular theories have conceptualized deviance as a form of mental illness, thereby suggesting minimal personal responsibility and various forms of therapy as the proper societal response. (See Chapter Five for a discussion of the medical model.)

Contextual Constructions of Deviance. While ethnomethodologists are concerned with general collective definitions of deviance and their historical emergence, the thrust of the perspective is on how such general definitions are applied in specific situations—contextual constructions. A general theory of contextual constructions, however, is difficult to identify. This discussion is generally based on the works of Harold Garfinkel (1967), Harvey Sacks (1972), Aaron V. Cicourel (1968), and Jack D. Douglas (1967 and 1971).

Sacks (1972) discusses two cognitive rules which people use in organizing information to construct social reality: the rule of consistency and the rule of economy. The former suggests that once people have categorized events and persons, they organize past information and future perceptions consistently with these categories. For example, upon defining someone as a homosexual, people tend to search for and remember confirming cues. They may note a male's "feminine walk," high-pitched voice, smooth skin, lack of female companionship, style of dress—all of which would have been ignored and organized differently had they not initially categorized the person as a homosexual. The economy rule refers to a tendency to "lock in" categories. That is, once a general category is selected for interpreting a situation, people tend not to reorganize situational cues to test the application of alternative categories. Upon deciding that a person is a homosexual, for example, people are not prone to consider alternative interpretations of a "feminine walk."

As a special case of this cognitive process, ethnomethodologists have been particularly interested in retrospective interpretation—a cognitive process whereby a person's past behavior is reinterpreted on the basis of present typifications. For example, upon classifying someone as a homosexual, people are prone to reinterpret his or her past behavior in a consistent manner. Events which were ignored as meaningless (standing close to people of the same sex, patting people of the same sex on the knee and kissing people of the same sex goodbye) take on a new significance. Harold Garfinkel (1956:421−22) states:

> The other person becomes in the eyes of his condemners literally a different person. It is not that the new attributes are added to the old "nucleus." He is not changed; he is reconstituted. The former identity, at best, receives the accent of mere appearance . . . the former identity stands as accidental; the new identity is the "basic reality." What he is now is what, "after all," he was all along.

Deviant intention—the extent to which a deviant act is planned and intended—is also important in defining a person as a deviant. Unintended deviant acts generally are not a basis for inferring a deviant identity. Edward E. Jones and Keith E. Davis (1965) argue that in attributing intentions to others, people are sensitive to whether or not their acts seem to be caused by external forces (social pressure and accidents). If external forces are not apparent, people tend to attribute acts to choice and impart motives, dispositions, and intentions to the actor. For example, homosexual behavior in a constrained single-sex environment (a prison) may not result in a homosexual label; rather the person may be defined as a heterosexual without choice.

People are not always pleased with being labeled a deviant and frequently resist the label. The end social product or definition is frequently the culmination of extensive negotiations and bargaining. For example, Yarrow et al. (1955) report that defining a family member as mentally ill is preceded by a long period of accommodation during which the disturbing behavior is normalized, or explained away; only after a long period of negotiation and redefinition is the disturbing behavior defined as a sign of illness. Goffman (1963) discusses the interpersonal manipulation involved in this process, and the techniques of information control people use to manage their public identities. Ethnomethodologists are particularly concerned with accounts in this negotiation process. Marvin B. Scott and Stanford M. Lyman (1968:46) define an account as ". . . a linguistic device employed whenever an action is subject to valuative inquiry." They discuss two types of accounts (excuses and justifications). Excuses are verbalizations which mitigate responsibility for an action. For example, an individual may explain his or her wayward action as a manifestation of an uncontrolled biological drive, as an unintended and unforeseen accident, or as a result of misinformation. Justifications are verbalizations which emphasize the positive consequences of an act, particularly under certain situations, while recognizing its negative properties in principle. Scott and Lyman (1968) state that techniques of neutralization (denial of injury, denial of victim, condemnation of the condemners, and appeal to higher loyalties) often function as social justifications. (See Chapter Four.) Consider again the homosexual example. A person identified as a homosexual may contest the label by excusing acts of homosexuality as caused by social pressure while on a sea cruise, or may justify them as neither injurious nor involving a victim.

To summarize, ethnomethodologists study the techniques (methods) used by people (ethnos) to construct reality (categories of deviance and deviant people). Being defined as a deviant is thought to be situationally problematic and the end product of a social process. Concern is focused on the role of typifications, lay theories, retrospective interpretation, and negotiation in this process.

Organizational Constructions. As organizations (police, hospitals) are instrumental in defining deviance, ethnomethodologists (Cicourel, 1968; Emerson, 1969; Douglas, 1967) have studied organizational constructions and construction processes.

Richard Hawkins and Gary Tiedeman (1975) argue that the constructions used by social control organizations are shaped by organizational needs for efficiency, perpetuation, and accountability. Efficiency requires a stable and simple categorical system in terms of which the complex world can be organized and described. As the business of social control organizations increases, demands for efficiency cumulate in more general and abstract typifications of deviance. The details and intricacies of individual cases must be ignored if they are to fit into organizational categories and routines. The need for accountability frequently results in unique and esoteric categorical systems (such as the categorical systems of psychiatrists) by which organizations manifest their unique contribution to social problem solving. Organizational categorical systems also reflect the professional and semiprofessional socialization of organizational participants. In law school lawyers learn to view the world through a legal model and in medical school psychiatrists learn to view the world through a medical model. (See Chapter Five for a discussion of the medical model.) See Figure 6.1.

In applying typifications to specific cases, social control agents function like everyone else, although within organizational constraints. Certain combinations of cues are used to categorize cases. Once categorized, through rules of consistency and economy, perceptions are ordered and information is collected to confirm the original categorization. For example, ethnomethodologists study biography building, a process whereby social control agents search into an individual's past for events which confirm the present label. In constructing the biography of a person classified as paranoid, a psychiatrist might note and record that he always locked the doors of his residence, accused his teachers of unfair grading, and divorced his wife for cheating; and in constructing the biography of a person diagnosed as a suicide, a psychiatrist might note and record that she was depressed and recently lost her job. These events and actions may be quite normal within various social contexts, yet when compiled selectively they can suggest abnormality.

Finally, the statistics of social control organizations (rates of crime and mental illness) are conceptualized and studied by ethnomethodologists, not as indicators of underlying "real" rates, but as indicators and reflections of organizational properties and routines.

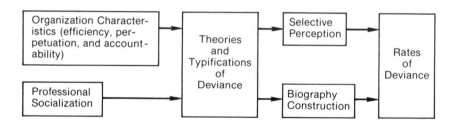

Figure 6.1. Organizational Construction Processes. Organizational characteristics and professional socialization influence organizational typifications and theories of deviance, which influence perception and biography construction, which in turn influence the official rates of deviance.

RESEARCH

Ethnomethodologists argue that to infer people's constructions, researchers must come to know people's methods or tools of reality construction—language, typifications, common sense theories, etc. This cannot be accomplished through the standard techniques of data collection, such as official records and standardized questionnaires. The latter categorize the constructions of people in terms of the constructions of sociologists; and the former categorize the constructions of people in terms of the constructions of social control agencies, and then in terms of the constructions of sociologists. Sociologists are thus two steps removed from people's constructions. Researchers are implored to experience reality as people experience it—to "go native." Participant observation (whereby the researcher becomes involved with the people studied) is advocated. The participant observer experiences what subjects experience, and thereby comes to construct reality in their terms. As participant observation is frequently neither practical nor possible (as with homosexuality and alcoholism), nonparticipant observation (whereby the researcher observes the action directly or firsthand, but does not actually become involved) is also recommended. Other techniques are used (such as interviews and sometimes even questionnaires) as needed; but in using them ethnomethodologists remain concerned with the problem of imposing their own constructions on the constructions of people studied.

This section describes three research areas: cultural typifications, methods of construction used by social control agents, and organizational products.

Stereotypes/typifications: Homosexuality

In the first of three studies, Jerry L. Simmons (1969) asked eighty-nine students in a social problems class to describe homosexuals, political radicals, beatniks, adulterers, and marijuana smokers. Although a questionnaire was used, open-ended questions allowed students to use their own descriptive categories. About two-thirds of the students wrote very stereotyped descriptions of each type, from which Simmons abstracted seventy traits.

In the second study these traits were included in a closed-ended questionnaire. One hundred thirty-four adults, selected to maximize variation on age, education, sex, and race, were asked to circle the five traits they felt most accurately described each of the five deviant types. The numbers in Table 6.1 refer to the percentage of respondents who selected the trait. Note that while the image of each type is different, for the most part each is described negatively. For example, the beatnik is described as sloppy, a nonconformist, an escapist, immature, and individualistic, and the homosexual as sexually abnormal, perverted, mentally ill, maladjusted, and effeminate. Those who used negative stereotypes to describe one deviant type also used them to describe the others, a tendency related to low education and a general attitude of social intolerance.

Table 6.1. TRAITS USED TO DESCRIBE EACH OF FIVE DEVIANT TYPES

Marijuana Smokers	%	Beatniks	%	Adulterers	%	Homosexuals	%	Political Radicals	%
Looking for kicks	59	Sloppy	57	Immoral	41	Sexually abnormal	72	Ambitious	61
Escapist	52	Nonconformist	46	Promiscuous	36	Perverted	52	Aggressive	47
Insecure	49	Escapist	32	Insecure	34	Mentally ill	40	Stubborn	32
Lacking self-control	41	Immature	28	Lonely	32	Maladjusted	40	Nonconformist	32
Frustrated	34	Individualistic	27	Sinful	31	Effeminate	29	Impulsive	28
Excitement seeking	29	Lazy	27	Self-interested	29	Lonely	22	Dangerous	28
Nervous	26	Insecure	26	Lacking self-control	28	Insecure	21	Individualistic	26
Maladjusted	24	Irresponsible	20	Passionate	24	Immoral	16	Self-interested	23
Lonely	22	Self-interested	18	Irresponsible	22	Repulsive	14	Intelligent	22
Immature	21	False lives	16	Frustrated	21	Frustrated	14	Irresponsible	21
Weakminded	17	Artistic	16	Immature	16	Weakminded	12	Conceited	15
Irresponsible	15	Maladjusted	14	Sensual	14	Lacking self-control	12	Imaginative	14
Mentally ill	13	Harmless	13	Over-sexed	13	Sensual	11	Excitement-seeking	9
Pleasure-loving	11	Imaginative	12	Sexually abnormal	12	Secretive	11		
Dangerous	11	Lonely	11	Pleasure-loving	12	Over-sexed	10		
		Imitative	10	False lives	11	Dangerous	10		
		Frustrated	10	Maladjusted	11	Sinful	10		
		Happy-go-lucky	9			Sensitive	10		

The numbers refer to the percentage of respondents who selected each trait.

A third study was undertaken to further explore the latter. Two hundred and eighty respondents, again selected to maximize diversity, were asked to respond "yes" or "no" to the following items about each of fifteen deviant types and five ethnic groups.

1. I would marry or accept as a close relative
2. I would accept as a close friend
3. I would accept as a next door neighbor
4. I would accept in my school or church
5. I would accept in my community but would not have contact with
6. I would accept as a resident of my county but not in my community
7. I would not accept at all even as a resident of my county

Table 6.2 shows the average social intolerance or distance for each deviant type; the level of acceptance is highest for intellectuals (low distance score) and the lowest for homosexuals (high distance score). As in the second study, people can be divided into those who are generally tolerant of deviants and ethnic groups and those who are not; again, the intolerant tend to be older and less educated than the tolerant. Additionally, the level of social intolerance relates to common sense theories about the causes of deviance and to policy recommendations. The intolerant and the stereotyper tend to believe in biological causes and to recommend severe social reactions to deviance.

Generally, Simmons's (1969) work provides us with some knowledge of the images people hold of various deviant types and the extent to which these images relate to common sense theories of deviance and social policy recommendations. There are two problems with this work: the sample is limited to the Western United

Table 6.2. AVERAGE SOCIAL DISTANCE TOWARD VARIOUS DEVIANT CATEGORIES

Simmons (1969)	Mean	Ward (1979)	Mean
*Homosexuals	5.3	Prostitutes	3.2
Lesbians	5.2	Homosexuals	2.7
*Prostitutes	5.0	Alcoholics	2.7
*Marijuana smokers	4.9	Political radicals	2.6
*Political radicals	4.3	Marijuana smokers	2.3
Adulterers	4.1	Ex-mental patients	2.1
*Alcoholics	4.0	Exconvicts	1.7
Beatniks	3.9		
Gamblers	3.6		
Exconvicts	3.5		
Atheists	3.4		
*Ex-mental patients	2.9		
*Intellectuals	2.0		

The range of Simmons's social distance scale is 1−7; the range of Ward's social distance scale is 1−5.

*Refers to the deviant types also studied by Ward.

States (California), and the data were collected in 1965, making the results somewhat dated.

Turn now to the work of Russell Ward (1979), who attempted to replicate Simmons's results in an Eastern city in 1976. A sample of 413 people was interviewed and asked to describe seven deviant types by circling the five of thirty-four traits (selected from Simmons's seventy traits) which most describe each type.

Table 6.2 compares Ward's results in the East in 1976 to Simmons's results in the West in 1965. Since Simmons used a seven-point social distance scale and Ward used a five-point scale, it is difficult to compare absolute scores between the studies; however, an examination of the items used in both scales suggests that social distance is lower in Ward's sample. Interestingly, the relative order of Ward's seven types and of the same seven types in Simmons's research is similar. Homosexuals and prostitutes show the highest level of social distance; alcoholics, political radicals, and marijuana users show middle levels; and ex-mental patients and ex-convicts the lowest levels. Also, similar to Simmons, Ward's data show social tolerance to decrease with age and to increase with education.

In terms of stereotypic descriptions, unfortunately, Ward reports only the homosexuality data. Again, the similarity with Simmons's data is noteworthy. Of the eight stereotypes most selected to describe homosexuals by Simmons's sample (see Table 6.1), seven were also the most selected by Ward's sample; and with a few exceptions the order of the first eight ranks is also similar. There are some differences as well. Generally, Ward argues that the image of the homosexual as sinful and lustful in Simmons's sample is not at all apparent in his sample. The homosexual is still viewed as sick, although less in a moral and more in a medical sense. This difference between Simmons's and Ward's findings may reflect a general shift in the United States from moral/immoral vocabularies to healthy/sick vocabularies in describing deviance.

Construction Methods: Police

Perhaps the major thrust of ethnomethodological research is the examination of the methods used by social control agents for constructing or labeling acts as deviance and actors as deviant. This section is based on two well-known studies of police (Piliavin and Briar, 1964; Cicourel, 1968). Their work shows how cognitive methods (typifications, common sense theories, retrospective interpretation, etc.) are used by police to construct everyday reality, thus affecting who is arrested and prosecuted. Both studies used field observation methods. Irving Piliavin and Scott Briar's research consists of a nine-month observation study of all juvenile officers (approximately thirty) in one police department. Aaron V. Cicourel's research consists of a two-year participant observation study of police and probation departments in two cities.

Aaron V. Cicourel, born 1928, received his B.A. in 1951 and his M.A. in 1955 from the University of California at Los Angeles, and his Ph.D. in 1959 from Cornell University, and presently is a Professor of Sociology and Medicine at the University of California at San Diego. He is well known for his work *The Social Organization of Juvenile Justice*, 1968, on ethnomethodology and deviance. (Courtesy of Aaron V. Cicourel, reprinted by permission.)

Cicourel reports that police employ five categories of delinquency: dependency cases, family and juvenile problems, minor misdemeanors and normal delinquency, normal misdemeanors, and serious offenses and felonies. Both Circourel's and Piliavin and Briar's findings suggest that two broad categories underlie these distinctions: "good" and "bad" youths. The first four categories refer to different types of essentially good youths who, for one reason or another, commit bad or delinquent acts. These acts are not viewed by police as cues or signs of an underlying immoral character; they are viewed as reflecting circumstances. On the other hand, some youths are viewed by police as basically bad. Their delinquent acts are seen as cues and signs of an underlying immoral character; consequently, unless something is done, police assume that they will continue to get into trouble.

These typifications of "good" and "bad" youths are enmeshed in theories of delinquency. Cicourel's data suggest that police view character development as a response to family and neighborhood disorganization or deprivation. Disorganized families (unemployed father, working mother, divorce, separation) and disorganized neighborhoods (unemployment, high crime rate) are thought of as causing troubled and trouble-making youth.

Both Cicourel and Piliavin and Briar examine the cues which police use in classifying youths as essentially good or bad. Offense behavior (burglary or truancy) is, of course, important. However, for inferring a youth's underlying character, offense behavior is only one among many cues and not always the most important. Police also scrutinize a youth's demeanor (body motion, facial expression, voice intonation, dress, walk, mannerisms, attitude, grooming). Demeanor is particularly important in field decisions, as police do not have access to official files to check a youth's past record and cannot check a youth's family or school performance. Police are sensitive to noncooperative and defiant youths, who are fractious, nonchalant, wear soiled jeans, leather jackets, and show little remorse over their offense. They are generally viewed as "tough guys" and "punks" who deserve severe sanctions.

These general images appear to affect arrest decisions. In their field study Piliavin and Briar (1964) classified youths as cooperative and noncooperative based on their responses to police questions, the respect and deference shown toward the police, and officers' assessments. Of the cooperative youths, only two of forty-five were arrested; but of the non-cooperative fourteen of twenty-one were arrested. (See Box 6.2.) Piliavin and Briar further suggest that as blacks more closely fit the typification of a "bad" youth, they are more likely to be arrested than are whites.

When someone is arrested, decisions have to be made about the nature of the charge and whether or not prosecution is warranted. At this stage in the decision-making process considerable background information is frequently available to the police, such as the youth's past record, family status, and school performance. Cicourel tries to show how this information is used by police to decide if the delinquent act is incidental to a moral character or is a manifestation of an immoral character and thus a sign of future trouble. To capture the flavor of Cicourel's analysis, two contrasting case studies are described.

In Smithfield's first encounter with the police for a $6.97 theft from the school cafeteria a court petition was filed; over the following three years he compiled an extensive record of one-half dozen law violations (including burglary). As a ward of the state his record was thoroughly compiled and updated, and his school performance and family were thoroughly investigated. Cicourel shows how this information was perceived and recorded by the investigators so as to confirm their original decision (biography construction). The following, for example, is a recorded quote from one of his teachers.

> "Smithfield does not appear to be interested in improving his educational status. He constantly expresses his dislike for school. He does not complete his assignments because he wastes his time. Smithfield enjoys participating in disturbances, whenever anyone else starts one. He also enjoys starting disturbances. Smithfield has no respect for authority. When asked to do something he often is recalcitrant and sits and pouts. He does not get along well with his peers."

In the investigative report the family was described as disorganized: his older brother was a ward of the court; his father was not residing at home and only partially employed; his mother lacked the ability to be firm; and the family was on welfare. In terms of police typifications and theories, Smithfield's behavior, school performance, and family show him to be an underlying delinquent from whom future trouble can be expected; firm action is thus required.

Donald's offense record was also extensive; rather than property offenses, his record consisted of a series of personal assaults. These resulted in no formal action other than warning and releasing him to his parents, until one assault with a deadly

Box 6.2 PILIAVIN AND BRIAR'S RESEARCH

The following excerpts from Piliavin and Briar's observational notes illustrate the importance of demeanor in police dispositions.

Case One: The interrogation of "A" (an eighteen-year-old upper-lower-class white male accused of statutory rape) was assigned to a police sergeant with long experience on the force. As I sat in his office while we waited for the youth to arrive for questioning, the sergeant expressed his uncertainty as to what he should do with this young man. On the one hand, he could not ignore the fact that an offense had been committed; he had been informed, in fact, that the youth was prepared to confess to the offense. Nor could he overlook the continued pressure from the girl's father (an important political figure) for the police to take severe action against the youth. On the other hand, the sergeant had formed a low opinion of the girl's moral character, and he considered it unfair to charge "A" with statutory rape when the girl was a willing partner to the offense and might even have been the instigator of it. However, his sense of injustice concerning "A" was tempered by his image of the youth as a "punk," based, he explained, on information he had received that the youth belonged to a certain gang, the members of which were well known to and disliked by the police. Nevertheless, as we prepared to leave his office to interview "A," the sergeant was still in doubt as to what he should do with him. In the interrogation, however, three points quickly emerged which profoundly affected the sergeant's judgment of the youth. First, the youth was polite and cooperative; he consistently addressed the officer as "sir," answered all questions quietly, and signed a statement implicating himself in numerous counts of statutory rape. Second, the youth's intentions toward the girl appeared to have been honorable; for example, he said that he wanted to marry her eventually. Third, the youth was not in fact a member of the gang in question. The sergeant's attitude became increasingly sympathetic, and after we left the interrogation room he announced his intention to "get 'A' off the hook," meaning that he wanted to have the charges against "A" reduced or, if possible, dropped.

Case Two: Officers "X" and "Y" brought into the police station a seventeen-year-old white boy who, along with two older companions, had been found in a home having sex relations with a fifteen-year-old girl. The boy responded to police officers' queries slowly and with obvious disregard. It was apparent that his lack of deference toward the officers and his failure to evidence concern about his situation were irritating his questioners. Finally, one of the officers turned to me and, obviously angry, commented that in his view the boy was simply a "stud" interested only in sex, eating, and sleeping. The policemen conjectured that the boy "probably already had knocked up half a dozen girls." The boy ignored these remarks, except for an occasional impassive stare at the patrolmen. Turning to the boy, the officer remarked, "What the hell am I going to do with you?" And again the boy simply returned the officer's gaze. The latter then said, "Well, I guess we'll just have to put you away for a while." An arrest report was then made out and the boy was taken to Juvenile Hall.

weapon left the victim close to death. An extensive investigation followed. Donald's involvement in the boy scouts was noted and his school performance was described as normal with grades above average and with no conduct problems. The investigation of the family revealed it to be intact, socially active, upwardly mobile, and middle-class. The mother, for example, was a member of various social clubs in which the wife of the probation officer on the case was also a member. Generally, Donald's school performance and respectable family suggested that the assault was more a function of peer association or circumstances than an expression of an underlying immoral character. In addition to being a source of information about a juvenile's character, parents may defend and protect their offspring from social control agencies. This is revealed in the ability of Donald's family to persuade the presiding judge to ignore the probation officer's report recommending that Donald be sent to a county ranch. Prior to the hearing Donald's parents removed him from public school and enrolled him in a Catholic school; the new principal then forwarded a letter to the judge describing Donald's good adjustment and good academic progress. Subsequently, the judge decided to keep Donald at the Catholic school rather than send him to the county ranch as recommended by the probation officer. During the course of his probation, Donald violated the rules of probation many times, about which nothing was done.

These two cases provide an interesting contrast. Smithfield stole an item valued at $7.00; yet, in terms of police typifications and theories, his general behavior, school performance, and family suggested that the behavior was a sign of an underlying immoral character and thus a sign of future trouble. He was dealt with firmly. On the other hand, Donald's offense was very serious; yet, in terms of police typifications and theories, his general behavior, school performance, and family suggested that the offense was incidental to his underlying moral character; additionally, his parents had the resources to negotiate a minimal societal reaction.

Construction Methods: Psychiatrists

The general typifications (diagnostic categories) of psychiatrists are imbedded in the medical model, whereby people are generally classified as sick or healthy, although the specific typifications depend on the specific psychiatric theory of mental illness (psychoanalysis or behaviorism). This section examines how these general typifications or constructions are applied in specific cases, and how they influence the organization of past information (biography reconstruction) and future information (selective perception), thereby "locking in" a construction of reality. The discussion relies on the research of Thomas Scheff (1964) and D. L. Rosenhan (1973). Both studies use observational techniques, and although separated by approximately one decade, both studies draw similar conclusions.

As a nonparticipant observer, Scheff studied the involuntary commitment procedures in a Midwestern state. At the time of the study this state required a psychiatric examination by two court-appointed psychiatrists in all commitment proceedings. Based on these examinations and the patients' official records, the examining psychiatrists were asked to make one of the following recommendations to the court: release, commit for thirty-day observation, or commit indefinitely. As the official records were frequently incomplete, for the most part these recommendations were based on the examinations.

Scheff observed twenty-six such examinations. They were quickly conducted, averaging only ten minutes each and ranging from five to seventeen minutes. Two lines of questioning were pursued. One line attempted to establish the circumstances which led to the patient's hospitalization and the other attempted to establish the patient's orientation and capacity for abstract thinking. As to the latter, patients were rapidly asked a series of questions concerning the date, the President, and the Governor, and to solve various arithmetic problems. One examiner asked rapidly, "What year is it? What year was it seven years ago? Seventeen years before that?" etc. Only two of the patients were able to answer the questions. Another examiner asked "In what way are a banana, an orange, and an apple alike?" The patient answered, "They are all something to eat." The examiner thought the answer inappropriate, manifesting concreteness of thought, sometimes viewed as a sign or symptom of mental illness. In the examiner's own words, "She wasn't able to say a banana and an orange were fruit. She couldn't take it one step further, she had to say it was something to eat." Based on a variety of these type of questions only two of the twenty-six cases were recommended for release; eighteen were recommended for commitment; and six were recommended for commitment for a thirty-day observation period. Based on the patients' records and behavior during the examination, Scheff argues that only about eight of the twenty-six met the legal criteria for commitment.

This tendency to over commit may be explained by the typifications and theories of mental illness held by most doctors (the medical model of mental illness) and the organizational constraints under which they work. The medical model suggests that mental illness deteriorates rapidly without treatment, that effective treatments are available, that there are few negative consequences associated with psychiatric treatment, and that mental disorders can result in harm to the patient and to others. Hence, when in doubt, like physical illness, it is safer to over commit (treat a few people who need no treatment), than to under commit (not treat a few people who need treatment). Furthermore, the examination salary schedule (a flat fee per examination) makes it financially advantageous for doctors to spend as little time as possible with each patient. Under these circumstances doctors are frequently uncertain of their diagnosis, predisposing them to make the medically safe decision.

Once a person is committed to a mental hospital and defined as mentally ill, information about his or her life is frequently reorganized, and perceptions of present behavior are selectively structured consistent with the present diagnosis. This, of course, is not a conscious effort on the part of medical personnel to justify their original diagnosis; rather it is part of the normal methods by which people construct social reality.

A recent study by D. L. Rosenhan (1973) provides information on these processes. He conducted an experiment in which eight psychologically normal people gained admission to mental hospitals located in five different states. The eight pseudopatients varied socially: one was a psychology student, three were practicing psychologists, one was a pediatrician, one a psychiatrist, one a painter, and one a homemaker. Each pseudopatient called the hospital for an appointment, and at the appointment complained of hearing voices. Other than these symptoms and providing a false name and vocation, no other incorrect information was given. The pseudopatients correctly described their own life situations, including their troubles and satisfactions; all eight people would be considered to have led quite normal lives. None of the pseudopatients was detected, and all were admitted to the hospital. Rosenhan reports on their experiences and on the biography reconstruction that subsequently occurred.

Although all of the pseudopatients led normal lives, this is not how their lives were interpreted psychologically. Their lives were interpreted consistent with their psychiatric diagnosis. For example, one patient had a close relationship with his mother and a remote relationship with his father during childhood; during adolescense and adulthood the relationships reversed. His relationship with his wife was generally close and warm, with an occasional argument, and his children were rarely spanked. The following is the case summary of the patient:

> This white 30-year old male . . . manifests a long history of considerable ambivalence in close relationships, which began in early childhood. A warm relationship with his mother cools during his adolescence. A distant relationship to his father is described as becoming very intense. Affective stability is absent. His attempts to control emotionality with his wife and children are punctuated by angry outbursts and in the case of the children, spankings. And while he says that he has several good friends, one senses considerable ambivalence imbedded in those relationships also . . . .

Hospital behavior was also frequently interpreted within the context of diagnostic categories. For example, the pseudopatients were asked by the researcher to take extensive notes on their observations and experiences. This behavior was not questioned by the hospital staff; in fact, it was barely noticed. When noted (three patients), it was interpreted pathologically as compulsive behavior, a symptom of various forms of mental illness. Another patient, for example, who was pacing a long hospital corridor, was asked, "Nervous, Mr. X?" "No, bored," he replied.

Generally, the work of Piliavin and Briar, Cicourel, Scheff, and Rosenhan suggest that the general images or typifications of delinquency and mental illness held by social control agents are intermeshed in general common sense theories of delinquency and mental illness. These theories suggest cues through which general typifications are applied to specific cases. Through processes of retrospective interpretation, biography reconstruction, and selective perception past and present behavior is reorganized to reinforce or lock in initial definitions of reality (arrest and diagnostic decisions). (For an example of the processes of construction used by friends and acquaintances, see Box 6.3.)

Box 6.3 INFERRING HOMOSEXUALITY

John I. Kitsuse (1962) illustrates the variety of situational cues used to infer homosexuality and the role of retrospective interpretation in this inferential process. In a study of seven hundred students, seventy-five indicated that they had known a homosexual. These respondents were asked the following questions: "When was the first time you noticed (found out) that this person was a homosexual? What was the situation? What did you notice about him (her)? How did he (she) behave?" The following excerpt from a male respondent about an encounter with a stranger in a bar is illustrative of the findings:

I: What happened during your conversation?

R: He asked me if I went to college and I said I did. Then he asked me what I was studying. When I told him psychology he appeared very interested.

I: What do you mean "interested?"

R: Well, you know queers really go for this psychology stuff.

I: Then what happened?

R: Ah, let's see. I'm not exactly sure, but somehow we got into an argument about psychology and to prove my point I told him to pick an area of study. Well, he appeared to be very pensive and after great thought he said, "Okay, let's take homosexuality."

I: What did you make of that?

R: Well, by now I figured the guy was queer so I got the hell outta there.

Upon defining someone as a homosexual, people frequently reinterpret past behavior in terms of this categorization. For example, a female respondent said in an interview:

I: Will you tell me more about the situation?

R: Well, their relationship was a continuous one, although I think that it is a friendship now as I don't see them together as I used to; I don't think it is still homosexual. When I see them together, they don't seem to be displaying the affection openly as they did when I first realized the situation.

I: How do you mean "openly?"

R: Well, they would hold each other's hand in public places.

I: And what did you make of this?

R: Well, I really don't know, because I like to hold people's hands, too! I guess I actually didn't see this as directly connected with the situation. What I mean is that, if I hadn't seen that other incident [she had observed the two girls in bed together] I probably wouldn't have thought of it [hand-holding] very much . . . Well, actually there were a few things that I questioned later on that I hadn't thought really very much about . . . I can remember her being quite affectionate towards me several times when we were in our room together, like putting her arm around my shoulder. Or I remember one time specifically when she asked me for a kiss. I was shocked at the time, but I laughed it off jokingly.

Organizational Products: Suicide Statistics

Ethnomethodologists argue that being labeled a deviant (delinquent, homosexual, mentally ill) is more a function of the methods of reality construction employed by social control agents than of rule breaking. Consequently, the records or statistics of social control organizations can be understood as emergent products of these methods. These statistics tell us less about the level and distribution of norm violations among social units than about the level of distribution or organizational activities among social units.

For example, official statistics show that delinquency is higher in urban than rural areas and in lower-class than upper-class neighborhoods, and that it has increased over the last few decades. These differentials may be the product of differentials in the operations and routines of different juvenile justice systems. Police may be more active in urban than rural areas, for in rural areas informal processes of social control still operate to some extent. Police may also be more active in lower-class than upper-class neighborhoods, as the lower-class lacks the resources to resist police intrusions. And as the world has become urbanized, informal processes of social control have become less effective, and formal control systems have expanded. Therefore, studies using official records to assess trends over time will show an increase in delinquency.

Statistical studies also show that mental illness is higher in urban than rural areas (Srole et al., 1962) and among the lower class than the upper-class, and that it has generally increased in the United States since World War I. These differentials may be a product of differentials in the operations and routines of mental health professionals. As mental health professionals tend to practice in urban areas and as their presence generates business, official statistics will show that the rate of illness is higher in urban than in rural areas. Since the upper class uses private psychiatrists and resists involuntary commitments (Krohn and Akers, 1977), official statistics (generally hospital records) will show that the rate of mental illness is higher among the lower class than the upper class. And as the United States has become urbanized, the number of mental health professionals per capita has increased; therefore, studies using official records to assess trends over time will show an increase in mental illness.

The work of Jack D. Douglas (1967, 1971) on suicide statistics nicely illustrates the linkage between organizational routines and official statistics. Douglas (1971) reports that coroners and medical examiners, generally unaware of legal definitions of suicide, tend to employ the common sense definition, "intentional taking of one's own life." The following six criteria are used:

1. the initiation of an act that leads to the death of the initiator
2. the willing of an act that leads to the death of the willer
3. the willing of self-destruction
4. the loss of will

5. the motivation to be dead (or to die) which leads to the initiation of an act that leads to the death of the initiator

6. the knowledge of an actor that actions he initiates tend to produce the objective state of death.

An inferential problem consists of deciding what evidence is necessary to demonstrate the presence of these criteria in individual cases. Generally, coroners and medical examiners use common sense ideas or theories about the nature of the act (position of the wound), the nature of the person (depressive type), and the nature of the social situation (unemployed) to infer suicide intention, but vary considerably in the amount of evidence collected, which dimension is emphasized, and how the data are interpreted. Consider the act itself and the immediate situation prior to the act. Was a suicide note left? If not, how much weight should be given to this? Douglas (1967) reports that in one city a suicide is not recorded unless a note is present. What is the position of the wound? Was alcohol present? Was there a family quarrel? These immediate factors may be interpreted in relation to other factors, such as the personality and background of the victim. Was the person depressive? How long was he or she unemployed? Additionally, Douglas notes that as suicide carries a negative connotation, families frequently pressure examiners and coroners not to classify deaths as suicides.

Douglas' study of the decision making of coroners and medical examiners suggests that classifying an act as a suicide is inherently and situationally problematic. Thus, to a large extent, the suicide rate of a county reflects the routines by which coroners and medical examiners collect and interpret information to infer suicidal intention.

In comparing the suicide rates of one county over time or the suicide rates of various counties at any point in time, two types of errors are important: random errors and systematic errors. The former refers to errors in the decision-making process, which do not bias suicide rates in one direction or another. Because decision-making rules are clumsy, cumbersome, and ambiguous, some nonsuicides may be classified as suicides and some suicides may be classified as nonsuicides; these errors, however, balance each other out. While they result in some wrong decisions about individual suicides, they produce valid rates. Douglas is concerned about problems generated by systematic errors, that is, errors which distort suicide rates, either over- or underestimating them. These errors can vary from jurisdiction to jurisdiction so that in one jurisdiction the suicide rate is overestimated and in another it is underestimated. They are particularly troublesome when related to conditions hypothesized as causing suicide. If the hypothesized causal conditions are present in jurisdictions where suicides are overestimated and not present in jurisdictions where suicides are underestimated, the causal theory of suicide may appear to be valid when it is not.

Douglas (1967) examines Emile Durkheim's theory of suicide in this light. (See Chapter Two for a discussion of Durkheim.) Durkheim hypothesized that social disintegration and deregulation cause a high rate of suicide. Hence, as Catholic countries are more integrated than Protestant countries, he argued that they should show lower suicide rates than Protestant countries—a proposition generally supported by suicide statistics. Douglas argues that this pattern may reflect systematic measurement error. Since suicide is more negatively evaluated in the Catholic than the Protestant religion, Catholic families make greater efforts than Protestant families to conceal suicides and to exert pressure on coroners not to classify their loved ones as suicides. Hence, fewer unexplained Catholic than Protestant deaths may be classified as suicides, thereby lowering the official suicide rate of Catholics. Durkheim also argued and marshaled evidence showing that during social crises (such as economic depression) suicides increase. Douglas argues that this pattern may also reflect systematic measurement error. During social crises, when people are psychologically depressed, suicide is likely to be considered as a motive for unexplained deaths.

Contemporary extensions of Durkheim are subject to similar interpretations. Andrew F. Henry and James F. Short (1954) argue that as the upper class has the most to lose, it should be the most affected by a depression; thus, its suicide rate should be the most sensitive to economic cycles. If this logic is also assumed by coroners, during a depression they may be more prone to classify unexplained deaths of the upper class than the lower class as suicides, thereby generating the statistics which appear to validate the theory. A. L. Porterfield (1952) argues that low social integration in urban areas accounts for the high suicide rate in those areas. Again, if coroners also assume this theory, they may be more prone to classify unexplained deaths in urban than rural areas as suicides. Additionally, municipalities employ professional medical examiners and purchase the equip-

---

Box 6.4 CAUSAL STRUCTURE GENERATING OFFICIAL STATISTICS

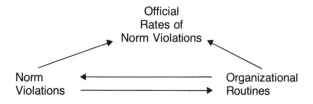

Official
Rates of
Norm Violations

Norm
Violations

Organizational
Routines

Official statistics reflect both norm violations and organizational routines. Traditional theories of norm violations assume that the effect of organizational routines is minimal or does not differ among social units. Thus, differences in official rates of norm violations among social units are assumed to reflect underlying differences in norm violations. Ethnomethodologists sensitize us to the link between official statistics as an emergent organizational product and organizational routines.

ment necessary to diagnose suicide; rural coroners may not have the expertise and facilities necessary to contest the pressures of relatives not to classify unexplained deaths as suicides.

Douglas (1967, 1971) is not arguing that the findings of Durkheim and his contemporaries have been generated by systematic errors in the decision making of coroners and medical examiners. Rather, he is arguing that we do not know; but, given what we do know about the social and psychological processes which underlie the decision making of coroners and medical examiners, systematic error is as plausible as the theories of Durkheim and his contemporaries as an explanation of the regularities and stabilities in suicide rates.

To summarize, ethnomethodological research generally focuses on the questions: what is labeled deviance and who is labeled deviant? This section has examined research on the general images or categories of deviance held by the public, on the decision-making processes by which police and psychiatrists apply general categories of delinquency and mental illness in everyday situations, and on the link between the everyday decision making of coroners and the validity of suicide statistics.

SOCIAL POLICY

Discussions of social policy implicitly assume 1. an objective world in which social problems are located, 2. that the world is knowable even though such knowledge may be less than perfect and difficult to obtain, and 3. that some parts of the world can be defined as problematic, although good people may disagree upon the criteria to be employed in making such judgments. For the most part, the structural/functional, Chicago, and social control (and to a lesser extent labeling) perspectives make these assumptions. They assume that norm and law violations exist in the world, that sociologists using research techniques can identify violators and the rate of violations, and that violations constitute a social problem.

Ethnomethodologists do not clearly make these assumptions and in some cases explicitly deny them. In regard to the first assumption, they suspend reality, arguing that for purposes of study reality can be ignored; they are concerned with people's constructions of reality, not reality in any objective sense. As to the second assumption, some ethnomethodologists deny that even the constructions of people are knowable in any ultimate or objective sense. Hugh Mehan and Houston Wood (1975), for example, argue that the theories of sociologists are no different from the theories of lay people. Neither has more creditability than the other, both are constructions. As to the third assumption, some ethnomethodologists argue that sociologists should not evaluate the world, defining some states of the world as desirable and others as problematic. David Matza (1969) has explicitly argued that evaluating the world detracts from adequately describing the constructions of people. Sociologists should concentrate on the latter.

What, then, does social policy mean within an ethnomethodological framework? Does it make sense to talk about changing a world which theory and research have suspended? Does it make sense for sociologists to formulate social policy to change a world, if their constructions do not reflect that world any more accurately than do the constructions of lay people? The policy recommendations of sociologists are thus no better or worse than the policy recommendations of anyone else. To ethnomethodologists, defining some state of society as a problem about which something should be done is itself a subjective construction. Ethnomethodologists are more interested in studying that construction than the "objective" state to which it refers, as the latter is suspended for purposes of research. They examine how methods of constructing reality (typifications and lay theories) lead to social problem constructions, and how different groups with different social problem constructions negotiate a commonly agreed upon construction. In the study of rape, for example, ethnomethodologists may focus on how and why rape is constructed as a social problem. What are the underlying typifications, lay theories, and negotiation processes? The problem of rape is "solved" when people no longer construct it as a problem.

Ethnomethodology encompasses a variety of subschools (Zimmerman, 1978), not all of which fully embrace the tenets of phenomenology. If some of the phenomenological assumptions are relaxed, ethnomethodological research can lead to more traditional social policies. For example, labeling theorists argue that the medical model of mental illness (a construction) leads to societal reactions which stabilize mental illness (residual deviance). Ethnomethodological studies of the medical model as a social construction (its historical development and situational applications) could be useful in formulating policies to alter professional and public conceptions of mental illness. Ethnomethodologists might also direct attention to the validity of people's construction based on the findings of sociological investigations (such as the constructions of police about lower-class black Americans), and direct social policy toward eradicating incorrect constructions, especially if they lead to harmful outcomes. If reality is suspended, however, such questions and concerns are meaningless.

CRITIQUE

Microlevel Orientation. Ian Taylor et al. (1973) argue that in viewing social structure as constantly emerging or as a fluid manifestation of microprocesses, ethnomethodologists ignore the structural forces which shape and order microlevel processes of reality construction. For example, Piliavin and Briar (1964) and Cicourel (1968) focus on how police construct law violations and violators in everyday situations, but ignore how these constructions are influenced by social structural forces. Taylor et al. argue that the police are not "self-organizing," but that their constructions and organizational routines represent the interests of a ruling class.

General Propositions. Ethnomethodologists criticize contemporary sociological concepts (such as anomie) for not reflecting the concepts people use to construct their worlds. They argue that the concepts of sociology should be formulated in terms of people's concepts, or at the very least should be translatable into them or be compatible with them. People's contextual and situational meanings must be captured in sociological concepts. The ethnomethodology strategy ties sociological concepts to the unique constructions of everyday situations. Yet, if sociology is to formulate abstract propositions and generalizations, uniform and general concepts are required for the orderly description of the variations in people's constructions and construction processes. Some ethnomethodologists (Cicourel, 1968) are sensitive to this problem, although they have not seriously addressed it: how can the contextual constructions of people be translated into the general concepts of sociologists?

Explanation and Prediction. Because of the paucity of general concepts for describing reality, explanation as a deduction of specific observations from general propositions is, of course, not possible (see Chapter One). Additionally, in conceptualizing people as actively constructing their environment, ethnomethodologists do not identify explanation with causal structures or processes. To ethnomethodologists, explanation is generally equated with "understanding." Actions are said to be understood when the researcher "knows" the actors' constructions; these constructions in turn are said to be understood when the researcher "knows" the actors' techniques of construction. This definition of explanation differs from that used by the other perspectives; and as it is not based on general and abstract concepts, it does not lead to prediction.

Research. Because of their concern not to distort the constructions of people, ethnomethodologists have avoided structured techniques of data collection (questionnaires, interviews, official records), which express the constructions of people in terms of the constructions of sociologists. Instead they have emphasized direct observation, particularly participant observation, which presumably allows researchers to experience reality somewhat like that of the subjects, thereby insuring that the constructions of researchers are not too different from those of the subjects.

While useful for just this reason, participant observation has limitations. Certain positions in social control organizations require considerable training and experience; thus, the constructions of people in those positions are not accessible to most participant observers. How is the participant observer to study the constructions of judges and prosecutors? Nonparticipant observation has somewhat similar limitations, for the behavior of social control agents is frequently invisible to most observers. Agents frequently go to extremes to avoid public visibility, and when researchers are present they may alter their behavior. The major problem of field observation, particularly participant observation, is observer reliability. Without techniques for structuring observations, different observers construct reality differently. How are we to weigh or evaluate the validity of these different constructions? Ethnomethodologists are insensitive to this problem. In fact, some (Mehan and Wood, 1975) ignore the problem, arguing that sociologists are not different from lay people. Different lay people have different understandings and constructions of reality; hence, different sociologists have different understandings and constructions of reality. If we accept this thesis, what is the special province or mission of sociology?

As a consequence of this style of research little research accumulation has occurred. Research does not test theories, it illustrates them. The research of Piliavin and Briar (1964), Cicourel (1968), Scheff (1964), Rosenhan (1973), and Douglas (1967) tends to illustrate rather than "prove" or "test" ethnomethodological theory.

Social Policy. Policy implications of ethnomethodology are vague and have not been explicated. After all, what are the policy implications of a perspective which suspends reality?

REFERENCES

BECKER, HOWARD. *Outsiders: Studies in the Sociology of Deviance* (New York: Free Press, 1963).

CICOUREL, AARON V. *Method and Measurement in Sociology* (New York: Free Press, 1964).

————. *The Social Organization of Juvenile Justice* (New York: Wiley, 1968).

DOUGLAS, JACK D. *The Social Meaning of Suicide* (Princeton: Princeton University Press, 1967).

————. *American Social Order* (New York: Free Press, 1971).

EMERSON, ROBERT. *Judging Delinquents* (Chicago: Aldine, 1969).

GARFINKEL, HAROLD. "Conditions of successful degradation ceremonies." American Journal of Sociology, 61 (March 1956): 420–24.

————. *Studies in Ethnomethodology* (Englewood Cliffs, N.J.: Prentice-Hall, Inc., 1967).

GOFFMAN, IRVING. *Stigma* (Englewood Cliffs, N.J.: Prentice-Hall, 1963).

HAWKINS, RICHARD and GARY TIEDEMAN. *The Creation of Deviance* (Columbus, Ohio: Charles E. Merrill, 1975).

HEEREN, JOHN. "Alfred Schutz and the sociology of common sense knowledge," in Jack D. Douglas (ed.), *Understanding Everyday Life* (Chicago: Aldine, 1970).

HENRY, ANDREW F. and JAMES F. SHORT. *Suicide and Homicide* (New York: Free Press, 1954).

JONES, EDWARD E. and KEITH E. DAVIS. "From acts to dispositions: The attribution process in person perception," in L. Berkowitz (ed.), *Advances in Experimental Social Psychology, Vol. 2,* New York: Academic Press, 1965).

KITSUSE, JOHN I. "Societal reactions to deviant behavior," Social Problems 9 (Winter 1962):247–56.

KROHN, MARVIN and RONALD L. AKERS. "An alternative view of the labeling versus psychiatric perspectives on societal reaction to mental illness," Social Forces 56 (Dec. 1977):341–61.

LIPPMAN, WALTER. *Public Opinion* (New York: Macmillan, 1922).

MATZA, DAVID. *Becoming Deviant* (Englewood Cliffs, N.J.: Prentice-Hall, Inc., 1969).

MEHAN, HUGH and HOUSTON WOOD. *The Reality of Ethnomethodology* (New York: Wiley, 1975).

NUNNALLY, JUM C. *Popular Concepts of Mental Illness* (New York: Holt, Rinehart & Winston, 1961).

PILIAVIN, IRVING and SCOTT BRIAR. "Police encounters with juveniles," American Journal of Sociology 69 (Sept. 1964):206–14.

PORTERFIELD, A. L. "Suicide and crime in folk and in secular society," American Journal of Sociology 57 (1952):331–38.

ROSENHAN, DAVID L. "On being sane in insane places," Science 179 (Jan. 1973):250–58.

SACKS, HARVEY. "An initial investigation of usability of conversational data for doing sociology," in David Sudnow (ed.), *Studies in Social Interaction,* (New York: Free Press, 1972).

SCHEFF, THOMAS J. "The societal reaction to deviance: Ascriptive elements in the psychiatric screening of mental patients in a Midwestern state," Social Problems 11 (Spring 1964):401–13.

SCHUR, EDWIN M. *Labelling Deviant Behavior* (New York: Harper & Row 1971).

SCHUTZ, ALFRED J. *Collected Papers I: The Problem of Social Reality* ed. by Maurice Notanson. (The Hague: Martins Nijhoff, 1962).

———. *Collected Papers III: Studies in Phenomenological Philosophy* ed. by I. Schutz. (The Hague: Martins Nijhoff, 1966).

SCOTT, MARVIN B. and STANFORD M. LYMAN. "Accounts," American Sociological Review 33 (Feb. 1968):46–62.

SCOTT, ROBERT A. *The Making of Blind Men* (New York: Russell Sage, 1969).

SIMMONS, JERRY L. *Deviants* (Berkeley, Calif.: Glendessary Press, 1969).

SROLE, LEO, THOMAS S. LANGNER, STANLEY T. MICHAEL, MARVIN K. OPLER, and THOMAS A. C. RENNIE. *Mental Health in the Metropolis* (New York: McGraw-Hill, 1962).

STINCHCOMBE, ARTHUR L. "Institutions of privacy in the determination of police administrative practice," American Journal of Sociology 69 (Sept., 1963):150–58.

TAYLOR, IAN, PAUL WALTON, and JOCK YOUNG. *The New Criminology* (London: Routledge & Kegan Paul, 1973).

TOWNSEND, J. MARSHALL. "Cultural conceptions, mental disorders and social roles: A comparison of Germany and America," American Sociological Review 40 (Dec. 1975):739–52.

WARD, RUSSELL. "Typifications of homosexuals," Sociological Quarterly 20 (Summer 1979):411–23.

YARROW, MARIAN R., CHARLOTTE GREEN SCHWARTZ, HARRIET S. MURPHY, and LEILA CALHOUN. "The psychological meaning of mental illness in the family," Journal of Social Issues 11 (1955):12–24.

ZIMMERMAN, DON H. "Ethnomethodology," The American Sociologist 13 (Feb. 1978):6–14.

CHAPTER SEVEN

THE CONFLICT PERSPECTIVE

THEORY

Contemporary conflict approaches to the study of deviance and crime can be traced to the work of Karl Marx and more recently to the work of Ralf Dahrendorf. Observing nineteenth century Europe, Marx argued that conflict between social classes is the basic social process in society—*the* key to understanding other social processes and structures. In industrial societies, Marx argued, there are two major economic classes of people: those who own the means of production (capitalists) and those employed by the owners (laborers). Marx argued that the economic interests of capitalists and laborers are diametrically opposed. As labor is an element or resource in the process of production, it is in the interest of capitalists to maintain low wages, which makes them more competitive on national and international markets. On the other hand, the cost of labor to capitalists is income to laborers. Thus, it is in the interest of labor to increase the cost of labor. Marx argued that in accordance with the laws of competition the ranks of labor would swell with unsuccessful capitalists, artisans, and farmers. Being less competitive, the standard of living of laborers would decrease, and, thus, social conflict would accentuate.

Marx also argued that the system of economic relationships affects the political, cultural, and religious institutions of society. Capitalistic societies are prone to develop laws, religions, and science—which protect the interests of capitalists. For example, in Western societies, governments protect the property of capitalists and Christianity supports the capitalist order by diverting the energies of laborers toward the hereafter rather than toward their earthly miseries. Marx referred to Western religion as the "opiate" of the people.

Ralf Dahrendorf's work (1958, 1959) is sometimes described as an adaptation of Marx to twentieth-century industrial society. Whereas Marx emphasized ownership of the means of production, Dahrendorf emphasizes power as the major social division; and whereas Marx argued that power is derived from ownership of the means of production, Dahrendorf argues that in contemporary industrial society power is frequently divorced from ownership of the means of production and is based on institutional authority. Dahrendorf focuses on the division between those who have and those who do not have authority to control behavior in institutional structures. Economic structures are important but not central. Additionally, Dahrendorf argues that authority relationships in one institution (economic) do not necessarily overlap with authority relationships in other institutions (education, religion, government). Social conflict is fractured.

Neither Marx nor Dahrendorf wrote much about crime. Marx viewed crime and criminals as somewhat irrelevant to the social forces which shape society and history (Taylor et al., 1973). He described criminals as parasites who use the goods and services of society without making a contribution to society. He did not view crime as political behavior and did not view criminals as concerned with social change, only with self preservation. In fact, he argued that crime may retard social change. Since criminals are drawn from the ranks of labor, they weaken the forces of labor. Furthermore, high crime rates increase the size and strength of the police force, which is used to support the capitalist social order.

Conflict criminologists have not tried to develop or expand Marx's or Dahrendorf's few specific ideas on crime. Rather they have derived theories of crime from Marx's and Dahrendorf's general concepts of social conflict. Specifically, they have focused on the following questions:

1. Why are the norms of some social groups or classes transformed into law, thus making criminals out of conflicting groups or classes?
2. Why are some laws enforced but not others, thus making criminals out of those who violate some laws but not others?
3. Why are laws enforced against certain groups and classes but not others, thus making criminals out of some law violators but not others?

Generally, conflict criminologists study the social and political processes by which crime and criminals are created, "the politics of crime." The concept most important in the study of politics, "power," is then central to the study of crime. In respect to the above three questions, conflict criminologists argue that social power determines what norms become laws and what laws are enforced against what classes of people.

The work of three conflict criminologists (George B. Vold, Austin T. Turk, and Richard Quinney) will be discussed. Vold provides a transition from the Chicago school (see Chapter Three) to the new conflict criminologists; and Turk extends the work of Dahrendorf, and Quinney extends the work of Marx to the study of crime.

Cultural Conflict (George B. Vold)

The cultural conflict thesis developed within the early Chicago school. In their studies of urban life the Chicago researchers observed cultural differences among different ethnic immigrant groups. They conceptualized cultural diversity as a cause of deviance and crime through two processes. One, residents of culturally diverse areas are exposed to a social environment of normative ambiguity and conflict, which reduces social controls and generates stress, and thereby leads to deviance and crime (see Chapter Three). Two, as the norms of ethnic groups frequently conflict with the law, those who adhere to traditional ethnic norms frequently violate contemporary laws (Sellin, 1938). The latter approach to the relationship between cultural conflict and crime provides a link between the Chicago school and the new conflict criminologists.

George B. Vold (1958), emphasizing this approach to cultural conflict, argues that criminal behavior is frequently an expression of values which clash with the law. When one group has the power to transform its values into laws, it has the power to make criminals out of those who behaviorally express conflicting values. Conscientious objectors, for example, hold values inconsistent with the behavior required during wartime. Thus, during wartime—only during wartime— conscientious objectors become criminals. Delinquents can also be conceptualized as a minority group whose values violate laws; in fact, juvenile gangs sometimes take on the characteristics (group loyalty and division of labor) of warring nations. Vold also argues that people sometimes violate the law as well as their own values in an effort to achieve higher values. For example, crimes of theft, homicide, and sabotage are sometimes committed in the name of revolution. If the revolution fails, those committing the actions are defined as criminals; if it succeeds, they become heroes and the traditional authorities become the criminals. Some leaders in the United States civil rights movement have advocated open violence, deemed to be wrong in principle but necessary in the struggle for human rights.

Vold's work shifts attention away from understanding crime as individual law violations to understanding crime as group struggles. However, he makes only the initial step. For the most part, he uses conflict theory to understand crimes which have traditionally been ignored by criminologists—the "leftovers" (racial disturbance, industrial strife, and conscientious objection), and to understand evanescent conflicts —those which are temporary (union strike), or those where the minority group either can easily change its status (conscientious objectors) or will change its status with age (delinquents). He does not focus on the stable conflicts in industrial societies, such as those based on social class or race.

Pluralistic Conflict (Austin T. Turk)

Austin T. Turk's (1969) book, *Criminality and the Legal Order,* was one of the first efforts to formulate a general conflict theory of crime. Following Dahrendorf, Turk focuses on conflict between those who have power (authorities) to control behavior and those who do not (subjects) in coordinated relationships (institutions). Like Dahrendorf, Turk does not attempt to link authority to ownership of the means of production or even to positions in the economic order and he examines authority-subject relationships within institutions with little concern for overarching or overlapping authority-subject relationships across institutions. Within this general framework, Turk focuses on legal conflict and criminalization. Specifically, he asks the following two questions:

1. Under what conditions are authority-subject cultural and behavioral differences transformed into legal conflict?
2. Under what conditions do those who violate laws (norms of the authorities) become criminalized? In other words, under what circumstances are laws enforced?

Concerning the first question, Turk specifies three conditions under which behavioral and cultural differences between authorities and subjects result in conflict.

Proposition 1: Conflict between authorities and subjects occurs when behavioral differences between authorities and subjects are compounded by cultural differences.

If cultural or value differences between authorities and subjects are not reflected in behavior, or if behavioral differences between authorities and subjects do not reflect important value differences, conflict will be minimal. This proposition is somewhat obvious, for people rarely struggle over abstractions or behaviors which are insignificant. Yet, in formulating a general theory of group conflict it must still be stated.

Proposition 2: Conflict is more probable the more organized are those who have an illegal attribute or engage in an illegal act.

The concept ''organized'' means that the act in question is part of a general cultural complex, and/or that the subjects involved can marshal forces to resist authorities. Compare, for example, homosexuality today and in the 1950s. In the 1950s homosexuals were somewhat isolated from each other, and homosexuality as a social issue was isolated from other social issues. Although a homosexual may have known a few others, few homosexuals were open, ''out of the closet,'' about their homosexuality, and few homosexuals were engaged in organizational and political activities to legitimize homosexuality. Hence, in the 1950s the cultural

Austin T. Turk, born 1934, received his B.A. in 1956 from the University of Georgia, his M.A. in 1959 from the University of Kentucky, and his Ph.D. in 1962 from the University of Wisconsin, and is presently a Professor of Sociology at the University of Toronto in Canada. He is best known for his work in conflict theory, such as *Criminality and Legal Order*, 1969. (Courtesy of Austin T. Turk, reprinted by permission.)

and behavioral differences between homosexuals and heterosexuals (subjects and authorities, respectively, in Turk's terms) were not a source of conflict. Conflict occurred in the 1960s when homosexuals came "out of the closet," linking homosexuality with other social issues, and organized for political purposes.

Proposition 3: Conflict is more probable the less sophisticated the subjects.

Subjects are defined as sophisticated when their knowledge of the strengths and weaknesses of authorities enables them to manipulate authorities, thereby allowing them to violate authority norms without open conflict. For example, organized criminals (racketeers) and professional criminals (pickpockets) are frequently able to manipulate authorities so that their illicit activities can continue, whereas the draft evaders and antiwar resisters of the 1960s openly fought with authorities.

Turk's second question concerns criminalization. Given some state of social conflict, under what conditions will legal norms (laws) be enforced and some people be defined as criminals?

Proposition 4: The probability of enforcement of legal norms increases as the congruence between the cultural and behavioral norms of authorities increases.

In other words, the legal norms that are culturally significant to authorities are the most prone to be enforced. Thus, the probability of becoming a criminal in the United States is higher for violating burglary than price-fixing laws. The former violates the legal and cultural norms of authorities, while the latter violates only the legal norms of authorities. The police subculture is also important. Police are authorities' first line of defense and have considerable discretion in deciding what legal norms to enforce and when to enforce them. Legal norms which are consistent with the police subculture may be strongly enforced (laws on homosexuality), whereas legal norms which are inconsistent with the police subculture may be only weakly enforced (laws on civil rights).

Proposition 5: The lower the power of the resisters (subjects), the higher the probability of enforcement.

This is a simple but important proposition, asserting that laws are most rigorously enforced against those who have the least power to resist. Turk argues that enforcement agencies carry out their functions so as to minimize their efforts. Consequently, they focus attention on the powerless, who have few resources to resist, rather than the powerful, who have resources to purchase the best legal assistance, in many cases better than enforcement agencies can afford.

Proposition 6: The lower the realism of the norm violators (resisters), the higher the probability of enforcement.

Realism, the counterpart of sophistication, refers to aspects of a violation which affect the probability of enforcement; a realistic violation decreases the probability and an unrealistic violation increases it. For example, violators frequently behave so as to draw attention to their violations; thus, enforcers cannot ignore them, even if they wish to. Flagrant abuses of laws, such as a draft resister who burns his draft card before the media, a prostitute who propositions customers on the doorsteps of city hall, and a homosexual who involves partners under age, bring the attention of authorities to the violation.

To summarize, Turk specifies the conditions when group differences generate group conflict, and when legal norms (laws) are enforced. He points to struggles over legal norms in societies, and argues that criminalization depends on the outcomes of these struggles. Conflict between authorities and subjects is most probable when both cultural and behavioral differences exist between authorities and subjects, when subjects are organized, and when subjects are unsophisticated. Laws are most likely to be enforced when they are consistent with the behavioral and cultural norms of authorities, when the violators are powerless, and when the violations are unrealistic.

Radical Criminology (Richard Quinney)

Richard Quinney's work can be divided into that published approximately before and after 1971. His early work, similar to Turk's, conceptualizes society in terms of competing interests; his later work, the subject of this discussion, is more explicitly Marxian. Contrary to pluralistic or multiple interest theorists, Quinney argues that an underlying basic social conflict exists between those who own and control the means of production and those who do not. Those who control economic relationships constitute a ruling class which also controls social relationships in other institutional spheres. Political, educational, and religious authorities serve their interests. The following propositions, taken from *A Critique of Legal*

Richard Quinney, born 1934, received his B.S. in 1956 from Carroll College, his M.A. in 1957 from Northwestern University, and his Ph.D. in 1962 from the University of Wisconsin, and is presently affiliated with Boston College and Brown University. He is well known for his numerous articles and books on conflict criminology, such as *Class, State, and Crime,* 1977. (Courtesy of Richard Quinney, reprinted by permission.)

Order (1974) and further developed in *Class, State and Crime* (1977), describe Quinney's theory.

Proposition 1: Criminal law is an instrument of the state and ruling class to maintain and perpetuate the existing social and economic order.

This proposition asserts that law is a political instrument and that people become criminal because a ruling class has the power to create criminal laws and apply them. Quinney defines the ruling class as those who own and control the means of production (the capitalists), and thus argues that laws in contemporary America and, generally, the Western world reflect the interests of those who own and control capital. While one can agree with Quinney that numerous laws clearly represent the interests of those who own and manage capital, numerous laws also seem to represent the interests of labor (such as the New Deal legislation of the 1930s and 1940s) and other groups. Quinney is, of course, aware of this and retorts by arguing that in reality these laws, too, assist the ruling capitalist class. Without some reform legislation, like the New Deal, a more radical change would occur in the economic order. These laws, by reforming the most exploitive economic relationships, in actuality function to preserve the capitalist order.

In addition to law formulation, Quinney argues that the interests of capitalists determine when and to whom laws are applied. Laws are selectively enforced against those people who threaten the interests of those who own and control the means of production; when members of the ruling class violate laws, they are not rigorously enforced. To some extent this may be true, because the ruling class tends not to violate the laws of property that are rigorously enforced (laws of burglary, robbery, and theft); they violate the laws of property that are not rigorously enforced (antitrust, stock manipulation and environmental protection).

Crime control bureaucracies focus on those laws consistent with the interests of those who own and control the means of production, whereas laws which directly conflict with these interests are not rigorously enforced (consumer and environmental protection laws). Thus, much discrimination in law enforcement is in effect discrimination in what laws are enforced. Yet, even when members of the ruling class violate laws which are generally enforced (laws of theft and personnel safety), these laws are not as rigorously enforced against them as they are against the lower class (see research section). Much of this differential is accounted for by the capacity of the ruling class to resist law enforcement.

> *Proposition 2:* Crime control in capitalist society is accomplished through a variety of institutions and agencies established and administered by a governing elite, representing ruling class interests, for the purpose of establishing domestic order.

In addition to the government, Quinney argues that various institutions (education, religion, and mass media) and agencies are organized to represent the interests of the ruling class. He is particularly concerned with the development and perpetuation of a moral order which legitimizes the capitalistic legal order, and with the role of various institutions in articulating that order. For if those who neither own nor control the means of production come to accept capitalist definitions of morality, they will pattern their behavior to conform to these definitions, and thus to the interests of the ruling class rather than to their own interests.

Quinney criticizes the mass media for disseminating capitalist definitions of crime. He argues that the mass media (newspapers, magazines, radio, movies, and television) focus on lower-class crimes and ignore the crimes of big business and the state unless they constitute special events. The success of the media, according to Quinney, is evidenced in the fact that within the last decade the public has begun to view street crime as one of the most, if not *the* most, serious problem facing society (Furstenberg, 1971). He also criticizes the mass media for emphasizing the "rule of law," the doctrine which stipulates that whatever the law, people are obligated to obey it. Since law represents the interests of the ruling class, the

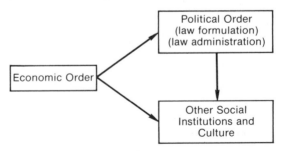

Figure 7.1. Causal Structure Underlying Quinney's Propositions One and Two. Quinney's propositions one and two are part of a general Marxian framework in which social institutions (education) and culture (moral definitions of right and wrong) are said to reflect the political and economic orders, and the political order in turn is said to reflect the economic order.

doctrine protects the interests of the ruling class and constitutes part of its ideology.

Quinney also takes to task the intellectuals who generate and articulate this ideology. He points to religious leaders who support the capitalist system by adhering to and advocating the rule of law, and who condemn from the pulpit crimes of the lower class against the property of the ruling class. He also criticizes social scientists (criminologists and sociologists) whose theories and research on crime (generally lower-class crime) are used by the ruling class to justify unequal social arrangements and to control the behavior of the lower class.

Proposition 3: The contradictions of advanced capitalism . . . require that the subordinate classes remain oppressed by whatever means necessary, especially through the coercion and violence of the legal system.

Quinney (1977) argues that the United States and the Western world in general are entering an advanced stage of capitalism where the "inherent contradictions" of capitalism are very severe. In advanced capitalism, competition among capitalists culminates in the failure of many capitalists, thereby increasing the ranks of the proletarian class. Quinney argues that in the contemporary United States 80 percent of the adult population are working class, 18.5 percent are petite bourgeoisie (lower middle class), and only 1.5 percent are capitalists. Also, in advanced capitalism the economic order becomes increasingly technological and cyclical, thereby increasing the surplus population (that portion of the population which plays no useful economic role—the unemployed). Both the large proletarian class and surplus population constitute a major threat to the established social order.

Basing his argument partially on James O'Connor's (1974) work, Quinney avers that the ruling class attempts to control this threat by increasing social welfare and coercive control expenditures and bureaucracies. He cites the growing expenditures of the criminal justice system to support his thesis (1977). Federal expenditures for the criminal justice system, for example, have increased from $0.5 billion in 1967 to $3.5 billion in 1977. These increases are not just a function of inflation; the proportion of gross national product allocated to the criminal justice system has also increased sharply.

The post-1971 work of Quinney (1974, 1975, and 1977) can be summarized in terms of three propositions. While they cannot capture completely the complexities of his work, they do describe its flavor and thrust. To reiterate, laws are formulated and administered to serve the interest of those who own and control the means of production; the state and other institutional arrangements (mass media, religion, and education) serve the interests of those who own and control the means of production; and as the capitalist system matures, a greater proportion of its resources is expended on coercive social control. Quinney and other radical conflict theorists shift our attention to a set of issues not normally studied by criminologists. They emphasize the political nature of crime. Rather than studying why people violate the legal order, Quinney focuses our attention on the legal

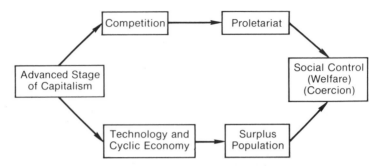

Figure 7.2. Approximate Causal Structure Implied in Quinney's Proposition Three. Quinney argues that advanced capitalism increases competition and generates a technological and cyclical economy, which, respectively, increases the size of the proletariat and the surplus population. Threatened by the latter, authorities respond by increasing social control bureaucracies.

order itself as the subject of study. While many sociologists may not agree with his theory about the legal order, it is important that the legal order be studied. Specifically, it is important that we study the relationship between ownership or control of the means of production and the formulation and administration of criminal laws, and the extent to which institutional arrangements and scholarship function in the service of special interests.

Summary

This section discusses the conflict theories of Vold, Turk, and Quinney. Vold (1958) might well be considered the first conflict theorist to have some impact on the contemporary study of deviance and crime. Generally, he argues that some crimes can be understood in terms of cultural conflict. Groups conflict over what is proper behavior; and some groups have the power to transform their cultural norms into laws. By the mid-1960s conflict theories became quite prominent. The work of Turk is representative. He endeavors to explain when group differences eventuate into open conflict and when the violators of legal norms are criminalized. Quinney addresses the same general questions from a Marxian framework, arguing that law formulation and enforcement reflect the interests of those who own and control the means of production.

RESEARCH

Many of the specific propositions of conflict theories have been the subject of research. This section examines the general relationship between group or class interests and law formulation and enforcement.

Law Formulation

The study of law formulation endeavors to explain why some rules of conduct become law—specified by the state, subject to sanction by the state, and enforced by specially authorized personnel of the state. Contrary to consensus theories, which view laws as reflecting the rules of conduct most widely agreed upon and intensely supported in society, conflict theories assume that power differentials between groups determine which rules of conduct become laws, or which group interests become transformed into the interests of the state.

Business Interests. Business laws refer to laws governing the ownership, management, and transfer of property. It might be instructive to begin with a discussion of the origin and development of some contemporary business laws.

Jerome Hall (1952) has extensively researched the historical development of the contemporary law of theft, and the group and class interests which affected its development. Prior to the fourteenth century in Europe it was a crime to forcibly take from people their own property while it was in their possession. However, there was no law governing the ownership of property entrusted to a person for transportation or other reasons who absconded with the property. It was an owner's responsibility to select trustworthy carriers. This legal arrangement was consistent with authority-subject relationships of the feudalistic social structure. Communities were mainly agricultural and somewhat self-sufficient, making the transportation of property between communities an exception to daily life. Also, the relationships between authorities and subjects (at least between authorities and their immediate subordinates) were enduring and more of a primary than secondary nature. Thus, selecting trustworthy persons as carriers was probably not the problem it is today.

With the commercialization and industrialization of the fifteenth century, this social arrangement changed. Communities became less self-sufficient, commercial trade developed between communities, and some communities emerged as trade or commercial centers; with the geographical movement of people, social relationships became less enduring. Consequently, while owners of property had a great need for trustworthy carriers, they had great difficulty finding them. This change in social conditions and the emergence of a new business class created a new interest: the protection of property while in transit.

A legal change occurred with the Carrier case in England in 1473. A person, employed to carry bales to Southampton, transported them to another area, broke the bales, and absconded with the contents. He was later caught and charged with a crime. What crime? The carrier had legally obtained possession of the goods. No law had been broken. The judge at the time argued as follows: "Breaking the bulk" ended the arrangement between the owner and carrier, and the goods legally reverted back to the possession of the owner. The carrier thus illegally acquired the goods.

In sum, the commercial revolution created a new powerful economic class with new legal interests (secure trade). It was just a matter of time before their interests were reflected in the law. This law (judicial decision) provided the foundation for contemporary laws that govern the management and transportation of property.

Another excellent example of historical research on the relationship between economic interests and the origins and development of law is William J. Chambliss' study (1964) of the development of vagrancy laws. Vagrancy laws exist in just about all states and tend to be used either to arrest "undesirables" who have violated no other laws or to force "undesirables" to leave the community. Chambliss' research suggests that the social conditions in England around the twelfth century in conjunction with the interests of the landed aristocracy explain the origin of these laws. The Black Death plague and the Crusades reduced the labor supply by 50 percent; industrialization and commercialization made urban areas more attractive to serfs; and the Crusades impoverished many of the landed aristocracy. Vagrancy laws were an effort of the landed aristocracy to control their labor supply in a time of need. In effect, the laws made it illegal to travel and to accept or give charity, thus providing a ready and cheap supply of labor to the landed aristocracy. Incidentally, the vagrancy laws were also in the interests of the Church of England. At the time, partially because of the Crusades, the church was in financial straits. With the passing of the vagrancy laws, the church could dismiss its traditional social obligation to help the poor. After some time, the labor supply increased and the administration of the laws was relaxed. By the sixteenth century the laws were revived to protect the interests of the new commercial class to conduct trade in a safe and orderly manner. The laws were used to rid the community and countryside of undesirables, people who, because of their character and lack of regular employment, were potential thieves and sources of disruption.

During the twentieth century various laws have been passed, presumably in the interests of labor, consumers, and the general public, which regulate business and

William J. Chambliss, born 1933, received his M.A. in 1960 and his Ph.D. in 1962 from Indiana University, and is currently a Professor of Sociology at the University of Delaware. He is well known for his research on conflict theory. (Courtesy of William J. Chambliss, reprinted by permission.)

commercial interests. Quinney has argued that these laws do nothing of the kind, because they are not effectively enforced. Furthermore, because they provide the illusion that business interests are being regulated, they are, in effect, in the interests of business! This subsection examines some of the research on the enforcement of laws governing price fixing and false advertising.

The Sherman Anti-Trust Act of 1890 makes it illegal to contract or conspire to restrain trade. A 1970 survey asked the presidents of the 1000 largest manufacturing corporations in the United States if, in their minds, many corporations engage in price fixing. These are the people who should know. Of the largest 500 corporations, 47 percent answered "yes;" of the next 500, 70 percent answered "yes" (McCaghy, 1976:209). Assuming these figures are rough estimates of the degree of price fixing, why do so many corporations violate the law? The answer is simple. Such law violations are profitable and the law is only minimally enforced.

The heavy electrical equipment conspiracy case (Geis, 1967) provides an instructive illustration. Starting in the mid-1940s, manufacturers of heavy electrical equipment (including General Electric and Westinghouse) conspired to fix prices on contract bidding. The twenty-nine corporations involved controlled 95 percent of the market. They fixed prices by deciding which corporation would submit the lowest bid for an individual contract and what that bid should be. Thus, that corporation could not be underbid and could set its bid at the level of profit it wished to make on the contracted work. Clearly, this was a violation of the Sherman Anti-Trust Act. The corporations involved knew it. As revealed in the trial, the corporations went to extremes to avoid detection. For example, the corporate representatives involved met in obscure places, communicated with each other at their homes rather than places of business, used public rather than their private telephones, and used coded communications.

To understand why this went on, one need only examine the enforcement of law. Twenty-nine conspirators were convicted. Seven were sentenced to thirty days in jail and twenty-one were given thirty-day suspended sentences. The companies were fined 1.8 million —not very high considering that the cost of the conspiracy to the public was estimated at $1.7 billion over seven years. Additionally, the IRS allowed the companies to deduct these fines plus legal expenses from their taxes as regular expenses of doing business.

This, of course, is a dramatic example, and it is presented here as just that; but it illustrates the extent to which laws meant to regulate the interests of business corporations are weakly enforced. Recent research shows that this case is indicative of the enforcement of the Sherman Anti-Trust Act. McCormick (1977) reports that from 1890 to 1969, 1551 antitrust prosecutions were initiated of which 45 percent were criminal cases (all could have been) and 35 percent led to criminal convictions; however, less than 2 percent (twenty-six cases) resulted in served sentences, which rarely exceeded six months with an average of approximately three months. Of these twenty-six cases the first eleven involved union and labor defendants, and twenty-three of the twenty-six involved labor misconduct or

Box 7.1 PORTRAIT OF AN OFFENDER—THE ELECTRICAL CONSPIRACY

The highest paid executive incarcerated was a General Electric vice-president, earning $135,000 a year. He was born in Atlanta, graduated from Georgia Tech, received an honorary doctorate degree from Sienna College, was married, and is the father of three children. He served in the Navy during the Second World War, rising to the rank of lieutenant commander, and was a director of the Schenectady Boys' Club, a trustee of Miss Hall's School, and a member of Governor Rockefeller's Temporary State Committee on Economic Expansion. Employed by General Electric shortly after graduation from college, he rose rapidly through the managerial ranks, was mentioned as a possible president of General Electric, and was described by the president as "an exceptionally eager and promising individual."

In 1946 he was introduced to competitors by his superior and told that he "should be the one to contact them as far as power transformers were concerned in the future." The meetings were erratic and problematic with numerous disagreements between the participants, and were not disclosed to "the manufacturing people, the engineers, and especially the lawyers." This was easy "because commercial transactions remained unquestioned by managerial personnel so long as they showed a reasonable profit." The price-fixing meetings continued from 1946 until 1949. At that time a federal investigation of the transformer industry sent the conspirators into seclusion. "The iron curtain was completely down" for a year, and salespeople at General Electric were told not to attend meetings of the National Electrical Manufacturers' Association, where they had traditionally planned and schemed with competitors. Meetings resumed, however, when his superior decided that "the market was getting in chaotic condition" and that they "had better go out and see what could be done about it." He was told not to inform Robert Paxton, "an Adam Smith advocate" and the plant works manager, about the meetings, because Paxton "don't understand these things."

Upon being promoted to general manager in 1954, he was told by the president of General Electric "to comply with the company policy and with the antitrust laws, and to see that his subordinates did so too." However, his more immediate superior told him, "Now, keep on doing the way that you have been doing but just . . . be sensible about it and use your head on the subject." The price-fixing meetings therefore continued; however, in the late 1950s foreign competition often forced the American firms to give up price fixing and be more competitive.

In 1957 the witness was promoted to vice-president and again lectured by the company president about price fixing. This time he decided to discontinue his involvement in price fixing, and issued orders to his subordinates that they no longer attend meetings with competitors for the purpose of "stabilizing" the market. However, as he had rarely obeyed such orders, neither did the salespeople in his division.

In responding to a U.S. Senate investigation, the former General Electric vice-president viewed his situation philosophically. As to his resignation from the company, it was "the way the ball has bounced." He hoped that he would have "the opportunity to continue in American industry and do a job," and he wished others who had been dismissed "good luck." "I want to leave the violence. It was not until the electrical conspiracy case in 1961 that business people were imprisoned for price fixing and monopolization under the Sherman Anti-Trust Act. McCormick refers to these sentences as so light as to be viewed as a "reasonable license fee for engaging in illegal conduct." Cases such as these suggest that if any criminals are being "coddled" by the criminal justice system, it is the middle-class criminals violating laws meant to regulate business interests.

The violation of false advertising laws also appears to be epidemic. The chief of the Food and Drug Administration has stated that one-third of United States manufacturers of prescription drugs are violating federal laws prohibiting false and misleading advertising. If this charge is true, why is it the case? For the same reason that corporations participate in price fixing. False advertising is profitable (or at least corporations believe that it is), and the relevant laws are not enforced. Marshall B. Clinard and Richard Quinney (1973) report on a series of cases. For example, in 1970 the Food and Drug Administration notified the manufacturers of various mouthwashes to stop advertising that their products "effectively destroy bacteria that causes bad breath," and "combat cold symptoms and minor throat irritations." The mouthwashes were found to be ineffective in living up to their therapeutic and preventive claims. The manufacturers were given thirty days to reply, otherwise the FDA would remove the products from the shelves. Similar cases have involved various manufacturers of toothpastes, automobile tires, and detergents. Generally, the replies requested by the FDA are made and the proceedings drag on for years, while the advertising frequently continues. Charles H. McCaghy (1976) reports on an instructive case. In 1974 the Federal Trade Commission charged Sunoco with running false advertisements from 1969 to 1972 about the capacities of its gasoline, and ordered Sunoco to stop, "to cease and desist." The "cease and desist" order is illustrative of how many laws are frequently enforced against big corporations. They are asked to stop breaking the law. There is rarely a jail sentence, sometimes a fine; but more frequently the corporation is only asked to sign a consent decree (a statement not admitting guilt but stating that the corporation will not continue the activity).

The extensiveness of corporate crime and the minimal level of government enforcement of the law is documented in a recent study by Marshall B. Clinard (1979) of the enforcement actions against the 582 largest publicly owned corporations in the United States (477 manufacturing, eighteen wholesale, sixty-six retail, and twenty-one service) in 1975 and 1976. During this time period, a total of 1365 enforcement actions were initiated against these corporations, although very few involved criminal proceedings. For example, there were 1258 enforcement actions against the 477 manufacturing corporations. Of the 66.4 percent which were sanctioned, 88.1 percent of the sanctions were administrative, 9.2 percent were civil, and only 2.7 were criminal. Rarely was a convicted executive imprisoned. Of the sixty-one convicted executives of parent corporations, 19 percent received probation, 10 percent a suspended sentence, 63 percent a fine, and only 8 percent were incarcerated. In nearly all of the latter cases the sentences ranged from one to six months.

To summarize, research shows the role of economic interests in the historical formulation of laws regarding theft and vagrancy, and that present laws formulated to regulate the behavior of economic interest groups (such as price fixing and false advertising) are minimally enforced. Generally, corporations make whatever profits they can from violating certain laws. When the government catches up to them (if it ever does), they must cease and desist and frequently use some of these profits to pay a fine. Thus considerable research supports Quinney's proposition, that what is crime and who is the criminal depends on the power of groups who own and control the means of production.

Governmental Agency Interests. Governmental agencies, like most organizations, seek to control their environment and expand their activities, thereby increasing their power. Donald Dickson (1968) argues that law enforcement agencies (Internal Revenue Service, Federal Bureau of Investigation, Central Intelligence Agency) regularly attempt to influence legislatures in the formulation of laws and the courts in the interpretation of laws. This section examines the Federal Narcotics Bureau, based on the research of Alfred R. Lindesmith (1965), Joseph R. Gusfield (1963), Donald Dickson (1968), and Howard S. Becker (1963).

In 1914 Congress passed the Harrison Act, designed to exercise some control over narcotics traffic, but mainly to make narcotics transactions a matter of public record. The act initiated an excise tax and required that all companies and persons handling narcotics be registered and pay nominal fees. Lindesmith's research suggests that narcotics use was not considered much of a social problem, and that Congress for the most part was not concerned with arresting drug traffic. The medical use of drugs was explicitly exempt from the Harrison act; the use of narcotics was not made illegal; and the agency to administer the act was set up within the IRS bureau of the Treasury Department, a department regularly involved with revenue collection, not crime.

Dickson's and Lindesmith's research shows that, like most agencies, the Narcotics Agency moved to expand its mandate. As this required a new law or a broader interpretation of the Harrison Act, the Agency began a campaign to change public attitudes toward narcotics use and addiction. They issued reports and newspaper articles decrying the use of drugs and addiction, linking the use of drugs to crimes and various immoralities, and portraying the addict as generally depraved and immoral. At the same time they initiated a series of court test cases to broaden the meaning of the law. Dickson reports that the Narcotics Agency carefully selected cases in which physicians flagrantly issued narcotics. Their campaign was successful. In Webb v. United States, the Supreme Court stated that a physician could not supply drugs to a person unless he or she was treating the person; and in Behrman v. the United States the Court went further, stating that a physician could not issue drugs to a person even if he or she was trying to cure the person. Yet in Linder v. the United States the Court reversed itself and stated that the Harrison Act says nothing about addiction and does not attempt to regulate the practice of medicine; it specifically warned the Narcotics Agency about over-extending its mandate. Both Dickson's and Lindesmith's research shows that the Agency simply ignored the latter decision, and, based on the former decisions, launched a campaign against doctors treating patients with narcotics and narcotic clinics. Few doctors were willing to violate the Narcotic Agency's policy, thereby risking imprisonment and loss of their medical practice, although the Supreme Court might eventually vindicate them.

In effect, the Narcotics Bureau expanded its mandate and transformed narcotic users into criminals. The success of its campaign was reflected in increased budgetary appropriations from Congress. In 1918 the Agency's budget was $325,000, but by 1925 it grew 400 percent to $1,329,440.

A similar situation surrounds the passage of the Marijuana Tax Act of 1937. Becker (1963) reports that the Narcotics Agency had little interest in marijuana until Harry Anslinger became the commissioner. Anslinger regarded marijuana use as immoral and campaigned to have Congress pass an act giving the Agency the power to control it—again enlarging the scope and power of the Agency. During the 1930s the Agency initiated a campaign to convince the public and Congress that marijuana smoking is linked to crime, disease, and immorality, and generally constitutes a social problem about which something should be done. To document the Agency's influence, Becker counted the number of published articles on marijuana cited in the *Reader's Guide to Periodic Literature* before and after the passage of the act. From 1925 to 1935 no articles appeared; from July, 1935 to June, 1937 four appeared; but from July, 1937 to June, 1939 seventeen appeared. Within a few years after passage of the act, the number of articles dropped sharply. From July, 1939 to June, 1941 only four appeared. Of the seventeen articles which appeared directly before and during the passage of the act, ten acknowledged the help of the Narcotics Agency in either writing or collecting information for the article.

Dickson (1968) feels that Becker overemphasizes the role of the Agency's sense of morality in its marijuana campaign and neglects the role of power. He notes that in 1932 the Agency's budget reached a high point and then started to drop, and that the marijuana campaign was an effort to reemphasize the drug problem, thus expanding the functions of the Agency and creating a need for a larger budget.

While Becker argues that the motivation behind the Agency's campaign was morality and Dickson argues that it was power, both agree that the Agency was instrumental in the passage of the Marijuana Tax Act of 1937, which increased the scope of the Agency's functions. Recently, Galliher and Walker (1977) have questioned the evidence upon which both Becker's and Dickson's conclusions are based. They note that of the articles cited in the Reader's Guide to Periodic Literature, only five definitely appeared before the passage of the act in August, 1937. Of the seventeen which appeared between July, 1937 and June, 1939, sixteen appeared after the passage of the act. However, the fact that many of the articles appeared after the passage of the act may only reflect publication lag time. Many may have been prepared and written prior to the passage. Moreover, Galliher and Walker report that in the public hearings held by the House Ways and Means and the Senate Finance Committees, the Agency strongly supported the passage of the act.

Generally, these case studies suggest that the Federal Narcotics Agency, initially organized to enforce the Harrison Act, has been instrumental in formulating narcotics laws as they are enforced today. The Agency has transformed its interest into law, thereby affecting what is crime and who is the criminal. Similar issues have been raised about the behavior of the IRS, FBI, CIA, and various other governmental agencies in influencing legislation and court decisions and frequently in going about their business in violation of the law and court decisions.

Religious Interests. Religious groups, too, have interests and frequently the power to transform them into law. As a historical case, consider the Massachusetts Bay Colony, a Puritan community founded in 1630. While organized as a commercial venture, the Bay Colony had a religious mission. In Governor John Winthrop's words, the mission was to build ''a city of God upon a hill.'' George Lee Haskins (1960) and Richard Quinney (1970) argue that Biblical Scriptures served as a guide to the formulation of law, as evidenced in the crimes punishable by death: idolatry, witchcraft, blasphemy, bestiality, sodomy, adultery, rape, man stealing, treason, false witness with the intent to take life, cursing or smiting a parent, and stubbornness or rebelliousness of a son against his parents.

Sunday laws, which prohibit on Sunday behavior which is ordinarily legal, are additional examples of the power of some religions. These laws prohibit or restrict general economic and certain social activities (drinking and dancing) on Sundays, and sometimes make church attendance mandatory. They were taken very seriously not too long ago, and even today are partially enforced. This is clearly a case of conflict and power. For the laws restrict the behavior of those Christians who do not believe in them and clearly restrict the behavior of non-Christians and atheists. Note that Jews have not been able to get the same consideration for their Sabbath.

Another instructive case of religious influence is the national and local prohibition acts. Joseph R. Gusfield (1963) argues that rural Protestants were threatened by the post-Civil War and post-World War I Eastern and Southern European Catholic immigrants, who settled in urban areas and maintained a lifestyle quite different from that of rural Protestants. Alcohol became a symbol of the struggle between rural Protestants and urban Catholics for cultural and political dominance. Within the Protestant religion alcohol has a somewhat negative meaning and for some Protestant groups it is clearly a sign of immorality, whereas within the Catholic religion alcohol has little negative meaning and is considered a normal part of social life. The power of the rural Protestants prevailed and a series of antidrinking laws was passed in various states and towns, culminating in a national prohibition act.

Abortion is another issue in which the influence of religious groups is evident. The Catholic Church, for example, regards abortion as sinful and has been very influential in transforming its conception of morality into law. Church authorities have worked to influence hospital regulations, city ordinances, state laws, and federal court decisions, and have been very successful.

These cases can be multiplied at will. Religious groups have a history of transforming their interests into law. The Puritans of the Massachusetts Bay Colony, Protestants on the issue of alcohol, and the Catholic Church on the issue of abortion are cases in point. Thus, religious groups have also been instrumental in determining what is crime and who is the criminal.

Summary.   This section examines research bearing on the formulation and administration of the law. It examines the laws of theft and vagrancy as outcomes of the conflict between the landed aristocracy and the emerging commercial class in medieval Europe, and it examines laws which have been passed to regulate business interests but where enforcement is minimal. Various studies show that either no funds for enforcement are appropriated or the agencies charged with enforcement are composed of representatives of the industry they are charged to regulate. Hence, those who violate business laws in carrying out corporate interests are rarely imprisoned, although they may be reprimanded or possibly fined. The section also shows how governmental agencies use their power to expand their domain, such as the Federal Narcotics Agency's campaign to criminalize the medical and general use of narcotics. Finally, research shows that religious groups also work to transform their interests into laws, thereby creating crimes and criminals. The general point is clear: what is crime and who is the criminal frequently depend on group interests and political power.

Law: Its Selective Application

The latter section focused on what laws are formulated and enforced; this section focuses on discrimination in the enforcement of the law. Conflict theorists state that power plays a major role in determining what people are the objects of enforcement. William J. Chambliss (1969:84) states: ". . . those people are arrested, tried and sentenced who can offer the fewest rewards for nonenforcement of the laws and who can be processed without creating any undue strain for the organizations which comprise the legal system." Studies of selective enforcement have been reported for numerous laws, such as drinking, drugs, prostitution, and homosexuality.

Juvenile Justice System: Social Class and Race.   The juvenile justice system involves three important decision points: the decision to arrest a suspicious juvenile; the decision to prosecute an arrested juvenile; and the decision to incarcerate a prosecuted juvenile. For the most part the power to resist enforcement has been studied in terms of social class and race. For example, Howard S. Becker (1963:13) states that:

> The middle-class boy is less likely when picked up by the police to be taken to the station; less likely when taken to the station to be booked; and it is extremely unlikely that he will be convicted and sentenced. That variation occurs even though the original infraction of the rule is the same for the two cases. Similarly, the law is differentially applied to Negroes and Whites.

Perhaps the first critical legal decision is the decision to arrest a suspicious juvenile. A large number of studies can be located which strongly show racial and social class differentials at the arrest level (Williams and Gold, 1972; Hirschi, 1969; Gould, 1969; Black and Reiss, 1970). The first three studies collected information on a sample of juveniles from different areas and then checked with local police departments to determine what proportions of the lower-class, middle-class, white, and black juveniles had police records; and the Black and Reiss study employed observers who rode in the back seat of police patrol cars and recorded the proportion of black and white juvenile suspects who were arrested. To summarize, all four studies show black juveniles to be overarrested. Black and Reiss report a 13 percent differential, Williams and Gold a 6 percent differential, Hirschi a 24 percent differential, and Gould an 18 percent differential. Two of the studies examine social class and both show lower-class juveniles to be overarrested.

Once juveniles enter the justice system through an arrest, the relationships between social class or race and subsequent legal decisions can be estimated from police records. (See studies by Weiner and Willie, 1971; Meade, 1974; Terry, 1967; Thornberry, 1973; Ferdinand and Luchterhand, 1970; Goldman, 1963; Arnold, 1971; and Wilson, 1968.) Of the six studies that examine social class, all but Arnold report that lower-class juveniles are prosecuted at a higher rate than middle-class juveniles. Of the eight studies that examine race, all but Meade report that blacks are prosecuted at a higher rate than whites. For race the percentage differences are particularly substantial, with Thornberry showing a 20 percent difference, Ferdinand and Luchterhand a 16 percent difference, Goldman a 31 percent difference, Arnold a 15 percent difference, and Wilson a 16 percent difference.

Court statistics are used to estimate the relationships between social class or race and the severity of judicial dispositions. See studies by Terry, 1967; Thornberry, 1973; Ferdinand and Luchterhand, 1970; Arnold, 1971; Wheeler et al., 1968; Langley, 1972; Thomas and Sieverdes, 1975; and Scarpetti and Stephenson, 1971. To summarize, of the studies which examine social class, all but Thomas and Sieverdes (1975) report that lower-class juveniles receive the more severe dispositions. Thornberry reports a 10 percent differential, Arnold reports a 19 percent differential, and Scarpetti reports a 7 percent differential. Of the studies that examine race, all but Terry report that blacks receive the more severe dispositions. Thornberry reports an 18 percent differential, Ferdinand and Luchterhand a 9 percent differential, Arnold a 37 percent differential, Langley a 24 percent differential, and Scarpetti a 6 percent differential.

In total, studies examining social class and race at the arrest, prosecution, and judicial levels show that social class and racial differentials can be documented at each decision-making level.

In a recent review of this literature, Allen E. Liska and Mark Tausig (1979) demonstrate how even small social class and racial differentials at each decision-making level generate sizable accumulative social class and racial differentials. They argue that if "small" differentials at all decision points regularly favor white and middle-class adolescents over black and lower-class adolescents, the differentials "multiply" through the justice system, resulting in a homogeneous black and lower-class prison population. For example, for Thornberry (1973) 40.8 percent of the arrested blacks and 21.2 percent of the arrested whites are referred to a precourt hearing (a ratio of approximately 1.9:1); of these 58.2 percent of the blacks and 52.9 percent of the whites are referred to juvenile court (a ratio of 1.1:1); and of these 42.3 percent of the blacks and 24.6 percent of the whites are institutionalized (a ratio of 1.7:1). As a result of these three decisions 10.2 percent of the arrested blacks but only 2.7 percent of the arrested whites are institutionalized (a ratio of 3.8:1, substantially greater than the ratio at any one decision level). The accumulative product of the specific decision differentials can also be observed by examining the proportions of the arrested and institutional populations that are black. For Thornberry, blacks constitute 55 percent of the arrest population, but as a product of the racial differentials operating at each decision level, blacks constitute 82 percent of the institutional population.

Conflict theorists argue that these studies show that because lower-class and black juveniles lack the power to resist, they are more likely to be arrested, prosecuted, and given more severe judicial dispositions than middle-class and white juveniles. This interpretation, however, assumes that black, white, lower-class, and middle-class juveniles commit equivalent levels of delinquency. If lower-class and black juveniles commit more delinquent acts and/or more serious delinquent acts than do middle-class and white juveniles, they should show higher levels of arrest, prosecution, and incarceration than do middle-class and white juveniles. Hence, research must take into account a juvenile's level of delinquency involvement when estimating social class and racial differentials in the juvenile justice system.

The simplest method for doing this is to compare arrest, prosecution, and judicial disposition rates for lower-class, middle-class, black, and white juveniles who have the same level of delinquency involvement. Of the above studies only Ferdinand and Luchterhand, Arnold, and Thornberry match juveniles on past record and seriousness of present offense, while examining differentials in prosecution and judicial disposition. They suggest that a portion of the racial and social class differentials in prosecution and judicial dispositions comes about because lower-class and black juveniles commit more serious offenses and have longer prior records, although a significant portion of those differentials cannot be so explained. For example, Thornberry's data show that about 20 to 40 percent of the race and social class differences cannot be so explained; and Liska and Tausig (1979) report that upon controlling for past record and offense seriousness, substantial accumulative racial differences remain for all three of the above studies.

In summary, studies show that social class and racial differentials exist at the arrest, prosecution, and judicial levels of the juvenile justice system. Relative to their proportion in the population, more lower-class and black juveniles are arrested, of those arrested a higher proportion of lower-class and black juveniles are prosecuted, and of those prosecuted a higher proportion of lower-class and black juveniles are given more severe dispositions. Part of these differentials can be explained by legal considerations. Lower-class and black juveniles commit

---

Box 7.2 RACIAL DISCRIMINATION

William R. Arnold (1971) reports research on the extent to which prosecution and judicial decisions are affected by social class and race. The project examines the records of a sample of juveniles in a Southern city of about 250,000, born between September 1, 1947 and December 31, 1948. Each offense committed prior to April 9, 1964 is included. The findings show that 14 percent of the arrested Anglos, 22 percent of the arrested Latin Americans, and 29 percent of the arrested Blacks were prosecuted; and of those prosecuted 24 percent of Anglos and 71 percent of Latins and Blacks were given the more severe judicial dispositions. Are these racial differences a result of differences in the type of offenses and frequency of offenses committed by the Black, Latin, and Anglo juveniles? If the Blacks and Latins have longer prior records and have committed more serious offenses than the Anglos, then legally a higher proportion of the Blacks and Latins than the Anglos should be prosecuted and given the more severe judicial dispositions. Not to do so would be discriminatory. To control for the effect of these legal considerations, Arnold compared those Latins, Blacks, and Anglos with the same legal experiences (level of prior offenses and seriousness of present offense). For those with little legal experience, 9 percent of the Anglos, 5 percent of the Latins, and 6 percent of the Blacks were prosecuted, and 20 percent of the Anglos and 67 percent of both the Latins and Blacks were given severe dispositions. For those with considerable legal experience 21 percent of the Anglos, 40 percent of the Latins, and 61 percent of the Blacks were prosecuted, and 30 percent of the Anglos, 85 percent of the Latins, and 71 percent of the Blacks were given more severe judicial dispositions. Arnold's study thus shows that independent of prior offense record and the seriousness of the present offense, more Latins and Blacks than Anglos are prosecuted and given severe judicial dispositions.

more offenses and more serious offenses than do whites. Yet even when juveniles are matched on those legal characteristics, substantial racial and social class differentials still exist.

Conflict theorists argue that the capacity of white and middle-class parents to resist the enforcement of the law accounts for these differentials. At the arrest level the middle-class juvenile is cautiously handled because his or her parents have the capacity to make trouble for the officer, such as initiating false arrest and libel suits. At the prosecution and court levels the resources of the middle-class and white parents are even more evident. They can afford the best lawyers to bargain with the prosecutor or juvenile officer over charges and over what should be done with their child, and they can also afford private detectives and expert witnesses such as social workers and psychiatrists. They can also provide positive alternatives to legal prosecution. Rather than sending their child to an overcrowded facility and expose him or her to hardened delinquents, middle-class parents can suggest that their child be placed in their custody. They have the resources to provide professional help (psychiatric help and summer camps) or to change neighborhoods and schools. This may be very persuasive to a prosecutor or juvenile court judge.

Power (Social Class) and Psychiatrists.   A considerable amount of research (Dohrenwend and Dohrenwend, 1969) shows a reasonably strong relationship between admission to a mental hospital and social class. This relationship has traditionally been explained by assuming a higher level of stress in the social environment of the lower class than the middle and upper class (Dohrenwend and Dohrenwend, 1969). However, from the viewpoint of conflict theory it seems equally reasonable to argue that the lower class is hospitalized because it lacks the power to resist commitment. Undoubtedly, the relationship between social class and hospitalization is affected by differences in both stress and power. Research must isolate these two processes.

Rushing (1971), in addressing this issue, distinguishes between voluntary and involuntary commitment (court commitments). He argues that official coercion and the power to resist are most relevant in the latter, but that for voluntary commitment the social-class commitment relationship may well be explained by class-related stress.

Commitment procedures, varying somewhat from state to state, generally involve two or three people (including a relative, physician, psychiatrist, and law enforcement officer) who initiate and file a petition with a court alleging a person's mental illness. This leads to some type of court hearing in which the accused is examined by court-appointed medical personnel (not always psychiatrists). Using their reports and whatever other information may be available, an officer of the court (not always a judge) makes a decision to commit or release the accused. This is a very important decision carrying significant legal and social consequences. Upon being involuntarily committed a person is judged to be legally incompetent, and, depending somewhat on the state, cannot control his or her economic resources, cannot enter into valid contracts, cannot file for divorce, cannot operate a motor vehicle, cannot vote, and is generally deprived of civil liberties.

Involuntary commitment can be resisted in various ways. Perhaps the most effective form of resistance is to deter other people from filing a commitment petition. Social control agents are reluctant to file such petitions as the "petitioner is subject to both criminal and civil charges if his act is judged to have been malicious and careless" (Rushing, 1971:515). Rock et al. (1968) report that, while such reprisals are rare, their possibility frequently deters physicians, police officers, and representatives of social agencies from initiating commitment proceedings. Of course, the prospects of such legal reprisals depend upon the resources of the accused.

The resources of the middle and upper classes can be very effective if a hearing is initiated. They can afford their own psychiatrists and psychologists to testify in their behalf as to their mental health and to provide them with care and therapy without hospitalization, and they can afford lawyers to present an effective legal defense. The role of a lawyer has been studied by Wenger and Fletcher (1969). As nonparticipant observers, they observed eighty-one commitment hearings in a Midwest state. In the sixty-five cases in which no counsel was present, 91 percent were committed, but in the fifteen cases in which counsel was present, only 24 percent were committed. It might be argued that lawyers tend to be employed in cases where the accused is mentally healthy, for healthy people are more likely to secure legal counsel to maintain their freedom. Hence, the low rate of commitment of those people represented by a lawyer may be a function not of the fact that a lawyer is representing them but of the fact that they are mentally healthy. Wenger and Fletcher also examined this possibility. Using the observations during the hearings, they rated the cases by the extent to which they met the state criteria for commitment. While there is a relationship between securing a lawyer and not meeting the criteria, controlling for this relationship does not significantly alter the original relationship between the presence of a lawyer and commitment. For example, twenty-three people did not meet the criteria. Of the fifteen without a lawyer 66 percent were committed, while of the eight with a lawyer none were committed. Hence, it seems reasonable to conclude that the upper class, because of the resources available to them, are much better able to resist involuntary commitment than are the lower class.

William Rushing has studied this relationship by examining the ratio of voluntary to involuntary commitments. If the conflict interpretation is correct, the ratio should be inversely related to social class: it should be highest for the lower class and lowest for the upper class. In the first of two studies, Rushing (1971) examines this relationship for all first admissions (2262 involuntary and 1496 voluntary) between 1956 and 1965 for three state hospitals in Washington. Patients were classified into five social class categories by occupational prestige. The two upper-class categories show a ratio of one to one (one involuntary commitment for every voluntary commitment); but the lower-class category shows a ratio of over two to one. For individual occupations, for example, the ratio is 1:1 for professionals, 1.3:1 for craftsmen, 2:1 for laborers, 4:1 for farm laborers. While the data show that the ratio of involuntary to voluntary admission is highest for the lower class, this does not necessarily support the conflict perspective. It could be argued that the lower class, because of high levels of strain in its environment, is generally more impaired than the middle and upper class, and that the lower class, because of its conceptions of mental illness, tends to avoid voluntary commitment, making involuntary commitment necessary.

In a second study, Rushing (1978) tests this explanation. He examined all twenty- to sixty-four-year-old first admissions to six mental hospitals in Tennessee between 1956 and 1965. Using education as an index of social class, he again reports that the ratio of involuntary to voluntary admissions is highest for the lower class. Controlling for the effects of disorder severity, the relationship is tempered but still evident, and is strongest for those cases where the evidence of illness is most ambiguous (functional as opposed to organic illness, and mild as opposed to severe illness). Hence, Rushing concludes that when the evidence of illness is most ambiguous, the power to resist is most significant in determining who is involuntarily committed.

Summary.   Who is a deviant is affected not only by what norms are enforced but by the power to resist. Research suggests that social power, as measured by position in the social structure, affects who is arrested, prosecuted, and incarcerated for law violations, and who is involuntarily committed for mental illness. Research attempts to isolate the effects of social power from the effects of norm violations (law violation and mental impairment) on societal reaction (incarceration and hospitalization).

SOCIAL POLICY

Contrary to the structural/functional, Chicago, social control, and even labeling theorists, conflict theorists are not concerned with reducing the level of law violations; rather, they are concerned with changing the processes of law formulation and administration and the general structure of society. Specific policy implications are dependent on the characteristics of specific conflict theories.

Liberal Reform or Social Control

Turk's theory, focusing on group conflict and criminalization, has not provided clear policy implications; some sociologists have drawn liberal implications and others have drawn conservative implications from it.

Concerning conflict, if we assume that low levels of conflict are advantageous for most social groups (a somewhat debatable point [Coser, 1956], and a point on which Turk is not clear), social policy should be directed toward decreasing group conflict. According to Turk's theory, group conflict should decrease when authority-subject differences decrease. If authority-subject differences are to be reduced, which class is to be changed, authorities or subjects? It seems unlikely that authorities will sponsor policies and programs to change themselves. Hence, if authority-subject differences are to be reduced, social policy will probably be directed at changing (manipulating) subjects. Also, according to Turk's theory, group conflict should decrease when subject organization decreases. Do we wish to reduce social conflict by making it more difficult for subjects to challenge authorities? Because of these apparent implications, Turk's theory could be interpreted as a set of rules for authorities to control the behavior of subjects—a modern day Machiavellian manifesto (Taylor et al., 1973). Such an interpretation, however, seems somewhat unwarranted. The general body of Turk's work criticizes inequalities in law formulation and application, and advocates a balance of power between competing interest groups as the optimal social condition.

To reduce criminalization, Turk's theory suggests increasing either authority tolerance of subject differences or subject power (traditional liberal policies). In contemporary America, tolerance of subject differences has generally taken the form of decriminalizing crimes without victims (marijuana use, pornography, abortion, prostitution, drug use, gambling); and policies designed to increase the power of subjects have emphasized equal access to lawmakers and equality in law enforcement and resistance.

The latter, however, has been relatively ineffective. Although some laws exist which regulate access to the lawmaking process (lobbying, conflict of interests, and political campaign contributions), they are not rigorously enforced. Yet even if all groups have equal access to the lawmaking process, lawmakers would still be more receptive to the concerns and interests of some groups than others. The fact that lawmakers tend to be middle and upper class, white, lawyers, and males suggests that laws will be more beneficial to these classes and groups than others, if for no other reason than that lawmakers have difficulty understanding the interests of other classes and groups. Mechanisms must be institutionalized which insure a greater representation of interests in the law formulation process.

In addition to inequalities in the law formulation process, research shows inequalities in law enforcement. Some laws are enforced and some are not. What can be done? President Carter initiated a policy to arrest the regular exchange between service on government regulatory commissions and agencies and employment in the regulated business corporations. He asked government employees in certain critical positions to sign a statement pledging that upon terminating government service they will not accept immediate employment in corporations which they had been charged with regulating. While only an initial step, it is one in the right direction. The present relationship between regulatory agencies and the corporations they regulate is comparable to appointing people involved in organized crime to head the FBI. Research also shows that for laws which are enforced, the power to resist is differentially distributed. While certain programs provide limited legal assistance to the poor, such as Public Defenders, they have limited effectiveness. David Sudnow (1965) has argued that Public Defenders work closely with the District Attorney's office to facilitate processing cases through the legal system. Public Defenders do not resist.

Generally, programs designed to level power inequalities are rigorously opposed by established and organized groups. Thus, for the most part such programs have been ineffective. As discussed in Chapter Two, when the Mobilization for Youth program attempted to organize neighborhoods (rent strikes, demonstrations, lawyers for welfare clients, and collecting data on landlord violations), the program was rigorously attacked by local authorities whose power was threatened. Monies for the program were frequently impounded, the FBI initiated an investigation into the program, and program files were confiscated.

In sum, although Taylor et al. (1973) interpret Turk's theory conservatively, as a guide to social control, it can reasonably be interpreted as a special case of pluralistic interest theory, suggesting the reduction of inequalities in law formulation and administration processes. Thus far the implementation of such policies has been minimal and relatively ineffective.

Radical Change

Quinney argues that meaningful reforms in law formulation and administration cannot occur within the context of a capitalistic system. If law formulation and administration reflect power and if power reflects ownership and control of the means of production, equality in law formulation and administration requires equality in the control and ownership of capital. Past reforms have done nothing more than strengthen the capitalist system. Quinney clearly advocates some form of socialism, with equality in decision making and in the consumption of economic resources. He also argues that since the state represents the interests of the powerful, within an equalitarian society the state has no function and will disappear; hence, there will be no criminal law and consequently, no crime.

While Quinney's description of the future is admittedly vague and somewhat utopian, he is also somewhat vague on the more immediate stages in the long transition process. Generally, he advocates social action within the context of historical inevitability.

He argues that the transition to socialism is inevitable, emerging from the contradictions of capitalism.

Capitalism is transformed into socialism when capitalism is no longer able to reconcile the conflicts between the existing mode of production and the relations of production, when the contradictions of capitalism reach a point where capitalism can no longer solve its inherent problems. Ultimately capitalist relations become an obstacle to the further development of capitalism. New forms of production and social relations develop. The capitalist system finally fails to control the population; criminal justice ceases to be effective; and a new social life emerges (Quinney, 1977:150).

Some events and social relationships are central to this social process. As capitalism matures the following occur: one, competition among capitalists becomes more intense and failures among capitalists increase, thereby increasing the ranks of the proletariat; two, industrialization becomes centered in urban areas, increasing interaction among the proletariat, which in turn increases the proletariat's sense of exploitation and class consciousness; and three, technology expands and the economy becomes more cyclical, increasing unemployment (surplus labor). Within traditional Marxian theory a large class-conscious urban proletariat is viewed as the moving revolutionary force which transforms capitalism into socialism. Quinney (1977) has recently emphasized the role of unproductive labor in this transformation. He argues that as capitalism matures more capital must be expended on social control (welfare and criminal justice). This is unproductive, because it does not produce surplus value (the products of labor which are used for capital investment) by which the capitalist system expands. In fact, as the social control system expands the level of surplus value may not be adequate to even maintain a steady economic state. The strains of capitalism are further accentuated (unemployment, crime, proletarization), increasing the need for greater social control, which in turn further decreases the level of surplus value, and so on.

Within the context of this "inevitable" social process, emerging through the contradictions of capitalism, Quinney advocates social action programs to accelerate the transition to socialism. Who is to be involved in such programs? Clearly, the capitalists and upper-level bureaucrats (who benefit from the present order) are not going to advocate or participate in such programs. Quinney calls upon those exploited and intellectuals to organize themselves to that end. He criticizes intellectuals and academicians for constructing theories and doing research which legitimize and support the present social order, and calls upon them to formulate "critical theory," theory critical of the present order and which unmasks the inherent contradictions and inequities of that order.

To summarize, Quinney argues that the distribution of social power is inextricably tied to ownership and control of the means of production in a capitalist society. Hence, a meaningful reduction in the inequities in law formulation and administration cannot occur without radical change in the structure of society. The policy implications of his most recent work focus on the process of transformation from capitalism to socialism.

CRITIQUE

Theory

Turk's concepts and propositions are not clearly articulated. A major portion of Turk's theory deals with conflict; yet "conflict" is not clearly defined. Does it mean fighting in the streets, struggling in the legislative halls and courts, or a refusal on the part of subjects to obey authorities? Some parts of Turk's work suggest that the crime rate is an indicator of conflict. If so, then conflict refers to street crime, not legislative struggles. The link between conflict and criminalization is also not clear. Is conflict necessary for criminalization, or can people be criminalized without conflict?

Turk overemphasizes the role of cultural differences in understanding conflict and criminalization. Clearly, people frequently struggle over cultural goals and the proper rules for achieving them; however, as we live in a world of finite resources, even when people agree on what is important in social life, they frequently struggle over the distribution of these things. That is, conflict frequently occurs because people strive for the same things. In fact, some of the most intense struggles within and between societies have occurred between people and groups who agree on fundamental values.

In emphasizing cultural differences Turk does not articulate the role of economics in social conflicts. Taylor et al. (1973) argue that in Western industrial societies the major conflicts are between economic classes over the distribution of resources, and that most authority-subject relationships reflect the economic stratification system. Although we may not accept Quinney's exclusive emphasis on economic relationships, these relationships appear to be central in the distribution of social power, and thus should be given special consideration in the study of social conflict.

Most sociologists argue that a theory should be formulated so data can be marshaled to prove it either valid or invalid. Consider Quinney's proposition one: laws are formulated and enforced which are in the interests of those who control and own the means of production. Quinney does not clearly specify what is in their interests, and frequently ends up saying that all laws that are passed and enforced "must be" in their interests, otherwise they would not have been passed or enforced. For example, Quinney argues that the antibusiness legislation of the New Deal was "really" in the interests of owners and managers. Without these reforms a major social revolution would have occurred. This, of course, is mere speculation; there is no evidence that such a revolution would have taken place had the reforms not occurred. It is also a post hoc interpretation. Would Quinney have predicted the legislation prior to its enactment on the basis of what his theory deems to be in the interests of owners and managers? At the time the legislation was violently fought by owners and managers. Quinney must define clearly what is in the interests of those who control and own the means of production in order for researchers to observe whether there is the correspondence between interests, power, and law that Quinney purports.

R. Serge Denisoff and Donald McQuarie (1975) have criticized Quinney's proposition that owners and managers of the means of production control the state. They argue that owners and managers do not necessarily have the same interests, and that Quinney fails to consider the independent interests of the managers of capital (upper- and middle-level business managers). While using the term "own and control," for the most part he does not examine the relationship between ownership and control; he assumes either that those who own also manage, or that a homogeneity of interests exists between those who own and those who manage the economic system. Also, while Quinney (1977) acknowledges that in advanced stages of capitalism the state may develop some autonomy, he does not analyze the relationship between the interests of those who own and control the means of production and the interests of those who control the state. State bureaucrats are themselves an interest group working to translate their interest into the formulation and enforcement of the law.

Quinney, as well as many Marxists, takes a different view of theory from that of most sociologists and from that used in this book. He argues that the function of theory is to generate social equality and justice; in Marxian terms, to facilitate the transition to socialism by raising people's consciousness of their true interests, outlining and illuminating possible futures, and generally stimulating social action. However, from the viewpoint of most sociologists, Quinney is frequently more ideological than theoretical; he is more concerned with criticizing the structure of American society and bringing about social change than in validly explaining law formulation and administration in American society. Explanation and prediction as well as social action are valuable endeavors; yet frequently they can be antithetical. Emphasis on explanation and prediction can sometimes impede social action; and emphasis on social action can sometimes impede explanation and prediction. Quinney's work suffers from the latter. As he is less concerned with empirically testing his theory than with convincing others of its validity and of the need for social action, he frequently ignores counter evidence or construes it to fit his theory.

Perhaps some integration of Turk's and Quinney's theories may produce a more acceptable general conflict theory of law formulation and application. In constructing such a theory two issues must be considered. One, neither Turk nor Quinney deals with the process of law formulation. Quinney assumes that laws directly reflect the interests of those who own and control the means of production; and Turk assumes that laws reflect the interests of the powerful whoever they may be. Neither examines the processes by which the interests of the powerful are translated into law formulation and administration. (See Chambliss and Seidman, 1971, for discussion of these processes.) Two, conflict theory does not seem applicable to studying the formulation of many laws concerning personal violence (homicide, assault, suicide, rape, incest, and child molesting). While the administration of these laws frequently reflects power differentials, the laws themselves seem to reflect a general societal consensus (Rossi et al., 1974). They do not protect the interests of just one economic class or religion, but appear to protect the interests of people and society in general. Sociologists must come to grips with this issue, perhaps developing a typology or continuum of laws ranging from those that protect the exclusive interests of just some classes or groups, such as the owners and managers of capital, to those that reflect a societal consensus.

Research

Concerned with social change and justice, conflict sociologists have criticized Western society, particularly the unequal distribution of economic resources and power and other perspectives of deviance and crime, for not explicitly recognizing these inequities. They have criticized the structural/functional perspective for emphasizing areas of social consensus, and the labeling and ethnomethodological perspectives for being too concerned with the subjective worlds of lower-class deviants, thereby neglecting the objective realities of economic and power inequality. These endeavors are all useful and noteworthy; however, in pursuing them conflict sociologists have frequently had little intellectual energy left for systematic research. Studies are now starting to accumulate on the role of power in translating group or class interests into law. Many of the studies, however, are too illustrative. They are organized and designed to illustrate rather than test conflict theory. For example, the studies of the Federal Narcotics agency by Dickson (1968) and Becker (1963) illustrate how a federal agency can use its power to influence the formulation of the law, but do not rigorously test propositions concerning the transformation of the interests of governmental agencies into the formulation and administration of the law. Rigorous tests would require the systematic observation of a large number of governmental agencies—not just one or two selected to illustrate a theoretical proposition. Studies of power in resisting law enforcement have been more rigorous. They do not present only illustrative cases (upper-class juveniles who have successfully resisted enforcement of the law and lower-class juveniles who have not successfully resisted), but use large random samples to examine the relationship between power (social class or race) and law enforcement.

Social Policy

The policy implications and implementations of conflict theory are contingent upon the specific conflict theory. Turk's (1969) work, for example, does not explicitly consider social policy, although Taylor et al. (1973) have interpreted it as providing a manifesto for social control. This interpretation seems unwarranted. The work may be more reasonably interpreted as a special case of pluralistic interest theory, suggesting policies of tolerance and equality. For the most part, such policies have not been implemented. Efforts to increase the power of the poor (public defenders, legal aid, slum organizations) have been cosmetic in nature; serious efforts have been resisted by local and national authorities. Quinney (1974, 1977), perhaps as a reaction to this state of affairs, argues that radical societal change is necessary before meaningful legal change can occur. Yet his description of a socialistic state is vague and general, although understandably so, and his conception of the path to socialism waivers between the traditional Marxian inevitability thesis and social action programs to facilitate the course of history.

REFERENCES

ARNOLD, WILLIAM R. "Race and ethnicity relative to other factors in juvenile court dispositions," American Journal of Sociology 77 (Sept. 1971): 211–27.

BECKER, HOWARD S. *The Outsiders: Studies in the Sociology of Deviance (New York: Free Press, 1963).*

BERLEN, ADOLPH and GARDNER MEANS. *The Modern Corporation and Private Property* (New York: Macmillan, 1932).

BLACK, DONALD J. and ALBERT J. REISS. "Police control of juveniles," American Sociological Review 35 (Feb. 1970):63–77.

CHAMBLISS, WILLIAM J. "A sociological analysis of the law of vagrancy," Social Problems 12 (Summer 1964):67–77.

————. *Crime and the Legal Process* (New York: McGraw-Hill, 1969).

CHAMBLISS, WILLIAM and ROBERT B. SEIDMAN. *Law, Order and Power* (Reading, Mass.: Addison-Wesley, 1971).

CLINARD, MARSHALL B. "Corporate crime—testimony of Marshall B. Clinard before the Subcommittee on Crime, House Committee of the Judiciary, 1979."

CLINARD, MARSHALL B. and RICHARD QUINNEY. *Criminal Behavior Systems (2nd ed.)* (New York: Holt, Rinehart & Winston, 1973).

COSER, LEWIS. *The Functions of Social Conflicts* (London: Free Press, 1956).

DAHRENDORF, RALF. *Class and Class Conflict in Industrial Society* (Stanford, Calif.: Stanford University Press, 1959).

————. "Out of utopia: Toward a reorientation of sociological analysis," American Journal of Sociology 64 (Sept. 1958):115-27.

DENISOFF, R. SERGE and DONALD MCQUARIE, "Crime control in capitalist society: A reply to Quinney," Issues in Criminology 10 (Spring 1975): 109–19.

DICKSON, DONALD, "Bureaucracy and morality: an organizational perspective on a moral crusade," Social problems 16 (Fall 1968):143–55.

DOHRENWEND, BRUCE and BARBARA DOHRENWEND. *Social Status and Psychological Disorders* (New York: Wiley, 1969).

ERIKSON, KAI T. *Wayward Puritans* (New York: Wiley, 1966).

FERDINAND, T. N. and L. G. LUCHTERHAND. "Inner-city youth, the police, the juvenile court and justice," Social Problems 17 (1970):510–26.

FURSTENBERG, FRANK F. "Public reaction to crime in the streets," The American Scholar 40 (Autumn 1971):601–10.

GALLIHER, JOHN F. and ALLYN WALKER. "The puzzle of the social origins of the marijuana tax act of 1937," Social Problems 24 (Feb. 1977):367–76.

GEIS, GILBERT O., "White collar crime: The heavy electrical equipment antitrust cases of 1961," in M.C. Clinard and R. Quinney (eds.), *Criminal Behavior Systems* (New York: Holt, Rinehart & Winston, 1967), p. 139–51.

GOLDMAN, NATHAN. *The Differential Selection of Juvenile Offenders for Court Appearance* (New York: National Council of Crime and Delinquency, 1963).

GOULD, LEROY. "Who defines delinquency: A comparison of self-reported and officially-reported indexes of delinquency for three racial groups," Social Problems 16 (Winter 1969):325−35.

GUSFIELD, JOSEPH R. *Symbolic Crusade: Status Politics and the American Temperance Movement* (Urbana, Ill.: University of Illinois, 1963).

HALL, JEROME. *Theft, Law and Society* (Indianapolis: Bobbs-Merrill, 1952).

HASKINS, GEORGE LEE. *Law and Authority in Early Massachusetts* (New York: Macmillan, 1960).

HIRSCHI, TRAVIS. *Causes of Delinquency* (Berkeley, Calif.: University of California Press, 1969).

LANGLEY, MICHAEL H., "The juvenile court: The making of a delinquent," Law and Society Review 7 (Winter 1972):273−99.

LINDESMITH, ALFRED R. *The Addict and the Law* (Bloomington, Ind.: Indiana University, 1965).

LISKA, ALLEN E. and MARK TAUSIG, "Theoretical interpretations of social class and racial differentials in legal decision-making for juveniles," Sociological Quarterly 20 (Spring 1979):197−207.

MARX, KARL. *Selected Writings in Sociology and Social Philosophy,* ed. by T. B. Bottomore and M. Rubel (New York: McGraw-Hill, 1964).

MCCAGHY, CHARLES H. *Deviant Behavior, Crime, Conflict, and Interest Groups* (New York: Macmillan, 1976).

MCCORMICK, ALBERT E., JR. "Rule enforcement and moral indignation: Some observations on the effects of criminal antitrust convictions upon societal reaction processes," Social Problems 25 (Oct. 1977):30−39.

MEADE, ANTHONY. "Seriousness of delinquency, the adjudication decision and recidivism—a longitudinal configurational analysis," The Journal of Criminal Law and Criminology 64 (Dec. 1974):478−86.

MILLS, C. W. *The Marxists* (New York: Harcourt Brace, 1948).

O'CONNOR, JAMES. *The Fiscal Crisis of the State* (New York: Martin Press, 1974).

QUINNEY, RICHARD. *Criminology: Analysis and Critique of Crime in America* (Boston: Little, Brown, 1975).

———. *Critique of Legal Order* (Boston: Little, Brown, 1974).

———. *The Social Reality of Crime* (Boston: Little, Brown, 1970).

———. *Class, State and Crime* (New York: David McKay, 1977).

ROCK, RONALD, MARCUS A. JACOBSON, and RICHARD M. NANOPAUL. *Hospitalization and Discharge of the Mentally Ill* (Chicago: University of Chicago Press, 1968).

ROSSI, PETER H., EMILY WAITE, CHRISTINE E. BOSE, and RICHARD E. BERK. "The seriousness of crimes: Normative structure and individual differences," American Sociological Review 39 (April 1974):224−37.

RUSHING, WILLIAM A., "Individual resources, societal reaction and hospital commitment," American Journal of Sociology 77 (Nov. 1971):511–26.

———. "Status resources, societal reaction and mental hospital admission," American Sociological Review 43 (Aug. 1978):521–33.

SCARPETTI, F. R. and R. M. STEPHENSON. "Juvenile court dispositions, factors in the decision-making process," Crime and Delinquency 17 (April 1971): 142–51.

SCHUR, EDWIN M. *Crimes Without Victims* (Englewood Cliffs, N.J.: Prentice-Hall, Inc., 1965).

SELLIN, THORSTEN. *Cultural Conflict and Crime* (New York: Social Science Research Council, 1938).

SUDNOW, DAVID. "Normal crimes: Sociological features of the penal code in a public defender office," Social Problems 12 (Winter 1965):255–74.

TAYLOR, IAN, PAUL WALTON, and JOCK YOUNG. *The New Criminology* (New York: Harper & Row, 1973).

TERRY, ROBERT M. "The screening of juvenile offenders," The Journal of Criminal Law, Criminology and Police Science 58 (June 1967):173–82.

THOMAS, CHARLES W. and C. M. SIEVERDES. "Juvenile court intake: An analysis of discretionary decision-making," Criminology 12 (Feb. 1975): 413–32.

THORNBERRY, TERRENCE P. "Race, socioeconomic status and sentencing in the juvenile justice system," The Journal of Criminal Law, Criminology and Police Science 64 (March 1973):90–98.

TURK, AUSTIN T. *Criminality and Legal Order* (Chicago: Rand McNally, 1969).

VOLD, GEORGE B. *Theoretical Criminology* (New York: Oxford University Press, 1958).

WEINER, NORMAN L. and CHARLES V. WILLIE. "Decisions by juvenile officers," American Journal of Sociology 77 (Sept. 1971):199–210.

WENGER, DENNIS L. and C. RICHARD FLETCHER. "The effects of legal counsel on admissions to a state mental hospital," Journal of Health and Social Behavior 10 (March 1969):66–72.

WHEELER, STANTON, EDNA BONACICH, M. RICHARD CRAMER, and IRVING K. ZOLA. "Delinquency prevention and organizational relations," in Stanton Wheeler (ed.), *Controlling Delinquents* (New York: Wiley, 1968).p. 31–60.

WILLIAMS, J. R. and M. GOLD. "From delinquent behavior to official delinquency," Social Problems 20 (Fall 1972):209–28.

WILSON, JAMES Q. "The police and the delinquent in two cities," in Stanton Wheeler (ed.), *Controlling Delinquents* (New York: Wiley, 1968),p. 9–30.

CHAPTER EiGHT

SUMMARY

Chapters Two to Seven examine six theoretical perspectives of deviance. This, the concluding chapter, briefly summarizes each of the six perspectives, compares and contrasts them, and suggests directions for future research.

PERSPECTIVES

The Structural/Functional Perspective

Structural/functionalism assumes a high level of social consensus and integration in respect to values and goals, and analyzes the social structure (the persistent patterns of behavior which constitute society's organizations and institutions) in terms of its contributions to society's goals and values.

Within this general conceptual framework, Durkheim developed ideas about deviance. He argued that the division of labor, rapid social changes (such as economic contractions and expansions), and individualism, which emerge in urban societies, weaken the moral control of the community, and that norm violations are an outcome of a weak moral order. Variations of this theme have been developed by Gibbs and Martin (1964), Henry and Short (1954), Mizruchi and Perrucci (1968), and others. Merton (1938) is particularly noteworthy, because he tried to develop a general theory of deviance. Rather than focusing on breakdowns in the moral or regulatory order, Merton focused on disintegration within the general social order—inconsistencies between cultural goals and structural opportunities—as the cause of deviance. This theme has been developed and extended by Cloward and Ohlin (1964). Durkheim also argued that norm violations can be conceptualized as a vital component of the social order in that they can function to stabilize and maintain the social order. Erikson (1966) and others have developed this theme.

While only loosely related, these theorists can be conceptualized within the structural/functional perspective. Each assumes—sometimes only implicitly— that social order exists, and thus that norm violations are identifiable. Durkheim examines breakdowns in the social order; Merton and other contemporaries examine imperfections in the operation of the social order, and Erikson examines the role of norm violations in the stabilization and maintenance of the social order.

Structural/functionalism has generated a volume of research on a variety of deviant patterns. Durkheim reported data on suicide. His work has been continued by contemporary sociologists, suggesting that the nature of the social order is important in understanding suicide rates in the twentieth as well as the nineteenth century. Research directions have also been suggested by Merton's and Cloward and Ohlin's theories. Considerable effort, for example, has gone into showing that a discrepancy between aspirations and expectations is linked to the level of drug use. For the most part, little systematic empirical work has been generated by Durkheim's and Erikson's theories of the functions of deviance.

The policy implications and implementations of the structural/functional perspective to deviance are not always clear. Durkheim's and Merton's theories suggest changes in the structure of society—in some cases changes which violate social values and upset the present structure of social power. Hence, except for individualistic interpretations, these theories have not been a source of social policy. The same is true of Erikson's work. What are the policy implications of the proposition that deviance functions to increase social integration and clarify social norms? Should societies organize themselves to create a minimal level of deviance? Should a certain percentage of people be induced to violate social norms?

The Chicago Perspective

The Chicagoans were impressed with ecological analyses of the biotic world. They borrowed concepts like competition, struggle for survival, symbiosis, and natural area to describe social processes and order. Realizing also that man is a culture-bearing animal, they devoted much of their work to examining the link between ecological processes and culture, and to examining the extent to which cultural and ecological processes operate to produce social order. The Chicagoans identified certain ecological processes (competition, population movements, migration, immigration, and mobility) as disrupting processes of social control, thereby producing deviant behavior.

Believing that the social control processes of urban areas were disrupted, the Chicagoans frequently referred to urban areas as disorganized. For the most part, they did not measure the disruptive processes directly, but inferred them from what they believed to be their causes (urbanization) and their consequences (rates of deviance). Yet, while an area may show high rates of behavior that violate the norms of conventional society, this does not imply that the area lacks processes of social control and social order. Much of the behavior so precisely described by the Chicagoans, while deviant from the viewpoint of conventional society, may have reflected competing social orders—orders in conflict with conventional society, but orders nonetheless. In fact, social control processes probably operated to incorporate people into these orders. Acceptance of the conventional morality may have blinded the Chicagoans to these processes. Matza (1969), however, argues that they were far from blinded. Their research scrupulously described unconventional orders, although the implications of that research did not enter their theory at the abstract level. While describing unconventional orders, they conceptualized disorder or disorganization.

With the accumulation of these empirical studies, unconventional orders could no longer be conceptually ignored or denied. Although the social disorganization tradition continues to generate some research today, around the mid-1930s the Chicagoans began conceptualizing urban areas as differentially organized, characterized by various diverse and sometimes conflicting social orders, not always reflecting the conventional order. Note that such a conceptualization makes problematic the concept of deviance as norm violations, since that which constitutes a norm violation depends on what social order is assumed by sociologists. The Chicagoans resolved this issue by temporarily ignoring it. Rather than dealing with the question of social conflict, they implicitly assumed the normative perspective of middle-class whites (reflecting traditional rural American values and norms), and focused on the social psychological processes by which people become socialized into deviant social orders.

Sutherland's theory of differential association became the reference point for departure. Sutherland (1939) conceptualized the socialization process as symbolic learning occurring in immediate and intimate social relationships. More recently, Glaser (1956) has emphasized the role of referent others; Reckless and Dinitz (1967) have emphasized the role of self-concept; and Burgess and Akers (1966) have attempted to reconceptualize the socialization process in behavioristic terms. While differing as to the nature of the socialization process into deviance, Sutherland, Glaser, Reckless and Dinitz, and Burgess and Akers implicitly assume the perspective of middle-class whites from which the behavior of other groups is conceptualized as deviant.

Socialization research has developed rigorously. Studies have been conducted on most patterns of deviance (homosexuality, drug addiction, alcoholism, political radicalism, and prostitution), using case study, field observation, and survey techniques. Research testing differential association theory shows that the level and pattern of a person's deviance is related to the deviance of peers, and that the subjective attachment of deviant associations and self-concept modulate peer influence. Since the late 1960s various researchers have closely examined the causal processes which underlie the link between peer deviance and the level of a person's deviant involvement. While the data support the socialization process specified by differential association theory, they also suggest the importance of social selection and interpersonal social control processes.

Both social disorganization and socialization theories suggest social policies. The former suggests building conventional organizations to exercise social control, exemplified by the Chicago Area Projects. In terms of reducing deviance, the results of these projects are unknown, although they do show the feasibility of building community organizations in the inner city. Socialization theories shift policy from building community organizations to building links between deviants and the existing conventional community. The success of such programs has also been limited. Either the constructed linkages are weak (detached worker programs), so that they have little or no effect on a deviant's interaction patterns, or they are so encompassing (Synanon) that most deviants avoid involvement.

The Social Control Perspective

Like the structural/functional and Chicago perspectives, the social control perspective assumes that a conventional order can be identified, making norm violations relatively simple to define and an appropriate subject of study. The perspective sharply differs, however, from both the structural/functional and Chicago perspectives concerning the role of motivation in deviant behavior. Both latter perspectives assume that deviants differ from conformists in terms of motivation. Structural/functionalism assumes that as a consequence of certain structural conditions some people experience frustration and stress which motivates or "pushes" them into norm violations; and the Chicago socialization perspective assumes that as a consequence of association in minority subcultures some people learn attitudes and values which motivate or "push" them into norm violations. Hence, both perspectives examine how some people but not others come to acquire these motivational dispositions. The social control perspective, to the contrary, assumes that norm violations are generally so attractive, exciting, and profitable that most people are motivated to violate norms. Thus, there is little need to explain deviant motivation; to the contrary, it is necessary to explain why so few people act upon their deviant motives. Social control theorists focus this issue in terms of the question: what controls (Hirschi, 1969) or contains (Reckless, 1967) most people from acting upon their deviant motives?

Two types of social control are discussed: inner and outer controls. The former is illustrated by people who conform to society's rules because they have internalized them as their own, and the latter by people who conform to society's rules because of social rewards foregone and social punishments experienced upon being socially identified as a norm violator.

Recently, interest has focused on deterrence theory. As a special case of social control theory, it assumes that people are motivated to violate norms but are constrained by social controls. It ignores inner controls and emphasizes punishment, particularly state-administered punishment, as *the* means of social (outer) control; consequently, it focuses on law violations rather than norm violations in general.

Two processes of deterrence (general and specific) and three dimensions of punishment (severity, certainty, and celerity) are emphasized. Specific deterrence assumes that punishment decreases the future level of law violations of those punished through punishment sensitivity. Studies on the effect of imprisonment have provided little supportive evidence. While imprisonment may increase the level of punishment sensitivity, which may decrease future law violations, it may also increase criminal socialization and social stigma, which may increase future law violations. Future research must attempt to separate the net relationship between imprisonment and future law violations into these component effects. General deterrence assumes that punishment decreases the level of law violations of those unpunished. Three types of studies have been examined: comparative studies of crime rates across jurisdictions; time series studies of the crime rate in one jurisdiction; and perceptual studies. Most of these studies do not suggest a severity effect, but consistently suggest a certainty effect. However, they do not clearly isolate the effect of certainty on law violations from the effect of law violations on certainty.

While the policy implications of deterrence theory are reasonably clear, research suggests caution. This has not arrested efforts at policy implementations. Efforts have been expended to increase the size of the criminal justice system with no noticeable increase in the level of certainty and celerity; and as research has not been very supportive of the severity of punishment thesis, extended prison terms have been rationalized in terms of incapacitation without seriously considering its long-range consequences.

The Labeling Perspective

During the 1960s numerous sociologists questioned the extent to which normative consensus and stability characterize most Western societies, and thus by implication the viability of theoretical perspectives built on these assumptions. Instead, they emphasized the emerging, changing, and conflicting character of social norms. This was an important milestone in the study of deviance. For without clear and stable reference points for judging behavior, normative violations are definitionally problematic. Hence, in the 1960s many sociologists began defining deviance as a social definition which some groups and people use to describe the behavior of others, and thereby redefining the subject matter of the sociology of deviance as the study of such social definitions. Theory and research have focused on two general questions: What is defined as deviance? Who is defined as deviant?

The first question has directed theory and research toward the study of the emergence of social norms and social categories for labeling people as deviant. In this book it is discussed under the ethnomethodology and conflict perspectives.

The second question refers to the study of how existing categories for describing norm violators and violations are applied in specific situations. Of all individuals who violate norms only some are socially identified and labeled by family, friends, colleagues, the public, and authorities; on the other hand, some conformists are falsely identified as norm violators. Various sociologists (Lemert, 1951; Becker, 1963) have argued that this is an important issue because of the psychological and social consequences of being publicly identified—correctly or falsely—as a norm violator. They have examined the extent to which being publicly labeled as a norm violator affects social relationships (such as family relations, friendship patterns, and economic opportunities), and the extent to which these in turn influence future norm violations.

Labeling research has been reported on a variety of norm violations, particularly crime and delinquency and mental illness. The findings, however, have been ambiguous. While studies suggest that being labeled a criminal or a delinquent reduces economic opportunities and self-esteem, research on the effects of labeling on future law violations is not clear and subject to various interpretations. One interesting observation seems to reoccur: whites appear more sensitive to official labeling than blacks. Perhaps, since blacks occupy a negative social status and are not well integrated into society, they may not be very sensitive to official societal reactions. As to mental illness, various studies have examined the effects of labeling on social rejection in hypothetical situations, the subjective experience of hospitalized patients, the social relationships of hospitalized patients, and the effect of hospitalization on future behavior. While simple conclusions are difficult to draw and much work remains to be done, it seems reasonable to conclude that labeling theorists have overstated their case. Labeling can be debilitating, but need not be. Hospitalization, the most visible indicator of being labeled mentally ill, can be restitutive and frequently has no effect at all.

The general policy implications of labeling theory are relatively clear: reduce negative social labeling, that is, reduce involvement in the criminal justice system for those accused or convicted of law violations, and reduce hospitalization for those showing signs of mental illness. Social policies vary from radical nonintervention (community tolerance) to various forms of nonincarceration and nonhospitalized treatment, such as diversion programs and community home-care programs, respectively. Because of program selection and attrition, evaluating these programs is difficult. At present there is little evidence showing that diversionary programs are more successful at reducing future law violations than are traditional forms of societal reaction; and there is little evidence showing that alternatives to hospitalization are more effective than short-term hospitalization. (The problems associated with long-term hospitalization have been more clearly documented.) On the other hand, if research does not show major differences in effectiveness between forms of societal reaction, then a good case may be made for the policies advocated by labeling theorists, as they are economically less costly and more humane to those involved.

The Ethnomethodology Perspective

Ethnomethodology is concerned with describing people's subjective perceptions and interpretations of the world, and the processes by which people construct their worlds. Ethnomethodologists argue that people construct their realities with a set of cognitive rules, such as typifications, common sense theories, metaphors, and analogies, and that to explain action, theories must capture people's constructions or at least must be consistent with them.

From the perspective of ethnomethodology, deviance is a social definition or construction of people, organizations, and societies. Ethnomethodologists are concerned with the emergence and formulation of constructions (what is defined as deviant in what social situations?), with the specific application of such constructions (who is defined as deviant in what specific social situations?), and with the methods people (public, family, and friends) and organizations (police and psychiatrists) use in constructing and applying definitions of deviance.

Ethnomethodologists argue that to infer people's constructions researchers must come to know and use people's methods or tools of reality construction—language, typifications, and common sense theories. This cannot be accomplished through the standard techniques of data collection, such as official records and standardized questionnaires, which conceptualize the constructions of people in terms of the constructions of sociologists. Sociologists are implored to experience reality as people experience it—to "go native." Participant observation is advocated as a research technique. The participant observer experiences what subjects experience, and thus comes to construct experience in their terms. As participant observation is frequently neither practical nor possible (homosexuality and alcoholism), nonparticipant observation is also advocated. Other techniques are also used (such as interviews and sometimes even formal questionnaires) as needed, but in using them ethnomethodologists remained concerned with the problem of imposing the constructions of sociologists on the constructions of the people studied.

Research has been directed toward a number of topics. 1. Studies have examined typifications or general images of deviance held by the public and authorities. They suggest, for example, that Americans are moving away from viewing deviance in moral terms (good versus evil) and are moving toward viewing deviance in illness terms (health versus illness). These general images are related to people's theories of deviance and policy recommendations. People who hold stereotypic images are prone to hold biological theories of deviance and to recommend severe societal reactions. 2. Research has also examined the cognitive and interactive processes by which social control agents apply general images of deviance in everyday situations. Studies illustrate and suggest the importance of cognitive consistency, cognitive economy, retrospective interpretation, and various situational cues (like demeanor) in this process. Demeanor, for example, appears to be an important cue in inferring whether or not a suspect's law-violating behavior is a manifestation of an underlying immoral character. 3. Upon noting the problems in identifying norm violations and violators, some studies have examined how the routines and decision-making processes of social control agencies affect norm violation statistics. Douglas, for example, has tried to show how differences in suicide statistics among social units reflect differences in bureaucratic decision-making routines among social units.

What does social policy mean within an ethnomethodological framework? Does it make sense to talk about changing an objective world which theory and research have ignored or suspended? To many ethnomethodologists, defining some state of society as a problem about which something should be done is itself a subjective construction. They are more interested in studying such constructions, the methods of reality construction (typifications and lay theories) which lead to social problem constructions, and the process by which groups with different social problem constructions negotiate a commonly agreed upon construction, than in studying the "objective" state to which the construction refers.

The Conflict Perspective

The conflict perspective emphasizes social conflicts and studies the social processes whereby some norms are converted into laws, some laws are enforced, and some people are criminalized. Rather than studying why some people violate the legal order, the conflict perspective focuses on the legal order itself.

Vold (1958) might well be considered the first conflict theorist to have some impact on the contemporary study of deviance and crime. Generally, he argued that some crimes could be understood in terms of cultural conflicts. Groups conflict over what is proper behavior; and some groups have the power to transform their cultural norms into laws. Conflict theory occupies only one chapter in Vold's book and focuses on those criminal acts which were ignored by contemporary criminologists (civil rights, labor disputes, and conscientious objectors).

By the mid-1960s the conflict perspective became quite prominent. The work of Turk (1969), focuses on the conditions when group differences generate group conflict and when legal norms (laws) are enforced. He argues that conflict between authorities and subjects is most probable when both cultural and behavioral differences exist between authorities and subjects, when subjects are organized, and when subjects are unsophisticated; and that laws are enforced when they are consistent with the behavioral and cultural norms of authorities, when violators are powerless, and when violations are unrealistic. In the late 1960s and early 1970s, conflict theory took on a Marxian orientation, emphasizing the link between the economic order and crime. Quinney's (1977) recent work is representative. He argues that laws are formulated and administered to serve the interest of those who own and control the means of production; the state and other organizations (mass media, religion, and education) serve the interests of those who own and control the means of production; and as the capitalist system matures, a greater proportion of its gross national product is expended on coercive social control.

Propositions concerning the relationship between group or class interests and law formulation and administration have stimulated considerable research. Numerous studies have been reported showing the power of business interests to affect the formulation and administration of law. They suggest that when laws are passed to regulate business interests, enforcement is minimal. Either funds are not appropriated for enforcement or the agencies charged with enforcement are composed of representatives of the industry they are charged with regulating. When these laws are enforced, those convicted are rarely imprisoned: they are reprimanded or fined. Numerous studies also have been reported on how governmental agencies and religious groups too work to transform their interests into laws.

Of the laws which are formulated and administered, people differ in the power to resist enforcement. Studies of juvenile delinquency, for example, show that more lower-class and black than middle-class and white juveniles are arrested, prosecuted, and given severe dispositions. Part of these differentials can be explained by legal considerations, for by present legal standards lower-class and black juveniles commit more offenses and more serious offenses than do middle-class and white juveniles; yet even when juveniles are matched by legal considerations, racial and social class differentials still exist. Conflict theorists argue that the capacity of white and middle-class juveniles (through their parents) to resist enforcement accounts for these differentials.

Conflict theorists have little direct concern with reducing the level of law violations; rather they are concerned with changing the structural characteristics of law formulation and administration. Turk's theory, interpreted as a special case of pluralistic interest theory, suggests the reduction of inequalities in law formulation and administration. Quinney argues that since the distribution of social power is inextricably tied to ownership and control of the means of production, meaningful change in law formulation and administration cannot occur without a radical change in the structure of society. He advocates a socialist society.

COMPARING THE PERSPECTIVES

Throughout this book various differences among the perspectives have been noted. This section draws attention to significant differences among the perspectives in terms of theory, research, and social policy.

Theory

Subject Matter of Study. The basic and most underlying division in the sociology of deviance is the subject matter of study. Traditionally, the field has been identified with the study of norm violations, which assumes societal consensus and stability as points of reference from which violations can be defined. Of the six perspectives, the structural/functional, Chicago, and social control/deterrence perspectives are most clearly identified with the study of more violations. All three to various degrees make these assumptions. Structural/functionalism explicitly makes them; in fact, it is oriented toward explaining the nature of society's normative order. The social control perspective also makes them, although more implicitly than explicitly. Even the Chicago socialization perspective, which assumes a pluralistic society, still assumes a dominant or conventional order from which behavior can be judged as deviant.

During the 1960s numerous sociologists, emphasizing the emerging, changing, and conflicting character of social norms, questioned the assumptions of normative consensus and stability, and thus by implication the viability of theoretical perspectives built on these assumptions. For without clear and stable reference points for judging behavior, normative violations are definitionally problematic. Hence, starting in the 1960s many sociologists have defined deviance as a social definition which some groups and people use to describe the behavior of others, and have thereby redefined the subject matter of the sociology of deviance as the study of these social definitions. Theory and research have focused on two general questions: what is defined as deviance and who is defined as a deviant?

Three somewhat interrelated perspectives have emerged. The labeling perspective assumes a pluralistic society (norms are flexible and changing but some minimal level of consensus can be defined) and studies how societal definitions of deviance emerge and pattern the course of norm violations. The ethnomethodology perspective ignores or suspends the objective social order for the purpose of research and focuses on the social and psychological processes whereby situational consensus emerges and some actions and people are defined as deviant. The conflict perspective assumes that society (contemporary Western societies) is characterized by conflict, not consensus, and focuses on the role of power in law formulation and administration.

Push versus Control Perspectives. Of the perspectives which focus on deviance as a norm violation, the structural/functional and Chicago perspectives conceptualize the social environment as "pushing" people into deviance. They suggest that certain environments (such as lack of opportunities and deviant peers) produce a motivational disposition which makes norm violations attractive, and thus "pushes" people into violating them. The social control/deterrence perspective, to the contrary, assumes that norm violations are intrinsically attractive. Sociologists need not explain the motivation or "push" to violate norms; rather they must explain why most people do not act on their deviant motives. What controls them?

Norm Violations as an Act or a Career. Traditional perspectives implicitly assume that norm violations constitute "discrete" acts; they assume that the conditions which explain an initial act also explain subsequent acts. For example, Merton's theory assumes that ends-means discrepancy explains the initial and subsequent acts; and the Chicago and social control perspectives make the same assumptions about deviant associations and bonds of control, respectively. To the contrary, labeling theory assumes that explanatory conditions operate sequentially; those that initiate norm violations are not necessarily those that sustain it over time. While various psychological and social conditions may initiate episodic norm violations, the reactions to norm violations generate the psychological and social conditions which sustain norm violations over time.

Passive versus Active Concepts of the Individual. Most traditional perspectives of norm violations conceptualize the individual as passive in relationship to the social environment (society); they emphasize the effect of the objective social environment on the individual. The structural/functional perspective emphasizes the effect of social organization; the Chicago perspective emphasizes the effect of social disorganization and deviant subcultures; the social control perspective emphasizes the effect of social control systems; some subschools of the labeling perspective emphasize the effect of social labels on people; and the conflict perspective emphasizes the effect of economic structure and power on legal definitions. While some subschools of these perspectives note the importance of subjective interpretations of the social environment (subjective interpretations of peer definitions, social punishments, social labels, and legal definitions), they do not conceptualize them as a focus of research. Only the ethnomethodology perspective conceptualizes the relationship between the individual and the social environment as active. It suspends the environment as an objective reality, and focuses on how individuals (and organizations) construct or interpret the social environment, specifically how individuals construct definitions of deviance and people as deviants.

In summary, these assumptions about the nature of society, the individual, and the relationship between the individual and society affect the subject matter of the sociology of deviance, the kinds of theoretical and research questions posed about this subject matter, and social policy recommendations.

Research

The six perspectives differ on the role of research in a theoretical perspective. Traditionally, sociologists have viewed research as theory generating and testing. Various methods concerning the representativeness of a sample and the validity and reliability of measurement (see Chapter One) have become institutionalized. For the most part the structural/functional, Chicago, social control, and labeling perspectives fall within this tradition.

Ethnomethodology does not. The concern not to distort the constructions of people has resulted in the avoidance of structured techniques of data collection and in the extensive use of direct observation, particularly participant observation, which presumably enables researchers to experience reality somewhat like the subjects, thereby insuring that the constructions of researchers are not too different from the constructions of the subjects. The major problem of such research is observer reliability. Without techniques for structuring observations, different observers construct reality differently. How are we to weigh or evaluate the validity of the different constructions? Ethnomethodologists are somewhat insensitive to this problem. In fact, some ignore the problem, arguing that sociologists are no different than lay people. As different lay people have different understandings and constructions of reality so do different sociologists. Hence, much ethnomethodological research does not prove or even test ethnomethodological theory in the traditional sense; rather, it illustrates the theory in the sense of providing concrete examples or cases where the theory does or does not apply.

Sociologists also disagree over the proper relationship between social research and social values. Research is frequently used and conducted to foster certain values. Most sociologists acknowledge this. Research is not value free; nor should it be. Values affect what we study and how we study it. Yet, within these limitations, most sociologists argue that research should describe reality and test and generate theories. To the contrary, various conflict theorists (Marxists such as Quinney) argue that social research should be more explicitly political. Theories should be formulated and research should be conducted so as to foster and stimulate social equality; and research should not be evaluated in terms of traditional concepts of validity and reliability, but in terms of its capacity to foster social equality.

In sum, this book has emphasized the theory testing and generating function of social research, reflecting the dominant position in contemporary sociology. Yet research can have other functions. Some ethnomethodologists, because of their assumptions about reality, have implicitly emphasized its illustrative function; and some conflict theorists, because of their commitment to social equality, have explicitly emphasized its political function.

Social Policy

The traditional perspectives (structural/functionalism, Chicago, and social control) conceive of social policy in terms of reducing norm violations, although they differ in their exact policy implications. Structural/functionalism suggests reducing cultural-structural dysfunctionalism in society, which for the most part has been translated into programs to increase opportunities for the poor. The Chicago socialization perspective suggests altering interpersonal networks, which for the most part has been translated into self-help programs for norm violators. The social control/deterrence perspective suggests increasing the bonds between individuals and society, which for the most part has been translated into more severe legal penalties for law violators.

The social definitional perspectives shift attention away from norm and law violations toward the social control system and society itself. The labeling perspective, although still concerned with norm violations, advocates programs to reduce discrimination in labeling and to reduce the overall level of labeling. The conflict perspective ignores norm (law) violations, and is concerned with inequalities in law formulation and administration. Some conflict theorists argue that social justice can be achieved by reforming the justice system. Others argue that the justice system reflects the distribution of economic power in society, and that in a capitalist society that distribution is so skewed that equality in the justice system cannot be achieved without equality in the economic system. Hence, they advocate radical changes in the economic system. The ethnomethodology perspective does not shift social policy questions; it obscures them. Assumptions which suspend social reality do not lead to clear social policies. In fact, some ethnomethodologists have argued that evaluating society detracts from studying it; and others have studied social policies and social problems as subjective constructions, arguing that social problems like rape are "solved" when people no longer construct them as problems.

In summary, the social policies advocated by the six perspectives differ substantially, reflecting differences in theory. The traditional perspectives assume a high level of social consensus and are concerned with reducing violations of that consensus. The labeling perspective assumes a much more pluralistic social order, and is concerned with increasing equity in societal labeling and in reducing the overall level of labeling. The conflict perspective assumes a high level of conflict over scarce resources and is concerned with a more equitable distribution of resources. The ethnomethodology perspective, by suspending reality for purposes of theory and research, obscures social policy questions.

THE NEXT DECADE

Trying to predict the direction of the sociology of deviance over the next decade would certainly be hazardous. Yet whichever perspectives dominate the next decade, the following questions should be addressed.

Perspectives concerned with norm violation must contend with two questions. One, they must explain the distribution of violations over social units, such as organizations, neighborhoods, cities, states, countries. Why are rates of violation high in some units and low in others, and why do they increase during some times and decrease during others. Two, they must also explain individual violations. Why do some people violate norms more than others? Perspectives concerned with social definitions must address parallel questions. One, they must explain the distribution of social definations of deviance over social units, why some acts are defined as deviant in some units but not in others. Two, they must also explain why some people are defined as deviants while others are not, and the consequences of being so defined.

While the six contemporary perspectives address these questions and provide tentative answers, there are certain areas of reality to which they have not been applied. In his presidential address to the twenty-fourth annual meeting of the Society for the Study of Social Problems, Stanton Wheeler (1975) noted that in recent years the study of norm violations has been overshadowed by the study of social definitions, and argued that future research should strike a better balance between these two areas of study. He also noted, however, that norm violations research should not just expand traditional research that has focused on the norm violations of lower-class adolescents while ignoring the norm violations of middle- and upper-class adults. This bias reflects the type of norm violations selected for study. Past research has focused on street crimes such as assault, robbery, burglary, auto theft, and vandalism—violations which fit the opportunity structure and lifestyle of lower-class young males. Future research should focus on those violations which fit the opportunity structure and lifestyle of upper-class adult males and females, such as embezzlement, bribery, fraud, corruption of public trust, and the violation of antitrust, monopoly, and consumer protection laws.

In addition, Wheeler argued that past research has emphasized individual norm violations. Even the studies of social units have emphasized those types of violations and units (such as neighborhoods) for which individual violations can be summed and studied as aggregate characteristics of social units. While these studies have frequently been insightful, they have ignored the study of social units that are legal entities and act in a legal sense, such as business corporations, political parties, governments, and religions. Of course, the violations are still physically committed by individuals, but legally they are committed by organizations and the consequences of them (wealth and power) are experienced by organizations. For example, we know little about the distribution of violations among business corporations and city governments. Do some corporations violate some laws (consumer protection or antitrust) more than others? If so, why? Do some city governments violate some laws (water and air pollution) more than others? If so, why?

The structural/functional, Chicago, and social control perspectives may be as applicable to the study of upper-class and organizational violations as they are to lower-class individual violations. Indeed, deterrence theory may be more applicable to the violations of upper-class individuals and organizations than lower-class individuals. Organizations have the resources to accurately estimate the certainty, severity, and celerity of punishments associated with various law violations, and they operate in a rational calculative manner in which monetary punishments are frequently thought of as just another cost of doing business.

Reemphasizing our concern with norm and law violations should not detract from our concern with social definitions. The study of social definitions has also traditionally focused on lower-class individuals as those most likely to experience social labeling. Yet the study of social labeling might well be enhanced by studying the labeling (or lack of labeling) of upper-class individuals and social units, such as economic and political organizations.

As described in Chapter Five, the labeling perspective purports that labeling affects structural opportunities (economic and political), interpersonal networks, and attitudes (particularly self attitudes), which in turn lead to secondary deviance. What about upper-class type crimes, like the tax evasion of businessmen and the fee splitting of doctors? Does conviction of tax evasion or the violation of antitrust laws affect self-concepts, interpersonal relationships, and economic opportunities in ways that lead to secondary deviance? Some research on physicians convicted of malpractice (Schwartz and Skolnick, 1962) and business executives convicted of violating antitrust laws suggests that such labeling does not decrease economic opportunities; indeed, this research suggests that it may actually increase them. Generally, we know little about this process for middle- and upper-class type law violations.

What about organizations? Does being labeled in court as a law violator affect organizations in ways that lead to secondary deviance? If so, what are the mediating processes? Organizations do not have self-concepts, strictly speaking, but they do have reputations. Some organizations have a reputation for honesty and integrity whereas others do not. The same is true of city, state, and national governments. Does having the reputation as a dishonest corporation or government increase the subsequent level of deviance? Organizations also differ in terms of opportunities for achieving their goals. How are these affected by labeling? Does being labeled by a consumer protection agency as a producer of faulty products (automobiles with defective gasoline tanks which ignite, or automobile tires which unravel with use) affect business opportunities? If so, does it lead to secondary deviance?

Who is labeled as deviant? This question has been rigorously studied for

lower-class type crimes, while upper-class type crimes and crimes of organizations have been ignored. We know next to nothing about the social processes by
which some people become labeled as tax evaders, fee splitters, plagiarizers,
embezzlers, and trust violators, and the processes by which some organizations
become labeled for violating antitrust, corruption, conspiracy, and price-fixing
laws. To what extent are principles of cognitive organization (cognitive consistency, cognitive economy, and retrospective interpretation) and processes of
negotiation applicable to the study of labeling organizations, as they appear to be
to the study of labeling individuals?

Given these concerns, issues, questions, and problems, the sociology of deviance should prove to be an exciting enterprise over the next decade.

REFERENCES

BECKER, HOWARD. *Outsiders.* (N.Y.: Free Press, 1963).

BURGESS, ROBERT L. and RONALD L. AKERS. "A differential association-
reinforcement theory of criminal behavior," Social problems 14 (Fall 1966):
128–47.

CLOWARD, RICHARD A. and LLOYD E. OHLIN. *Delinquency and Opportunity*
(N.Y.: Free Press, 1964).

DURKHEIM, EMILE, *Suicide: A Study in Sociology,* trans. by J. A. Spaulding and
G. Simpson. (N.Y.: Free Press, 1951).

ERIKSON, KAI. Wayward Puritans: *A Study in the Sociology of Deviance.* (N.Y.:
Wiley, 1966).

GIBBS, JACK P. and WALTER T. MARTIN. *Status Integration and Suicide/A
Sociological Study* (Eugene, Ore.: University of Oregon Books, 1964).

GLASER, DANIEL. "Criminality theories and behavior images," American
Journal of Sociology 61 (March 1956):433–44.

HENRY, ANDREW F. and JAMES F. SHORT. *Suicide and Homicide: Some Economic, Sociological, and Psychological Aspects of Aggression* (N.Y.: Free
Press, 1954).

HIRSCHI, TRAVIS. *Causes of Delinquency* (Berkeley, Calif.: University of California Press, 1969).

LEMERT, EDWIN. *Social Pathology.* (N.Y.: McGraw-Hill, 1951).

MATZA, DAVID. *Becoming Deviant.* (Englewood Cliffs, N.J.: Prentice-Hall,
Inc., 1969).

MERTON, ROBERT K. "Social structure and anomie," American Sociological
Review 3 (Oct. 1938):672–82.

MIZRUCHI, EPHRAIM H. and ROBERT PERRUCCI. "Prescription, proscription
and permissiveness: Aspects of norms and deviant drinking behavior," in
Mark Lefton, James K. Skipper, and Charles H. McCaghy (eds.), *Approaches
to Deviance* (N.Y.: Appleton-Century-Crofts, 1968).

QUINNEY, RICHARD, *Class, State and Crime*. (N.Y.: David McKay, 1977).

RECKLESS, WALTER C. *The Crime Problem*. (Englewood Cliffs, N.J.: Prentice-Hall, Inc., 1967).

RECKLESS, WALTER and SIMON DINITZ. "Pioneering with self-concept as a vulnerability factor in delinquency," Journal of Criminal law, Criminology and Police Science 58 (1967):515—23.

SCHWARTZ, RICHARD D. and JEROME H. SKOLNICK, "Two studies of legal stigma," Social Problems 10 (1962):133—43.

SUTHERLAND, EDWIN and DONALD CRESSEY. *Principles of Criminology* (Philadelphia: J. B. Lippincott, 1939).

TURK, AUSTIN T. *Criminology and Legal Order*. (Chicago: Rand McNally, 1969).

VOLD, GEORGE B. *Theoretical Criminology* (N.Y.: Oxford University Press, 1958).

WHEELER, STANTON. "Trends and problems in the sociological study of crime," Social Problems 23 (June 1975):525—35.

iNdEX